EVERY TRICK IN THE BOOK

OTHER BOOKS BY MARK SENAK

HIV, AIDS and the Law –
A Guide to Our Rights and Challenges

A Fragile Circle – A Memoir

EVERY TRICK IN THE BOOK

The Essential Lesbian & Gay Legal Guide

MARK SENAK

M. Evans and Company, Inc., New York

This book and its contents are not a substitute for a lawyer and do not create an attorney/client relationship between reader and author. This book is not dispensing legal advice and readers with legal questions should consult an attorney for such advice.

M. Evans and Company, Inc.
216 East 49th Street
New York, New York 10017

wwww.mevans.com

Library of Congress Cataloging-in-Publication Data

Senak, Mark S.
Every trick in the book : a lesbian and gay legal guide / Mark Senak.
p. cm.
ISBN 0-87181-953-5
1. Homosexuality—Law and legislation—United States. 2. Lesbian—Legal status, laws, etc.—United States. 3. Gays—Legal status, laws, etc.—United States. 4. Sex and law—United States. I Title.

KF4754.5 .S46 2002 346.7301'3—dc21 2002020245

Book design and type formatting by Bernard Schleifer
Printed in the United States of America
10 9 8 7 6 5 4 3 2 1

To Rodger with Thanks

ACKNOWLEDGMENTS

THIS EFFORT WOULD merely be an idea without pages if not for the following people.

A book is just a lot of well-meaning words, often rambling and disorganized, until a patient and thoughtful editor gets involved. I owe a debt of gratitude to PJ Dempsey for her work and effort. Similarly, thanks are owed to my agent, Laurie Harper, for seeing this project as something worthy of her time.

The cleverness of Rodger McFarlane is reflected in the title, as is his generosity in giving me permission to use it.

Writing this book took more than the professional support of my editor and agent and creative support of my friends. Special thanks are due to friends Brad Ferris and Ryan Obermiller, who provided comfort in the most consistent and thoughtful ways. I wish the world were made of people like them.

Gratitude also goes to two other friends who were both encouraging and thoughtful along the way: Joe Gleason and Brian Gaudet. Thanks also to Anne and Don Hannaford for the many islands of civilization they provided through the course of the writing process.

Most of all, overwhelming appreciation is due, not just from myself, but from all gay, lesbian, bisexual and transgender people, to people who are truly heroes and heroines, who work for great organizations and who have provided their insights, thoughts and experience in these pages. Matt Coles of the American Civil Liberties Union; Sam Garrison, an attorney in private practice in North Carolina; Sharra Greer of the Servicemembers Legal Defense Network; Frederick Hertz, an attorney in private practice in California; Lorri Jean, formerly of the National

Lesbian and Gay Task Force, Frank Kameny, long time activist for gays and lesbians in the military; Kate Kendell of the National Center for Lesbian Rights; Kevin Layton and Winnie Stachelberg of the Human Rights Campaign and Judy Moats, another attorney in private practice in Virginia. These are all people who have shared their time, knowledge and viewpoints to help me. More importantly, they have devoted their talented efforts and careers to bringing enlightenment, justice, and fairness where there has been darkness. They have each individually and together enriched the lives of everyone, gay and straight. They deserve my and your thanks now and for many years to come as we will all enjoy the fruits of their labors in living our daily lives – maintaining our partnerships, building our families, fighting discrimination and obtaining the right to be treated equally with others. These pages and my talents are too limited to thank them properly.

I also wish to thank the Washington, D.C., Metropolitan Police Department Gay and Lesbian Liaison Unit for their responsiveness and assistance with questions and resources.

Lastly, I want, as always, to thank my family – my mother Kathleen, my father Peter, and my sister Paula for raising me with values that included respect for people and a fervent appreciation for the rights of individuals.

CONTENTS

INTRODUCTION

There was a time when there were no books needed about lesbian and gay legal issues, because the only laws directly involving lesbians and gays were sodomy laws. Of these there were many and, as you will see in Chapter 8, Crimes of Passion, they have been with us for a long, long time. But not only was there a paucity of law, before 1869, when the term *homosexuality* was first coined, there was arguably no identifiable lesbian and gay community of people. Prior to that time, gay men and lesbian women were defined solely by the act of sodomy. There was no real "them" and "us" – there was not a gay culture in the sense that we know it today.

Rather, engaging in sexual relations with a member of one's own sex was something that occurred along a spectrum of human sexual activity. Men slept with men, women slept with women. Men slept with women. Men slept with girls. Men slept with boys. Boys slept with women. Some people had sex with people who were not alive. Some people had sex with animals. All in all, there was just a spectrum of complex human sexual behavior, and sleeping with a member of your own sex was simply part of the human repertoire, though not an entirely popular part with the masses and particularly with official religious folks, unless they were practicing in secret themselves. In other words, gays and lesbians were really straight people who had done something wrong.

Men who slept with men were called many things other than homosexuals: *faggots* (derived, of course, from a term for the logs used to burn people who engaged in bad, bad activities, which included men who slept with men), *sodomites, pederasts*, to name a few. Women who slept with women, when referred to at all, were *sapphists*. These were words to define the fact that people engaged in sexual behavior that fell somewhere along the spectrum. But the creation of the term *homosexual* had a far different effect. It defined those people who slept with members of their own sex as a distinct culture. We were no longer defined by a sex act, we were defined as a separate, rebellious, and even aberrant behavior. We were no longer straight people who misbehaved, we were homosexuals. The term created a "them" that was separate from "us" – an essential foundation for any act of discrimination.

And, after dividing the world into two sexual camps, the word "homosexual" provided a sturdy peg upon which to hang any number of associations, such as mental illness, inclinations as sexual predators, and things of that ilk. That, in turn, is the reason so many people prefer the term gay, or almost any other term, to describe people who are oriented toward sleeping with members of their own sex. The term *homosexual* was connotated with shock treatments and shocking treatment of gay people.

B.H. (before homosexuality), there were merely people who committed sodomy. Prior to 1869, the most you could write in a legal book for lesbian and gay people was this: the law forbids you to have sex.

However, A.H. (after homosexuality), gays and lesbians were, by virtue of having a term to define them, a more identifiable group than existed prior to the term coming into use. Arguably, this watershed event, innocent as it may seem, created a "them" (heterosexuals) and an "us" (homosexuals). Having the components of a "them" and "us," believe it or not, makes for a lot more law than if there was just an "us." What that means is that during the B.H. era, a book about lesbian and gay law would have been impossible. In the time of A.H., it has become a necessity.

The reasons for that are many. Since 1869, the term *homosexual* has been used in legislation that goes far beyond outlawing the act of sodomy, but which was designed to exclude or discriminate against those people who commit sodomy. Laws were passed on a host of topics from marriage to military service that affect "us" in a way that often keeps us from living and enjoying life in the same way that "they" do. Homosexuals were forbidden from doing certain things by specific acts of legislation – from entering the military for example. But legal problems are not confined to being specifically mentioned in legislation. Even more problems can occur when the term *homosexual* is not used in legislation, for example, when hate crime laws protect other classes of people but leave homosexuals out. Curiously, homosexuals are not mentioned in marriage laws. But if you try to use that loophole to wed the one you love, you will find that you cannot use it and, in fact, that most states have enacted laws to exclude you specifically from using marriage laws. The effect of being mentioned in some laws, while being left out of others, creates significant legal problems for you, and, if you have one, for your partner and any children you may have.

In other words, there is a growing need for law and a growing body of law that affects the way you go about the business of leading your life – whether you want it to or not, and whether you are in a closet or quite out of it.

We don't have to look very far in history for a vivid example of why it has become important to know and understand the law and its effects on you as a gay man, lesbian woman, or bisexual or transgendered person. As a volunteer lawyer at the Gay Men's Health Crisis in New York in 1982, and later the director of legal services there from 1985-88, I saw first hand the sufferings of the AIDS epidemic. It was a medical devastation, but medical events don't occur in a vacuum – there were serious legal consequences for those involved. People who hadn't considered the effects of the law before now found themselves in a situation that clearly demonstrated how harmful it can be when the law has left you out of its provisions. Couples who had lived together for years and years would find that they were barred from the hospital room when their lover became ill. When people died without a will, the partner would be left with grief, but no inheritance. When obvious disease dragged someone out of the closet at their place of employment, they found themselves fired. The list is quite lengthy. But the point is, that the AIDS epidemic taught the lesbian and gay community that, when it comes to legal matters, you have to know, understand and plan much more than do people who live as "them." In fact, when it comes to legal matters, gays, lesbians, and bisexuals have to understand how the law works or doesn't work much better than their heterosexual counterparts. So do transgenders. Consider the following:

- Heterosexuals do not have to plan for their partner's inheritance; you do.
- They can take for granted that their spouse will be able to make medical decisions for them should they fall ill; you can't.
- They can start a family without wondering if the state in which they live will allow them to have a child; you do have to wonder.
- They can adopt children anywhere. You can't.
- No one is fired from a job for being heterosexual.
- When heterosexuals serve their country in the military, they do not have to hide their sexual orientation. You do.
- When a heterosexual couple makes love in their bedroom at night, it is not illegal. When you do, it might be.
- People don't beat other people up because they are straight.
- If a heterosexual falls in love with a non-citizen of the United States, they have the power to make their lover a citizen. You have no such power.

- Straight folks can get married to the person they love. You can't.
- When they fall in love and get married, they get a tax break; when you fall in love, you don't.
- And speaking of taxes, whenever tax cuts are conceived by government officials, they are aimed at families, which, under most circumstances, you are not allowed to have – in other words, they target tax cuts for themselves.

That barely scratches the surface. And if you are transgendered, you know discrimination even more intimately. However, for all of this inequity, there have been enormous changes in the law and the way it treats gays, lesbians, and bisexuals. Consider that in the past twenty-five years:

- There have been dozens of anti-discrimination laws passed in various cities, counties, and states.
- Domestic partnership, a legal recognition of your relationship, was written into corporate policies and laws around the country.
- Hate crime legislation has passed in many jurisdictions.
- Laws have been passed that protect you from domestic abuse.
- New powers of attorney have been created that allow you to make medical decisions for your partner.
- Lawsuits have created the ability for a partner in a relationship to obtain "palimony."
- Your right to have your relationship legally recognized by a state has been written into law in one state, and perhaps others will follow.
- Some, though only a very few, jurisdictions have begun to recognize protections for people who are transgendered.

In other words, in the past twenty-five years, the legal landscape has changed drastically, mostly for the better. But while changing, it has also become more complex. It is sometimes difficult for any one of us to understand how all of us are affected by the current state of law. For example, the woman who has lost her job because she is a lesbian understands employment discrimination. The couple who want to be married understand the fact that they are legally forbidden to in most states, or simply take for granted the fact that their state does not allow marriage between people of the same sex. The man who loses his home because his lover died understands how he is left out of inheritance laws. The single lesbian who wants to adopt a baby will learn that she cannot in the state in which she lives. Transsexuals embarking on a transition may find themselves friendless and homeless, even shelters turning them away because of who they are. But just as each of these types of individuals understand how the law fails to work for them in their particular circumstances, it is important to understand how the law fails us as a community. It is essential to remember how pervasive discrimination can be and realize the true impact it has on our lives, whether we're gay, lesbian, bisexual, or transgendered. Complacency is a luxury we cannot afford.

That is why this is not a "how-to" book in the traditional sense, and you won't find forms or instructions on how you should do things. Rather, you will find the story that tells you why things are they way they are and why and what you need to do about it. The legal pain that I saw people suffer during the AIDS epidemic was not the result of not knowing how to write a will – it was the result of not understanding the need to write one in the first place. It wasn't a matter of know-how; it was a matter of know-why. So, in this book, you will not find forms to use or step-by-step instructions on how to write a will or a live-together agreement. There are other very good books out there to help you do that, and in the resources section of this book, you will be directed to some of them.

This book is intended as a guide. It is not a substitute for the advice of a lawyer, doctor, psychologist, or any other professional. You would not take home a medical book and then operate on yourself, nor should you take home this book and become your own lawyer. Nor is it a scholarly legal work for academics.

Rather, it is the intent of this book to provide you with context and parameters so that you know when you should see a lawyer. When you do go, whether to assist you in writing a will, having a child or battling discrimination, getting married, getting divorced, being discriminated against, having been beaten up, arrested – this book will give you some understanding of what you will need to have in order to help you along the way. It is also the intention of the book to help you find the resources that are going to be of help to you, because, as you will see, if you don't get the right help, you could get into serious trouble. When you do go to a lawyer, you will be in a position to become a better partner in your care with him or her.

Each chapter is divided into three sections. It is sometimes helpful in learning more about where you are to examine where you've been – the past provides a context for the present. Therefore, the beginning section of each chapter provides you with that context, with a brief history of how we got to where we are. Under the second section, entitled "Current Events," you will get the lay of the land as it currently exists, with an emphasis on what you need to be prepared and an outline of the law as it exists today. The last section, "Future Directions," will give you a brief overview of what developments can be expected in the future.

The changes of the last half of the twentieth century have been remarkable. From the formation of the first fledgling lesbian and gay organizations to the Stonewall riots to the first anti-discrimination ordinances to the first legal recognition of gay relationships in Vermont, the change has been nothing short of breathtaking. The progress of public opinion will continue to effect change.

One thing that you will discover in the following pages is that efforts to keep lesbians, gays, bisexuals, and transexuals from enjoying their full rights as human beings and as U.S. citizens have used every trick in the book against you. In response, with so much pervasive change happening so quickly, it is important that you also have a good idea of every trick in the book.

CHAPTER 1

Goin' to the Chapel—Legal Ceremonies

History and Perspective – Gays, Lesbians and Marriage

THERE IS A FUTURE for gay relationships that is unprecedented in American law, but exactly what that future is going to look like is no certainty. The advances that have occurred in just the last fifteen years of the twentieth century are equivalent to the speed of light in legal, political and social terms. Domestic-partnership recognition by companies and municipalities, and state recognition of gay relationships as legal entities, were goals that did not seem truly attainable in the 1970s. The "separate but equal" accommodations for gay and lesbian relationships allowed for in the Vermont Civil Union (the first legal recognition of lesbian and gay relationships that approaches legal marriage), while an advancement, may in the long run serve as a setback if such arrangements serve as a justification for not recognizing legal marriage among gays and lesbians. And, if "separate but equal" institutions exist for gays and straights, then is there a point, either practical or moral, to pursuing the marriage issue any further?

Lesbians and gays are not the only groups in American history to have been targeted for marriage discrimination. Slaves and even couples of different races have also been forbidden to marry by the laws of the United States. In fact, slaves developed their own ceremony for marriage in which a broom was placed in the middle of the floor and the couple together jumped over it in front of their friends and family. This makeshift ceremony meant that they were married.

For the gay, lesbian, bisexual, and transgender community, there has been significant progress. These changes are not confined to the law, but have occurred in religion as well: across the United States, thousands of gay couples have been joined in a union by clergy in a ceremony referred to as anything other than "marriage." They are "joinings," "bonds of holy union" or some other euphemism, and they too represent progress, if not legal recognition.

However, it is not without possibility that the same conservatives who passed defense of marriage acts in their own states will now launch efforts to block recognition of any same-sex union at all such as those allowed by the Vermont statute. None of the progress that has so far been seen can assure a better future, though it does appear that, given the social evolution seen during the last half of the twentieth century, the legal bonds available to gay and lesbian couples will continue to grow.

In the meantime, there are alternatives, however, that will help you build a marriage out of existing law. Domestic partnership declarations in your city, coverage of your partner by your insurance at work, live-together agreements, and, for those in Vermont, the option of civil unions all fashion some sort of marriage rights for you and your partner. But a single truth remains: until there is true marriage for lesbians and gays in committed relationships, we in the lesbian and gay community will have to settle for our own versions of jumping the broom.

The Heterosexual Monopoly on Marriage

The law only allows heterosexuals to get married. Ask them why. The answer is because they say so. They must think that they are very good at it, but the statistics demonstrate otherwise, with half of their marriages ending in divorce.

The only place on earth that recognizes legal gay marriage is the Netherlands, which in April of 2001, ended discrimination in its marriage laws. Almost everywhere else the specter of a gay union being called a "marriage" has inspired a highly emotional, almost hysterical yet firm-handed response among many in the heterosexual community. Marriage has traditionally been defined as the legal and spiritual union between one man and one woman. Why is it that way? Because, the response goes, that is the way it was intended by God, and because it is the "natural" way (for heterosexuals anyway). End of discussion.

That has often been the way the majority deals with issues of the minority throughout history – by invoking God. Why is there slavery? Because God gave dominion of the earth to the white man. Why are men more equal than women? Because God made Adam first and woman was made from Adam's rib. Besides, she also brought sin. Why shouldn't people of different races marry? You guessed it – because that is not the way God intended for things to be. God gets a heavy bum rap in all of this. But the involvement of God makes policy makers feel justified in their opposition to gay marriage. In fact, some legislators are so sure that marriage can only be between one man and one woman that they have gone out and passed laws to that effect, just to be sure and make it official. Now, it is not only God's law, it has our stamp of approval on it as well. This type of legislation, passed in several states, was inspired by the fear that courts, in their blind and unreasonable drive to be fair, might actually sanction gay marriages. If they did that, just imagine what would happen.

Well, what would happen? What is the deal with gays being married? What is there to be so afraid of? There is a fundamental, heartfelt belief among many in the heterosexual community that by admitting that a man can fall in love with another man, or a woman with another woman, and that the nature of that relationship is every bit as important as a heterosexual union, then such an admission will completely undermine all civilization as we know it, and the heterosexual union will be forever imperiled. That sounds paranoid, doesn't it? But gays and lesbians are cast in the unenviable role. Because they want to get married, they are seen as seeking to undermine the sanctity of the marriage contract between heterosexuals. Somehow, they have figured that our desire to be married causes them to be unmarried. Not only did state legislatures react to this "threat" by passing laws against gay and lesbian marriage, but so did the U.S. Congress. They didn't call it the Anti-Gay and Lesbian Marriage Act, they called it the Defense of Marriage Act (DOMA). They seem very threatened and this makes them feel that they can preserve their own marriages by denying marriage to the rest of us. What's that about?

With all of this talk of the sanctity of marriage and God's law, it is perhaps good to have some perspective. In the Middle Ages, any discussion about the roundness of the Earth – or worse – any hint that the Earth might not be the center of the universe – was considered heresy, plain and simple. It inspired popes to kill and imprison people for daring to challenge the widely held status quo. It is kind of that way with marriage today. One and one woman – any other attempt to define marriage is like saying that the world is not flat: it violates the sense of order. Civilization as we know it will end. The family, in some way that has never been explained, will be undermined. And then, of course, as if all of that isn't bad enough, God will punish us. Man often invokes God to justify unjustifiable positions – and like the flat-earth law, it eventually fails.

Throughout American history, there have been other examples of marriage laws that prohibit the joining of people who love each other. Some states prohibited the marriage of Asians, others prohibited slaves to wed, except as guided by their owner, and persons of mixed race were also forbidden to marry. In 1967, the Supreme Court struck down a Virginia law prohibiting interracial marriage, and as recently as 1999, the Alabama senate voted an amendment to the state constitution, which had disallowed any interracial marriage. In the case of slaves, slave owners were responsible for marriages and could cancel them for breeding or sale purposes. This led many to say that African Americans had many partners and were promiscuous. That should ring a disturbing bell.

How did past prohibitions break down? What happened in Hawaii that scared state legislatures so much? What do the anti-gay marriage laws mean, and should we all move to Vermont? Is it possible that courts will one day say that you cannot deny rights to one part of the population that you freely give to another? Rest assured, they have done it in the past.

The Rise and Fall of Laws Banning Marriage Between the Races

There was a time when it was the marriage of slaves that was not recognized by the majority white society. When the slaves were freed and the Fourteenth Amendment to the United States Constitution was passed, African Americans were guaranteed equal access to the laws of the country, specifically voting laws, but also marriage laws.

However, to prevent an intermingling of races, also regarded as distasteful to the conservative majority, states passed laws banning marriage between the white and black races. It is the states, not the federal government, that regulate the laws of marriage. Remember that, it will be important later on.

Over the course of time, these anti-miscegenation laws fell into disuse, were ignored and overturned. One of the last states to have a law on the books that banned such marriages was the Commonwealth of Virginia, ironically the home of Thomas Jefferson, who is believed to have sired children with one of his slaves (who then became slaves themselves). The Virginia statute made mixed marriages null and void in the state.

You would think that "null and void" was good enough punishment. But the Virginia lawmakers were really upset by the thought that anyone would choose do this, so they went one step further and stated that anyone who entered into a mixed marriage was subject to criminal prosecution and imprisonment.[1] Marrying a person of the "colored" race was a felony and called for a prison term of one to five years. In the commonwealth of Jeffersonian

1. "If any white person and colored person shall go out of this State, for the purpose of being married, and with the intention of returning, and be married out of it, and afterwards return and reside in it, cohabiting as man and wife, they shall be punished...."

heritage, sex between the races was apparently one thing, but marriage quite another.

In 1958, Virginia Jeter and Richard Loving, a couple of mixed race, celebrated a wedding in the District of Columbia and set up home in Virginia. Under Virginia's statute, the two were charged with a crime, and in early 1959, they plead guilty. The trial judge was not happy. He explained that his decision was based on the fact that what the Lovings did by getting married violated God's intentions for marriage. "Almighty God created the races white, black, yellow, malay and red and he placed them on separate continents. And but for the interference of man with his arrangement there would be no cause for such marriages. The fact the he separated the races shows that he did not intend for the races to mix."

The judge meant business, and for their crime he sentenced the Lovings to one year in jail. However, rather then send them to prison for their marriage, the judge suspended their sentence. That suspension was based on their *banishment* – the judge ordered that the couple must leave their home and not darken the landscape of the Virginia Commonwealth for a period of twenty-five years. This case had everything: love, sex, crime, punishment – even banishment. The only thing he didn't do was smite them.

The Lovings followed the judge's advice and left Virginia for the more welcoming confines of Washington, D.C., where in 1963 they set into motion a fight to set aside their sentence and judgment. When the case got to a state trial judge, he refused to set aside the sentences, and so everyone got up and went to the Supreme Court.

The Lovings said that the Virginia statute went against the Fourteenth Amendment by denying them, as an integrated couple, equal access to marriage laws. To read that amendment, you would think that it would be pretty difficult to argue against the Lovings. "All persons born or naturalized in the United States and subject to the jurisdiction thereof, are citizens of the United States and of the State wherein they reside. No State shall make or enforce any law which shall abridge the privileges or immunities of citizens of the United States; nor shall any State deprive any person of life, liberty, or property, without due process of law; nor deny to any person within its jurisdiction the equal protection of the laws."

But the state of Virginia argued that marriage is a state, not federal, matter, and therefore there was no jurisdiction over a matter of marriage by federal law. The state further stated that they did not violate the Fourteenth Amendment because the law punished both blacks and whites, not just blacks, and therefore it was being applied even-handedly. Apparently, someone thought that was logical. The Supreme Court did not. While the Court agreed with the fact that states do get to regulate marriage, they said that power was not unlimited, particularly with regard to the Fourteenth Amendment, which most certainly did apply in this case.

That decision came down in 1967, a full eight years after the Loving's marriage. Their bond was declared legal by the Supreme Court, and their criminal convictions were reversed. They were no longer convicts of love. It was a long journey for the Lovings and for justice.

The Lovings' story is important for gay men and lesbians interested in marriage, for many reasons. The first is that the Supreme Court has gone on record as saying that the Fourteenth Amendment to the Constitution does not preclude the federal government from stepping on the toes of the states' regulation of marriage where a matter of equal access is concerned. Will the courts then say that equal access means equal access by people of the same sex? The second important lesson of the Lovings is that the wheels of justice move slowly. We may have to wait many years to find out what the courts say about equal access to the rights of marriage by lesbians and gays.

The last state to have anti-miscegenation laws on the books was Alabama. The laws were not just statutes; the law was part of the Alabama constitution. In 1999 the state senate voted to amend the constitution by repealing that part of it, which occurred in the following year, 2000, just in time to welcome the twenty-first century. The Loving case occurred forty years before. In the meantime, what progress has there been towards allowing lesbians and gays to tie the knot?

Gays and Lesbians Sue for the Right to Marry

For many years, the legalization of gay marriage was debated in this country, but without any serious prospect that it might, in fact, happen. So no one was very motivated to do anything about it. After all, during most of the second half of the twentieth century, most gay people would not even publicly admit to being gay. Most people in the United States did not admit to even knowing a homosexual, much less knowing one who wanted to be married as one. Gay marriage of any kind, as much as fanatics on either side of the argument might talk and write about it, simply did not appear as a real issue. In short, it wasn't conceivable. No one seriously entertained the notion.

The first attempt to do so through the U.S. courts came in Minnesota, when two men applied for a marriage license and were denied. They made their case that they were being denied equal protection of the laws. The court, however, said that they were not being denied equal protection, because the law had been clearly drawn up with men and women in mind. Additionally, the court said, the purpose of marriage was to procreate – everyone knew that after all, it was as old as Genesis. Again, as always, it is up to God and many judges seem to feel that they are able to speak for God.

Following that early attempt, there were others in Kentucky and Washington, sometimes with differing approaches, but always with the same result: marriage was made for one man and one woman. Today, gays and lesbians stand virtually alone in the law's disrespect for our relationships.

Nevertheless, there has been an accelerating movement in the gay and lesbian community toward creating family units. The U.S. Census reveals that the number of gay and lesbian households engaged in domestic partnership has dramatically increased over the past decade, and there are increasing numbers of children in gay families. The families are forming in spite of the law – eventually the law is going to have to deal with them.

Dealing with them is just what happened in Hawaii. A little group of islands taken over by the United States and eventually annexed through statehood now threatened the shores of the very continent that took it over by launching an invasion of gay and lesbian marriages. It was payback time.

In December 1990, three couples in the state of Hawaii applied for marriage licenses. Naturally they were all denied the license on the basis that the applicant couples were of the same sex and licenses were only issued to persons of the opposite sex. Consequently they brought suit in 1991 and, as you might expect, their complaint was denied. The director of the Department of Health (the governing authority in Hawaii for marriage licenses) had made a motion to dismiss that was granted, and therefore the complaint was dismissed before getting to trial.

The couples then immediately appealed to the Hawaiian Supreme Court. That court vacated the 1991 decision to dismiss the case. The court stated that the burden of proof for the case was on the defendant (the director of the Department of Health) to show that the marriage statute of Hawaii was not unconstitutional. It was not, the court said, for the plaintiffs to prove that it was. This made a trial eventually necessary. The Hawaiian Supreme Court said that the defendants had to demonstrate that the law as it stood supported a compelling state interest and that it was narrowly drawn so as to demonstrate that there was not an infringement of constitutional rights.

Everyone then went back to the original court, and there they finally argued the case in 1996. The state health director, as defendant, argued that there was a compelling state interest to deny the couples their marriage licenses based on these reasons:

- The state must protect the health and welfare of children as well as "other persons";
- The state must "foster" procreation;
- The state must ensure that marriages made within its laws and jurisdiction are recognized by other states;
- The state must protect civil liberties from the effects of same-sex marriage

In particular, the defendant focused on the state's interest in protecting children and fostering procreation. However, even the state's witnesses admitted that homosexuals can be, and in fact are, good parents. On that point, there seemed to be little disagreement between the plaintiff's witnesses and the defendants.

The court found that there was no evidence presented that demonstrated any adverse effects resulting from same-sex marriages in Hawaii. They stated that, though there is an interest to protect the well being of children, the sexual orientation of the parent or parents does not in and of itself disqualify them from being a fit parent. They also said that while the issue of Hawaiian marriages achieving recognition in sister states was an important one, the defendant had not shown anything other than the Defense of Marriage Act in support of its contention that a vital state interest was at stake, and this was, by itself, not enough. In the end, the court said, the Department of Health had failed to present evidence that same-sex marriages threatened a state interest that required protection by the state. The court ordered that the refusal to issue a marriage license to a same-sex couple was in violation of the Hawaiian constitution and ordered the Department of Health enjoined from refusing to issue such licenses. That occurred on December 3, 1996, and for the first time signaled loudly and clearly that legal gay marriages were a real and distinct possibility. Now people got good and scared.

It would have saved a lot of time and money if that had been the end of the story, but naturally, the Department of Health appealed this ruling to the Hawaiian Supreme Court. The case, of course, took its time to get to judgment and it was December 1999 before a decision was rendered. In that time, however, politics moved with greater stealth than did the judicial process.

In the election of 1998, voters in Hawaii, as well as Alaska, approved a constitutional amendment that would block lesbian and gay marriages by reserving marriage to opposite sex couples. The measure was largely supported by religious institutions.

When the matter then came before the Supreme Court of Hawaii, there was no longer any case in existence. The lower court had found it unconstitutional to forbid same-sex couples from having a marriage license as a matter of discrimination: not allowing equal access to the laws, in this case the marriage laws – to all persons in the state of Hawaii. When the Hawaiian electorate passed an amendment defining marriage as the union of one man and one woman, the case became moot, because marriage was now constitutionally defined to exclude same-sex couples. In short, it was an extraordinary turn of events, as if a state had made it part of its own constitution to allow segregation of whites from other races.

The Hawaiian case is an example of just how far people will go to "protect" the institution of marriage and reserve its exclusivity to the heterosexual majority. What is still not clear is just what is scaring them so much.

The House that Roared – Passage of "Gay/Lesbian Marriage" in Vermont

A few days after the Hawaii Supreme Court, compelled by the state's newly amended constitution, put an end to gay marriage hopes there, the Vermont Supreme Court issued an opinion that would take the debate to a new level. It resolved issues somewhat, complicated them further, and gave hope to those who crave legal recognition for their relationships. Whereas state legislatures kicked it into high gear and stated that marriage had to be an institution restricted to one man and one woman, the courts in Vermont looked at it another way. There, the court decided to consider whether gays and lesbians as a class were being deprived of benefits given to married people – and if, therefore, gays and lesbians were not being treated equally, as required by that state's constitution.

Three couples in the state of Vermont brought a case that would come before the Supreme Court of that state in November 1998. They were not gay and lesbian activists; they were simply people who wondered why, if they were willing to make a commitment to one another, the law did not owe them the same respect that it did their parents.

Like the Hawaiian couples, they brought their suit after their applications for marriage licenses were turned down by their respective town clerks. The couples brought suit and, again to no one's surprise, just like in Hawaii, the court issued an opinion that sided with the town clerks. Their reasoning was based on the idea that marriage was intended for procreation and therefore these same sex couples could be denied marriage. This of course, does not address the fact that marriage is open to many heterosexual couples who are not capable of procreation. It was not a thoughtful decision.

When the matter came before the Supreme Court, the couples argued that the denial of a license to them violated the statute in Vermont that guided marriage as well as the clause of the Vermont Constitution that was called the Common Benefits Clause – a clause that conferred upon citizens of the state the equal protection of the law. In the United States Constitution there is a similar sounding clause, called the Equal Protection Clause of the Fourteenth Amendment. You should know, however, that the Vermont Constitution, enacted in 1777, pre-dated the United States Equal Protection Clause of the Fourteenth Amendment by almost 100 years.[2]

The Court looked first at the Vermont marriage statute and could find no hint that marriage, in its strict sense, was ever intended by anyone who wrote the statute, or by subsequent court decisions or laws affecting marriage, to be anything other than the marriage of one man to one woman. "These statutes," they said, "read as a whole, reflect the common understanding that marriage under Vermont law consists of a union between a man and a woman." That, they said, was the statutory law. Therefore, the couples were in error, and the statute guiding marriage law had not been violated when they were refused a license.

However, the court then looked at the constitutionality of the claim of the three couples – that they were not being treated equally with heterosexual couples. Married people were able to get certain benefits merely by virtue of being married: access to a spouse's medical life, and disability insurance benefits; hospital visitation; spousal support; inheritance without the existence of a valid will by virtue of the laws of intestacy; tax benefits; and many other protections of the law. By denying same sex couples in committed relationships the same access to those laws, they argued, there was a violation of the Common Benefits Clause of the Vermont Constitution. They were not getting equal access to the law.

On this point, the Vermont Supreme Court unanimously agreed. However, since they had already said that marriage was contemplated by their marriage statute to be an institution between one man and one woman, they did not direct that the couples should be able to become married. Rather, they compelled the legislature of the State of Vermont to find a way to extend these same privileges to all Vermonters, not just heterosexually married ones. The court did not say how this should happen – the "how" was up to the legislature. The "why" was up to the court.

In the wake of the court decision, the legislature of Vermont drew up a bill for consideration that would extend spousal benefits under a new institution, one that was not marriage, but a special, legally recognized domestic partnership

---

2. The Fourteenth Amendment to the United States Constitution was not part of the original document, but an amendment passed by states after the Civil War, and so it came 100 years after the Vermont version, which was part of the original Vermont Constitution in 1777.

between same-sex couples. This was not the kind of domestic partnership already passed in many of the nation's municipalities, but a nearly full-blown reflection of the institution of marriage. Six months later, in April 2000, the legislature passed such a law, as mandated by the court, and Vermont Governor Howard Dean signed the bill into law.

The bill's First Section is the most respectful language ever written into law regarding the status of gay and lesbian citizens. In Section 1, under enumerating legislative findings, the bill reads that

- The state has a strong interest in promoting stable and lasting families, including families based upon a same-sex couple.
- Without the legal protections, benefits, and responsibilities associated with civil marriage, same sex couples suffer numerous obstacles and hardships.
- Despite longstanding social and economic discrimination, many gay and lesbian Vermonters have formed lasting, caring and faithful relationships with persons of their same sex. These couples live together, participate in their communities together, and some raise children and care for family members together, just as do couples who are married under Vermont law.

At midnight on July 1, 2000, the law went into effect. In Brattleboro, Vermont, the town clerk opened her office. Shortly thereafter, Kathleen Peterson and Carolyn Conrad stood together before a justice of the peace and exchanged their vows. They then became the first same-sex couple in American history to gain the same recognition by a state government as a heterosexual couple, acquiring almost all of the rights conferred by a state to heterosexual married couples. This includes rights of inheritance, state tax filings, and medical decision-making, among others. It was a moment of enormous historical significance in the history of lesbians and gays.

Do Gays and Lesbians Need Marriage?

Is marriage in the gay and lesbian community needed? Many in the gay and lesbian community have questioned the need for any recognition of their relationships through marriage at all. Why emulate heterosexual institutions – why try to become what they are? Many feel we should create our own separate and distinct family units.

Judy Moats is an attorney in Fairfax, Virginia, with a large lesbian and gay clientele. She represents couples in devising live-together agreements and parenting documents and she sees all kinds of families developing. She questions whether conventional marriage is the kind of institution the lesbian and gay community needs. "If we really looked at what we want, we want to be treated as the primary person in the life of another – meaning we inherit, we can make medical decisions, that our retirement benefits go to the other. If we could define what we really want, do we really want marriage? When a couple enters into a marriage contract, it is really a hell of a lot of pages in a code book in every state. Those are conditions that people agree to and they don't even know it." She proposes that marriage might be more survivable if we could design it, rather than enter into a preset series of conditions drawn up in a one-size-fits all law.

"If we had a registry system that allowed you to check off what rights you want with your partner – that might be a good way to do it," she says. "There is a lot of evolution going in marriage. We should just tack onto it and let people enter into the kind of contract they want. They should extend the whole thing to be beyond two people. Families don't need to be two adults and children – it should extend to other adults who are part of the family and should be eligible for health-insurance benefits and the like."

Even in the heterosexual community, the 1960s saw a rapidly increasing number of people who did not feel that the mere validity offered their relationship by a marriage certificate stood for anything at all. Men and women began to live together in unprecedented numbers without marching down any aisle and without registering themselves with any governmental entity. By some, this was commonly referred to as "living in sin." Today, you would be hard pressed to find people who would use that phrase to describe two heterosexual people living together.

The last few decades have also seen a lack of commitment to marriage, as expressed through the divorce rate in the United States. In the 1960s, only one in four marriages ended in divorce. By the 1990s fully one-half of all marriages were dissolving. And that is the state of heterosexual marriage *without* the destructive influence of gay marriages. That's what they've managed all on their own. You would think that given that track record, conservative legislators would be thrilled to see people – any kind of people – agitating for the stabilizing institution of marriage. It is a mystery why they are fighting it so much – if they would stop and think about it, they'd realize that maybe they need our help.

But for many people it is a big deal. Marriage not only establishes legitimacy in the eyes of society – the statement that a relationship has the validity of law – but it also conveys important legal rights. There are benefits in areas of tax, joint ownership, inheritance, social security survivor rights, decision-making for the ill, as well as in the fact that a spouse has standing to sue on behalf of a married partner. For gay and lesbian couples, there is a lack of legal respect for their relationships that results not only in emotional hurt and damage, but serious consequences to their financial well being. Marriage is a legal contract that confers rights and responsibilities to the parties who enter that contract and provides benefits to them. Whether it is written by the legislature or configured in a way envisioned by Judy Moats, whether you think marriage is important or not, whether you want legal validity or not, any legal system that allows one group of people access to benefits denied to another group is discrimination plain and simple. It is a system that needs fixing.

Current Events – Marriage Lite

There are some similarities between laws against interracial marriage and laws that forbid persons of the same sex to marry, and there are also some big differences. The Loving case discussed earlier in this chapter pretty much did away with those anti-marriage laws. But for gays and lesbians, it is going to take more than one court case; it is going to take years of talent, resources, and dedication.

Today in the United States, there are only two legal ways for gays and lesbians to get some recognition under the law. Those two ways involve either formation of a domestic partnership or entry into a legally recognized civil union. But there are other ways for couples to gain some marriage rights, including writing live-together agreements. Some couples may feel quite married simply by writing mutual wills, powers of attorney, signing a live-together agreement and changing their names to a combined hyphenated name (for name change information, see Chapter 6). But none of these means of obtaining greater rights for your relationship, either alone or in combination, are on a completely equal footing with marriage. While a combination of these tactics may get you many of the rights that married people have, you will not have all of them. For now, you will just have to settle for Marriage Lite.

Domestic Partnerships and Legal Unions

The troubles caused to gays and lesbians by the forbidding of marriage became very clear during the 1980s. Among other things, the AIDS epidemic highlighted the plight of unmarried partners who needed to negotiate a medical system that was sometimes callous to their needs. A same-sex couple had no legal rights to visitation in a hospital, particularly in strictly enforced intensive-care wards, much less the right or opportunity to make medical decisions for a partner who had become incapable of making his own. This situation wasn't confined to HIV; it is true of lesbian women with breast cancer or of any gay or lesbian or bisexual partner who meets with a serious accident. But the AIDS epidemic accentuated it to an unprecedented degree. As a result of the massive upheaval in gay households wrought by the epidemic, and as a result of forward thinking people, small cracks in the opposition to gay unions began to appear when employers began to offer domestic partners the same benefits under insurance plans offered to married partners. There grew such a need that something had to be done.

It might seem like a crazy idea in the middle of an epidemic that brought catastrophic disease to gay households. On the one hand, it was very expensive for companies when employees suddenly fell ill with a devastating illness and insurance had to cover multiple hospitalizations and expensive medications. In fact, small employers who began to suffer high numbers of employees with AIDS had to face higher premiums and policy cancellations. There was a time when many insurers would not even offer insurance coverage to small businesses that were considered to be "at risk" – meaning that they had a substantial number of gay employees, such as florists or hairdressers. Why then would large companies suddenly act against all apparent logic and offer domestic-partner coverage to same-sex couples? Many were motivated to do so because they were in geographical areas that had been highly affected by the epidemic and they wanted to do something they felt was the right thing to do – an exercise of good corporate responsibility. However, other early pioneers were not in epicenters of the epidemic; they were merely doing something that they thought was right.

The movement to cover domestic partners under the insurance plans of gay employees began in the private sector. The New York paper *The Village Voice*, Ben and Jerry's ice cream, and Lotus software were some of the pioneers. There was not only surprise because of the controversial nature of extending coverage, but because it seemed counter-intuitive in some respects. At the height of an epidemic that was ravaging the gay community with a costly and deadly disease, the thought of extending coverage to include more gay people in your insurance plan while other companies were being sued for trying to dump expensive gay employees seemed positively ludicrous. However, companies discovered that the cost was actually not very high. While there was a higher cost associated with HIV care, there was also a high cost associated with childbirth in heterosexual couples. As the labor market tightened in the latter part of the 1990s, domestic partner coverage became a perk that many employers embraced, not out of philosophical conviction as much as because it helped with employee retention.

Types of Domestic Partnerships

Domestic partner coverage began on two levels: one in which an employer would extend coverage to an employee's unmarried domestic partner, and the other in which municipalities would extend domestic partner status to non-married co-habiting people. Each offered different types of breakthroughs with a different kind of privilege attached to them.

Employer-Sponsored Domestic Partnerships. To date, hundreds of employers, private companies, universities, labor unions, offer their gay and lesbian employees domestic-partner coverage. In fact, it is interesting to note that heterosexual corporate America offered domestic partner coverage before many gay and lesbian organizations and even before many AIDS service organizations. Beyond the private sector, universities, and municipal and county employers followed suit. Coverage is now so widespread that approximately one-fifth of the Fortune 500 companies offer domestic-partner coverage. By the late spring of 2000, General Motors, Ford and Daimler-Chrysler jointly announced that they would provide domestic partner health care coverage for their gay and lesbian employees, an action that sent a huge message in times of tight employment. While one may not think of the big three auto manufacturers as gay and lesbian enclaves, they are thought of as somewhat conservative in their employment approaches, and it is indicative of the fact that domestic partnerships have entered the mainstream employment market big time.

The benefits of employer sponsored domestic partnership will depend on the employer, but they can include all of the benefits that are available to a married spouse. This would potentially include

- insurance coverage
- pension benefits
- leave for bereavement
- family and medical leave

The existence of these benefits will vary. Remember that they are employer generated and are a perk, so what one employer offers may not be what another offers.

It also bears noting that just because an employer offers domestic partnership coverage doesn't mean that it will always be offered. Benefits offered are subject to change, especially if there is a merger of two companies with disparate policies on domestic partner benefits. A high profile example of this occurred when oil giants Exxon and Mobil merged to become ExxonMobil. After the merger, the domestic partnership program that had been offered by Mobil became dormant so that additional employees could not be added.

Civil Domestic Partnerships. The second type of domestic partner coverage came when various governmental jurisdictions, themselves often employers who began to extend insurance coverage for domestic partners, also began to allow unmarried couples to legally register as domestic partners – giving some limited legal status to the arrangement. The number of such cities offering this type of arrangement is small, but is not limited to gay meccas, such as Los Angeles or New York. In some cases, county governments offer domestic partnership as well as some state governments. On the other hand, in the wake of the Vermont Civil Union events, some states are itching to slate ballot measures that will outlaw civil unions or the recognizing of any form of legal gay relationship. Other cities, such as San Francisco, require it of the entities with which they contract for city business.

One of the primary effects of domestic partner registration within a municipality is to achieve a legal status that allows one partner to have hospital visitation rights with another partner. Prior to the HIV epidemic, a person in a hospital, particularly an intensive care unit, might find him or herself alone if estranged from their family, because the hospital might have a family members only policy. The restriction of domestic partners from hospital rooms is rare, but not unheard of and certainly not impossible. Therefore, registration as a domestic partner helps to limit that kind of possibility further.

There are other benefits to legal domestic partner arrangements. For example, in some municipalities, a legally recognized domestic partner can take over the lease of an apartment or have other limited rights that would automatically go to a legally married spouse.

There could be future benefits as well. In the summer of 2002, the California legislature passed a law that would permit domestic partners to inherit from one another under the laws of intestacy. If signed into law, it would be an important benefit for gays and lesbians, overcoming one of the most difficult circumstances faced by a survivor in a gay or lesbian relationship who's partner has died without a will. As gay and lesbian partners found out in the wake of September 11, dealing with the deficiencies of the law at a time when you are grief stricken can be daunting. For more information on intestacy and the how dying without a will affects a survivor, see page 124.

If you have access to the Internet, you can determine whether government sanctioned domestic partnerships are a possibility for you. Use a search engine to find the website for your municipal government. Domestic partnership information would most likely reside with the City Clerk's office. If you don't have access to the Internet, you will need to call or visit your town hall and ask the office of the City Clerk. If you live in an area with a lesbian and gay organization of any kind, you should also call them or visit their Web site.

The effects of the registration will vary greatly depending on where you live. In some jurisdictions, it may provide you with a partnership in name, but without any real effects. In others, it may mean a great deal more. For example, the city and county of San Francisco are very active in their support of domestic partnerships and require that contractors with the city offer similar benefits to domestic partners as to the spouses of employees.

Creating and Dissolving Domestic Partnerships

If you do choose to avail yourself of domestic partner status, the process for doing so is simple. If the coverage is with your employer, you simply register with your human resources department during open enrollment time.

If you are registering as domestic partners with a municipality, however, there may be a more formal registration process that entails filing an affidavit with the proper civil authorities. Use of the law will depend on how the city ordinance is drawn up, and you can get that information from the City Clerk's office. In general, you will have to file an affidavit of domestic partnership that will register your household as such. The affidavit will cover a brief overview of your domestic bliss, affirming that you

- live in a mutual relationship;
- share a residence or primary residence;
- that you are of the age of majority; and
- are a resident of the jurisdiction in which you are seeking partnership status.

You may also have to state that you are not related by blood, that you are not currently in another registered domestic partnership and that you are not married. There may be a waiting period between any previous Domestic Partnership arrangement and the one you are currently seeking. There may be other timing requirements. Some statutes, such as the ordinance for San Francisco Domestic Partnerships, may allow the county or city clerk to perform a ceremony for the couple, though it is not required.

Methods for dissolving a domestic partnership also vary by jurisdiction. Domestic partnership ends when one of the parties dies, when a certificate or affidavit of dissolution is filed, when a partner gets legally married, or when the residence is no longer shared.

Limitations and Drawbacks of Domestic Partnership

There are issues connected with using this coverage. One that is not so obvious has to do with the fact that there can be tax implications for covering a domestic partner. *If your employer is providing legal benefits that not only extend to you, but also to your partner, then those benefits can be taxed.*

For many who would like to use domestic partner benefits, there is the more obvious consideration that in order to cover your domestic partner, you have to be ready, willing and able to declare to your employer that you in fact have a domestic partner. For a lot of people, that means that you come out of the closet at work. For some people, this is easier said than done. And while it is unlikely that you have an employer who is enlightened enough to offer domestic partnership and yet fires you for being gay, it is conceivable that you may have a supervisor or co-worker who now treats you differently because it is known that you are using domestic partnership benefits. If you feel you are discriminated against as a result, you need to be aware that you may not be living in a jurisdiction where discrimination against gays and lesbians is illegal (see chapter 5). That may seem ironic – and the irony doesn't end there. Many companies or municipalities that offer domestic partner benefits reside in states where sodomy is illegal under state law. So while your partner can be covered by your insurance, your lovemaking may still be against the law (see chapter 8).

The biggest drawback of all, of course, is that domestic partnership is not marriage – it is not even marriage lite. Still, it has made religious conservatives nervous and caused boycotts of many of the companies who offered domestic partner benefits. But that was nothing compared to what was afoot in the courts when gay and lesbian couples dared to ask for a marriage license.

Domestic partner registration should in no way be confused with the Civil Unions that are possible under Vermont law. That is like comparing cutting your toe nails to major surgery. Still, the limited legal recognition that was offered early on by municipal governments was the first legal recognition by any jurisdiction in the United States for same-sex couples.

The Law for Civil Union

The State of Vermont is currently the only state in the Union that has offered something that is a marriage equivalent for gay and lesbian couples. The Civil Union law goes much further than any domestic partnership law and very nearly affords a couple any of the rights and responsibilities offered under marriage. Pure and simple, a civil union in Vermont has nearly all of the benefits of marriage, though there are some factors involved that keep it from being marriage in every respect.

It is generally recognized that states will recognize and enforce one another's laws, so that a heterosexual couple who marries in North Dakota is still recognized as married when they go to visit South Dakota. There is little question that the creation of civil unions in the state of Vermont will raise difficult and thorny questions for Vermont's forty-nine other colleagues in the United States, precisely for the reason that they do recognize each other's laws. For the present time, it is safe to assume that if you go to Vermont and obtain a civil union, when you leave Vermont, your beautiful cloak of union will magically turn back to the drab every day, garments you wore as singles, like Cinderella after the ball. What you get from the Vermont Civil Union law is the right to be "nearly" married, but only in the state of Vermont. This is a matter being litigated currently in some states where couples are suing to force their state to recognize their Vermont Civil Union.

But for gay couples who enter into a civil union and who live in Vermont, virtually all of the rights offered by the state to heterosexual marriages also apply to same-sex civil unions. That means that you can adopt, child custody matters will be decided accordingly, you may inherit from one another, you can jointly file state taxes, you can receive spousal benefits from state benefits programs, you will have to divorce to dissolve the union, you can jointly own property, and you can make medical decisions for one another, and have access to each other's medical records. In fact, even laws that keep spouse from having to testify against spouse in a criminal proceeding – all of these and more apply to couples who enter a civil union. Bottom line, the law that was signed into law was required by the court to afford lesbian and gay citizens all of the rights and responsibilities that heterosexuals have under marriage laws, except that they couldn't call it "marriage."

This is drastically different from any previous ability of gay couples to enter into domestic partnership arrangements with municipalities. It is not a light step into living together; it is marriage with all of the rights and responsibilities. If you do it, understand that you are undertaking a very serious legal obligation.

Creating a Civil Union. If you decide that this is for you, then doing it is pretty easy. You only have to file an Application for Vermont License of Civil Union and fork over $20. The form will ask for your names, residence, birthplaces, parents' names (don't worry, they won't call them), educational background, race, and whether either party has been married or has had a previous civil union. If you want a certified copy of your civil union certificate, you need to pay an additional $7. For all the emotional cost there has been to lesbians and gays in the past by not being able to get married, the cost to get married is now only $27. It's a bargain.

The steps to a civil union are:

- Apply for a license from a town clerk where either party resides, or if you are not a Vermont resident, then any port in a storm – any town clerk should issue a license;
- Go to a justice of the peace, judge or clergy member and have the license certified by them;
- Commit to one another before that official (in other words, have the ceremony) within sixty days after the license was issued by the town clerk – the officiating party will certify the license;
- File it – the officiating party must file the license.

There are no requirements for medical or blood tests and, as mentioned above, there currently are no requirements of long-term residency, though that may change at some point in the future. Current restrictions on civil unions are the same as they are for any other marriage. You have to be mentally competent, and you have to at least eighteen years of age and not under anyone's guardianship. You also cannot enter into a civil union with a member of your family (this, of course, is better known as incest).

For additional information about forming a civil union in Vermont, consult with the Secretary of State of Vermont Web site, which is listed in the Resources section of this book.

Dissolving a Civil Union. What would marriage be without divorce? Like marriage, civil unions can be dissolved, and the court that does so is the same as the court for marriage – the Vermont family court.

A note of caution for those out-of-staters who have rushed or will rush to Vermont in order to obtain a Vermont Civil Union. While your state may not legally recognize your union, Vermont will not legally recognize any dissolution other than their own. In addition, the state in which you reside may find that it lacks the legal authority to do away with a civil union granted in Vermont. In 2002, a couple in Connecticut tried to have that state nullify their union – it didn't work. It is certainly a quandary, because while your state may not recognize your union, it won't interfere by dissolving it either. In other words, this is not something you can just walk away from. Tearing up the papers doesn't tear up the union. You can only dissolve the civil union in Vermont if one of you are living there at the time of the union dissolution, and a long vacation there won't do the trick. In fact, to bring the dissolution, one party must have resided in the state for six months, and for the court to grant it, the party must have resided there for a year. Like a divorce, there will have to be a division of property and decisions about custody issues regarding children. You may want to set this out ahead of time by writing a pre-nuptial agreement. Or, like most other married couples, you may just trust that your love will last and that whatever happens, you will work it out. But dissolution of a civil union is not like dissolving or walking away from a domestic partner benefit at work, or registration with a municipality. Just like regular marriage, to end a civil union, you are going to have to get a divorce, in this case called a dissolution. By late 2002, nearly five thousand couples had sought and obtained a civil union under the Vermont law, with family courts having dissolved only ten. While those statistics rate better than for heterosexual marriages, like marriage, it is easier to get married than it is to get divorced. The Vermont legislature may amend the law at some point in the future to consider the complications for out-of-staters. For more on divorce, see chapter 3.

Limitations of the Law. The Vermont Civil Union law is an incredible development and is very nearly a state of marriage. However, it is not an institution that completely crosses the marriage line. There are still limitations that were not under the control of the state legislature when it passed the bill. It is worth repeating that the law is only valid in Vermont. If a couple is bound by civil union in Vermont, that relationship is not recognized as legal anywhere else – even if you both reside in Vermont. If, on the other hand, a heterosexual couple gets married in Vermont, that relationship is recognized everywhere – that is one very important difference between marriage and civil unions.

Does that mean that out-of-state folks can't go to Vermont and have a civil union? Hey, it's a free country – sort of! Yes, anyone can certainly go to Vermont and have a civil union ceremony under that state's law. However, when you go home, your state will not recognize that union. When a couple undergoes a civil union in Vermont and then goes to Niagara Falls for a honeymoon, guess what – they are single again when they get to Niagara Falls. If it were marriage, it would be recognized in other states. One necessarily wonders whether other states would be forced to recognize Vermont's law and this is a battle not yet fully determined. Certainly non-Vermonters can go and have a civil union ceremony there, but when they go home, their state will not recognize it without a legal fight, and even then, the case may be thrown out. No one has won such a case yet.

Another limitation involves taxes. The state legislature of Vermont cannot tell the federal government what to do. While state taxes may be jointly filed in the state of Vermont, when it comes to federal taxes, the couple will have no more rights than they had before their civil union.

Nevertheless, they will still have all of the other rights married couples have: the right to inherit from one another, make medical decisions, adopt, and yes, even the right to divorce.

On the day following the law's effect and the first ceremonies, on July 2, 2000, several town clerks and their assistants handed in their resignations, saying that they could not morally issue such a license. The law provoked an enormous reaction in Vermont and has become the subject of hot debate. Legislators who voted for it found themselves targeted by reactionary groups who worked to have them removed from office. The existence of the statute galvanized opponents of gays and lesbians throughout the state and beyond. There will most certainly be attempts to repeal the law, calling into question how those who entered into the civil union would be treated by the law were the institution to be repealed. The Vermont Civil Union law is a foothold in the struggle for equal marriage rights, but how strong a foothold remains to be seen.

But there is little question that the court case that occurred in Hawaii spurred an enormous amount of action and reaction. Real action took place in Vermont. Inevitably, reaction took place in Washington, D.C., and several state capitals.

Doomed by DOMA – The Defense of Marriage Act

> "No State, territory, or possession of the United States, or Indian tribe, shall be required to give effect to any public act, record, or judicial proceeding of any other State, territory, possession, or tribe respecting a relationship between persons of the same sex that is treated as a marriage under the laws of such other State, territory, possession, or tribe, or a right or claim arising from such relationship."
>
> Section 2 of DOMA

Under the United States Constitution, there is something called the "Full Faith and Credit" clause which requires states to recognize the "acts, records and proceedings" of other states in the union. Without it, there could be some degree of chaos, and we would be something close to the "Dis-United States" were there to be a failure of states to respect one another's laws. For example, the state of Virginia might not recognize the inter-racial marriage that was performed in Illinois. People married in one state would not be considered married in another. The driver's license that you got in Wisconsin could become invalid the second you drive over the state line. The Full Faith and Credit Clause keeps the lid on chaos and recognizes that there is a national interest in high levels of cooperation among the states.

However, the Defense of Marriage Act (DOMA) seeks to make an end run around this clause of the constitution by creating an exception. DOMA is a federal law passed by the United States Congress that ensures that states have the right to pass laws that refuse to recognize same-sex marriages that may have been performed in sister states. In this way, if the Hawaiian case had been decided in favor of the plaintiffs and the citizens of Hawaii had not amended their constitution with the prohibition against gay and lesbian marriages, then Hawaii would have recognized that persons of the same sex had the right to apply for a marriage license. Hawaiian gay and lesbian couples would then have been allowed to be married under the law of that state. Like other Hawaiians, when they left that state and traveled to California, their marriage would have to be recognized. This prospect was positively terrifying. Therefore Congress crafted DOMA, which would allow states to "opt out" from the Full Faith and Credit Clause of the constitution with respect the issue of gay marriage. Whether that is constitutional remains untested. It isn't really logical.

What would happen if a particular state suddenly passed a law that said it would no longer recognize the driver's licenses of gay people from any state and that, therefore, gay people were barred from driving through that state? Both driver's licenses and marriage are regulated by the states, and whatever romantic and holy notions heterosexual legislators attach to the state of marriage, legally it is no different from a driver's license. The notion that a state would cease to recognize driver's licenses of gay people from sister states strikes one as ridiculous. That's because it is. That is also why DOMA sounds ridiculous. Then why wouldn't it be considered unconstitutional? Logically, it should be, but the current U.S. Supreme Court is not immune from making decisions that are more political than legal when considering equal rights.[3]

3. History provides us with some sad examples – the Dred Scott decision in 1857 essentially declared that slavery was constitutional; the Koramatsu case of 1944 declared that the internment of Japanese-Americans into concentration camps was constitutional; the Hardwick case of 1986 declared that acts of sex of homosexuals were not private enough to be included in the right to privacy (though it said nothing about heterosexual sex), and then, of course, there is the recent case of *Bush v. Gore* which appointed George W. Bush as the president of the United States.

Even without DOMA, several states rushed to declare gay marriages illegal, with Utah crossing the finishing line first when it passed its anti-marriage law in 1995. Interestingly, of the ten states with the highest rates of divorce, nine of them had passed state laws protecting their shaky marriages against gays and lesbians. Of the ten states with the lowest divorce rates, there are only a few that have passed such laws.

On the whole, however, faced with the possible success of the court actions brought in Hawaii and Vermont, state legislatures became very active very quickly in legislatively defining marriage as an institution between one man and one woman only. This thereby precluded any necessity of having to recognize a marriage from another state as a legal marriage if performed between persons of the same gender. Given the political safety of taking such a position and the fierce attachment among the general public to the idea that marriage among same sex individuals is immoral, it is likely that the list will continue to grow. The following states have enacted laws refusing to recognize marriage as being in any other form than that between a single man and a single woman.

States Forbidding Same-Sex Marriages

Alabama	Kentucky	Pennsylvania
Alaska	Louisiana	South Carolina
Arizona	Maine	South Dakota
Delaware	Michigan	Tennessee
Florida	Minnesota	Utah
Georgia	Mississippi	Virginia
Idaho	Montana	Washington
Illinois	Nevada	
Indiana	North Carolina	
Iowa	North Dakota	*Source:*
Kansas	Oklahoma	*Human Rights Campaign*

DOMA tried to jump the gun on the possibility that any state would lose their legislative minds and pass a law authorizing gays and lesbians to marry by setting out to define the meaning of "marriage" as "a legal union between one man and one woman as husband and wife" and to define "spouse" as a member of the opposite sex. DOMA makes these definitions in order to ensure that any federal benefits that are open to married couples, such as the joint filing of taxes and social security survivors or veterans benefits, would not be open to people of the same sex who married under any state law that recognized same-sex marriage. The legislation was overwhelmingly passed in the House of Representatives and in the Senate by a vote of 84–14 on September 10, 1996.[4] President Clinton signed it into law. It should be noted that

Attorney General John Ashcroft, who was then a senator representing the state of Missouri, was one of the sponsors of the bill in the Senate. With DOMA and the state laws that were found legal under its auspices, there has not been so much government-sponsored hysteria and paranoia since the infamous McCarthy era of the 1950s, when government acted and overreacted to the possibility of communist infiltration and behaved in ways that today are regarded as nothing less than irresponsible.

The existence of DOMA leaves us with a begging question. If the Supreme Court could strike down anti-miscegenation laws in Virginia because they defined marriage as being a relationship only between one person of one race and one person of the same race, how can DOMA, defining marriage as being a relationship only between one person of one sex and one person of another sex? In other words, is it more illegal to discriminate against a couple because of race than it is to discriminate against a couple because of sex (as opposed to sexual preference)? The very last line of the Supreme Court's decision in the *Loving v. Virginia* case was as follows: "Under our Constitution, the freedom to marry, or not marry, a person of another race resides with the individual and cannot be infringed by the State." Substitute the words "another race" with the words "same sex."

Lorri Jean, former executive director of the National Gay and Lesbian Task Force (NGLTF) believes that DOMA may have been the greatest setback ever dealt to lesbian and gay rights. "DOMA gave 'permission' to the anti-gay initiatives that are currently under way. They started against gay marriage, but have broadened into all fronts, and this is taking away energy from all of our resources. It is not a question of whether we are included in equal protection laws. The truly damning effect of DOMA is that it enshrined anti-gay discrimination into the law."

DOMA leaves some serious questions as to how gay and lesbian unions will be undertaken when so many laws have been constructed to prevent them. The questions may take a while to resolve. Until then, there are other options for couples who seek the shelter of the law to protect their relationships.

Live-Together Agreements

Domestic partnerships, either in the civil capacity or at work, get you some limited legal rights. However, one area where your rights are undefined is in respect to your treatment of each other and how you run your household. Remember that

4. The 14 members of the Senate who voted against DOMA were Daniel Akaka (Hawaii), Barbara Boxer (California), Russell Feingold (Wisconsin), Dianne Feinstein (California), Daniel Inouye (Hawaii), Edward Kennedy (Massachusetts), Robert Kerrey (Nebraska), John Kerry (Massachusetts), Carol Moseley-Braun (Illinois), Daniel Moynihan (New York), Claiborne Pell (Rhode Island), Charles Robb (Virginia), Paul Simon (Illinois), and Ron Wyden (Oregon).

marriage is really nothing more than a contract that is sanctioned by the state. If that marriage dissolves, there is a ready formula in state law for how property gets divided. But when a gay or lesbian couple break up, there are no guidelines in law, at least none as specific as divorce laws.

However, Live-Together Agreements of this nature are not necessarily confined to matters of breakups; otherwise this discussion would have been moved to Chapter 3. Writing a Live-Together Agreement puts on paper what you each understand to be the nature of your relationship.

What Live-Together Agreements Accomplish. A Live-Together Agreement is a seriously non-romantic document that is just what it says it is. If marriage is a dressed up contract, a live-together agreement is the naked version. It is a contractual agreement between two people that states how they are going to live together and deals primarily with matters of finance. The act of putting together a Live-Together Agreement means that both parties to the contract go into it with a fairly certain expectation of one another, at least regarding finances. The function of an agreement is to spell out what you each expect from your relationship for the purpose of protecting one another should conditions change. In that respect, as much as possible, you will need to anticipate those changes should you decide to enter into one.

Even though you can address many aspects of your relationship within a contract and even consider future events, your contract will not be an institution of marriage. It may look like marriage, and it may smell like marriage, but if you need to go to court over your agreement, you will be going to civil court, not to family court. As you will learn in chapter 3, the two are very different.

Deciding if You Need an Agreement. Your first step in approaching a Live-Together Agreement is deciding whether you really need one at all. Not every couple needs to have one. It is often a function of your economic situation, how much you have, how much you each earn, and whether both of you are working. In large part, a Live-Together Agreement is simply about economics and trying to address economic disparities.

Frederick Hertz, an Oakland, is a legal expert and author on gay and lesbian relationships. “A live together agreement is not the be all and end all,” he says. “If a couple have economic lives that are very simple and they don’t have a lot of money, or if they are sharing everything fifty-fifty, a written agreement is generally not required.” An example of a very simple economic existence would be a couple renting an apartment who between them do not have a lot of assets. “However, if their situation changes and a couple begins to accumulate a significant amount of property, or is purchasing a house, or where their contributions to the household are anything other than fifty-fifty, then I strongly recommend a written agreement."

Another factor to consider is whether the earning parity between partners is unbalanced. When there is such a disparity between partners – for example if one is well off and earning the money, while the other is taking care of kids and staying at home or taking a part-time job, then a written agreement becomes potentially very important.

However, there are alternatives to agreements that Hertz recommends. "You can decide, for example, to create a reserve account that is in the name of a dependent partner that is contributed to over time by both of the partners. In that way, if there is a break up, the dependent partner walks away with funds with which he or she can start over. Or if a person is living in a house owned by another,[5] then a set aside of funding each month will provide an ability for the non-owner to relocate should the need ever arise."

The factors that make you decide whether you need an agreement are obviously going to inform the content of your agreement, as will the issues you want to address when you write the agreement.

What Goes into Your Agreement. There are many elements of domestic life that can be included. Like a Power of Attorney (see chapter 4), you can make an agreement that is very broad in its content, or very narrow and focused.

Most obviously, you will need to consider property. If you both own real estate, you can agree to either keep property jointly or separately. If you are pooling your assets to purchase items that fall outside of real property, such as a car, you may want to spell out how that property would be sorted out in the event of a break up. Or, it may be that one of you wants to buy the furniture that you use while the other purchases support for the house (e.g., utilities, and food).

Though an agreement can be about property, there are also rights and responsibilities that can be sorted out. In fact, you may not want to talk about property at all in your agreement, but rather to record your agreement about who is going to do what in the household. For example, you can agree that one of the members of the couple is going to be responsible for particular efforts – such as homemaking – as well as spell out the support that partner would receive from the other in return, such as funding for education. In particular, in making a major purchase, such as a home or an investment property, you may wish to spell out the ownership and maintenance of the property in writing.

---

5. Many times, when one partner moves in with another in an existing house that is already owned by one, there may be a temptation to put your lover's name on the deed of your house. Talk to a lawyer first! In some states, the house will be re-appraised for taxes and, in fact, you may have to pay a rather large transfer tax.

One thing that does not go into your agreement: sex. Mentions of sexual roles or duties can imply a contract that exchanges money or security for sex. That is called prostitution, and would be considered illegal.

How to Create an Agreement. If you and your partner decide that an agreement is something you want, you may find that this is one area of law where you can sit down and work out what you want yourself. This is, after all, a contract, and you enter into contracts all the time without consulting an attorney. In his book *A Legal Guide for Lesbian and Gay Couples*, Frederick Hertz has supplied forms for Live-Together Agreements for a variety of purposes. If, however, you feel that your situation may be complex, it may then be best to consult an attorney. This is particularly true if your situation involves children and rights and responsibilities that you want to address (see chapter 2, Parenting Agreements).

If you do decide that an agreement is best for your relationship, don't make it an oral agreement. Oral contracts are difficult to prove and can be colored by charged emotions. If you have a need for an agreement, put it in writing. At the time of a breakup, one of the parties may try to assert an oral contract, because there is nothing in writing. Though breakups are discussed in Chapter 3, you should know that Minnesota, New York and Texas require a written agreement in order to make a claim regarding the relationship (see chapter 3, Palimony).

If you decide to use a lawyer, you actually should have more than one – i.e., just as in a divorce case, each party needs to be represented by his or her own counsel. That may sound more complicated than it is worth, but it assures that you are each coming to the table as independent parties and keeps at bay any appearance that it was an unfair deal.

How Agreements Differ from Pre-Nuptials. Live-Together Agreements are similar to, but not the same as, another non-romantic document that straight people call a "pre-nup," short for prenuptial agreement. For a Live-Together Agreement, you are drawing up a document because you *can't* get married. For a pre-nup, you are drawing up a document because you *can* get married. Big difference.

A pre-nup basically anticipates any issue that arises as a result of splitting up the marriage, with that opt-out clause known as divorce. It spells out an understanding ahead of time regarding any division of property. Given that, the use of a pre-nup by gay and lesbian couples is necessarily limited. However, with the new Vermont Civil Union law available to gay and lesbian couples, the pre-nup is not confined to heterosexuality anymore. Couples entering into a Vermont Civil Union could theoretically enter into their own pre-nup before taking their vows. However, given the newness of the Vermont law and the fact that many of the couples who have utilized it are out-of-state U.S. citizens, it is highly unlikely that there has been a rush by Vermont lesbian and gay citizens to form pre-nups. It is safe to say that Vermont attorneys have little, if any, experience with writing pre-nups for lesbian and gay couples who are taking their vows.

Adopting Your Partner

Some people have strong reasons for wanting the respect of the law in all ways for their relationship, and they are willing to go to almost any means to get it. One of those ways is for one partner to literally adopt the other as his or her child. Adult adoption is not impossible, though not common, and while it solves one problem (getting the benefit of a legal relationship), it could potentially create others.

The adoption of another person has serious consequences and needs to be very carefully considered given the many other options. And, of course, there are the social implications – it would be a wee bit awkward to introduce your lover as your son or daughter as well. Ugh. All jokes aside, adoption does get the law's backing for a binding legal relationship that will recognize two lovers as family, something none of the legal substitutes, such as living wills, powers of attorney or anything else short of marriage or Vermont Civil Unions, will do.

Once you adopt another person as your son or daughter, that person has an automatic right to inherit your property, and in some states, it may be impossible to disinherit a child, even an adult one. Adoption is more effective at creating "family" than marriage, because adult adoption takes marriage a step further. Unlike marriage or civil unions, you can't undo it. There is no divorce in adoption. Therefore, while you may feel you are the most in love couple in the world's history when you undertake this legal status, you may find yourselves in a difficult situation when, two years later, you can't stand the sight of each other. No matter how much you love one another, the consequence of this can be quite ugly.

There is also the unlikely criminal aspect of it all. Remembering that sodomy is still illegal in many states, consider that you may live in a state where you are not only breaking sodomy laws, but incest laws as well.

A Word About Announcements

Who married who in the town where you live? If you want to read about heterosexual couplings, you need only open the newspaper and you can see pictures and descriptions of who wore what . . . but if you want to read the latest about the hottest gay couple, like everything else, it depends on where you live. There are an increasing number of newspapers around the country that have begun to carry announcements of same-sex unions. One of the most recent, and certainly major papers to make the switch is *The New York Times* ("All the News That's Fit to Print), which began running the announcements in September 2002, and was joined in 2003 by *The Los Angeles Times*. To see whether or not your paper will cover your union, consult the Gay & Lesbian Alliance Against Defamation at www.glaad.org.

Future Directions – Recognition of Gay Marriage

In the wake of the Vermont case and subsequent law, and the reaction of DOMA at the federal level, there is a great deal for the courts and legislatures to sort out. There will be out-of-state gays and lesbians who go to Vermont to get "wed" who may go home and attempt to force their states to recognize their unions. The Vermont legislature may someday repeal the law. If it is repealed, what happens to the unions made under the law as it existed? Other state legislatures or courts may embrace similar laws. A gay couple married in Vermont and living in that state may die without a will, invoking the laws of automatic inheritance called intestacy. Their out-of-state relatives may challenge those laws. There are enough lawsuits, angry voters, and mixed up legislators to cause some degree of confusion to reign for some time to come. The ruling of the Vermont Supreme Court and the subsequent law that resulted are not creating ripples in the pool of law, but rather tidal waves. That makes one prediction secure: lawyers on both sides will have plenty of employment for years to come.

The institution of marriage has been jealously guarded by heterosexuals. However, the formation of domestic partnerships and the Vermont Civil Union law signal a growing willingness to provide recognition for gay and lesbian relationships. And as determined as some have been to guard the institution of marriage, others are as determined to bring suits that will bring about greater recognition of gay and lesbian relationships. In 2002 a suit was filed in New Jersey to emulate the type of victory seen in Vermont. At the beginning of 2003, there were legislative proposals either banning or creating legal recognition for same-sex couples in several sates. Nevertheless, efforts to gain new rights will be a struggle even as there are efforts to repeal rights gained.

Even long-standing domestic partnerships should not be taken for granted.

In the past, there have been attempts to enforce restrictions on their very existence, prohibiting companies from extending them. This has occurred not only through threats and executions of boycotts on such companies, but through official channels where there have been court challenges to domestic partnership laws, as well as bans on the practice by state insurance commissioners. There are even ballot initiatives contemplated that would force the repeal and/or forbid the extension of such benefits. Simply because they are widespread does not mean that they cannot become targets for those opposed to gay and lesbian rights. Such efforts would be another example of the pattern that has established itself in reaction to the breathtaking advances in gay and lesbian rights during the last part of the twentieth century.

If the future were going to be perfect, the dissolution of barriers to marriage for lesbians and gays would come about in nearly the same way that the Lovings destroyed the prejudices constructed by hateful laws against their marriage. A couple would bring a lawsuit that would be heard in court. The sheer hatred involved in a law forbidding two people who love each other from marrying and premised on prejudice would be struck down by the Supreme Court and its decision would become the law of the land. Over the course of time, people would become just as embarrassed about the prohibition of gay and lesbian marriage as they should be today about laws that forbade whites from marrying blacks.

Unfortunately, the future does not appear that perfect. The struggle for gay and lesbian marriage is likely to face a far more difficult and less sudden transition, because, unlike the marriage of persons of mixed races, the notion of marriage between people of the same sex offends morality rooted in religious beliefs. That factor is potent fuel for those in opposition to marriage for gays and lesbians.

For example, there was an effort announced in July 2001 to change the Constitution of the United States so that gay and lesbian marriages would be banned forever. If, before the Lovings case could have gotten to the Supreme Court, an amendment to the Constitution was passed that said it was the supreme law of the land that interracial marriages could not take place, then by the time their case got to court, it would have been a moot point.

Could that be done with gay marriage? Without question, it is a possibility. To amend the Constitution, the United States Congress must pass an amendment. Once it is passed, the issue goes before the state legislatures of the fifty states. There, the matter will be debated and put up for a vote. When two-thirds of the states have passed the amendment, then it becomes Constitutional law.

While therefore possible, whether it is probable is an entirely different matter. But consider the fact that so many states passed laws that forbid the recognition of gay marriage, coupled with the fact that Congress passed the Defense of Marriage Act so overwhelmingly, and the probability of a constitutional amendment becomes a little more certain.

On the other hand, the regulation of marriage as a matter of law has always been within the power of the individual states to regulate, not the federal government. Such an amendment might give pause to conservatives who, while opposed to the notion of gay marriage, may in fact be more opposed to the federal government stepping in to usurp what has traditionally been a state right. But, in fact, one group called the Alliance for Marriage (www.allianceformarriage.org), located in Alexandria, Virginia, has organized to propose such an amendment.

In pre-Civil War America, the marriage of slaves was not viewed in the same light as the marriage of their owners. Like gays and lesbians today, marriage for slaves was a social marriage, but not a legal one. For those of us who have gone through bonds of holy union or other similar church "marriage" ceremonies, in which gay and lesbian couples exchange vows, that should sound familiar. While an enslaved couple could express their bonds of love and loyalty, no white minister would have been caught dead blessing that union in a church. There were no real laws to support the newly joined couple in their efforts to sustain a marriage. It was not in the interests of the larger society to support a marriage between enslaved people – it did not provide commercial advantage.

Naturally, gay men and lesbians do not suffer the same grievous history as slaves. But it is rare that an entire class of people is legally denied access to the institution of marriage.

The fact that the law did not recognize their relationships did not stop slaves from having them, and it did stop a slave couple from "marrying" by "jumping the broom," as described in the beginning of this chapter.

The law is playing catch-up to reality. The United States Census began counting lesbian and gay households in the 1990 census. When the 2000 census was taken, it reflected huge increases in the numbers of same-sex households in the country. Even large states that are known to have big gay and lesbian populations saw an increase. California, for example, increased gay and lesbian joint households by 152 percent. Many smaller states saw astounding increases, such as Alabama with a 659 percent increase and Idaho with 952 percent. These states barely reported any same sex households at all in 1990, and there is, of course, controversy in these numbers. The United States Census Bureau casts doubt on the real value of the numbers, which isn't really the role of a census bureau when you think about it – after all they are numbers the bureau itself collected. The truth probably exists somewhere between the discounted numbers offered by the census bureau and what the numbers actually appear to be saying. The bottom line is that there is an undoubted increase in gay and lesbian households. More people are out of the closet, and when they come out, more are settling into households. When the numbers get big enough, eventually the law has to catch up to the reality and manage the situation. Otherwise it will become irrelevant in some respects.[6]

There are many things that lesbians and gays can and should do to protect their relationships when living together. They may eventually go the same way as jumping the broom when one day, marriage rights are finally recognized for all U.S. citizens, not merely heterosexuals.

6. A good example of this exists in the not too distant past. In New York, there were no legal provisions that allowed for a person to appoint a non-family member as a medical power of attorney. However, so many gay men who were sick with AIDS did fill them out and present them to doctors that eventually the law caught up with reality, and a statute was passed to recognize the documents.

CHAPTER 2

And Baby Makes Three

History and Perspective – Our Changing Role as Parents

YOU ARE SAYING to yourself, having kids is the oldest trick in the book – people have been doing it for as long as there have been people. Well, that is an apt observation, but when we are talking about gays and lesbians having children, it is a whole different ballgame, because many heterosexuals consider gays, lesbians, bisexuals and transgenders by nature not to be fit parents. That complicates things quite a bit, socially, politically, and of course, legally. You may find that your kids from your former marriage are no longer allowed to see you, that kids you want to adopt are not available to you, and that your service as a foster parent is denied you because of the fact that you are gay, lesbian, bisexual, or transgender.

Kids In and Out of the Closet

Historically, there were a number of ways for gays and lesbians to become parents. There was, of course, the absolutely oldest way. Oscar Wilde serves as an example. In those days, a gay man or lesbian woman wanting to become a parent got married and had children the same way that straight people do – through a biological union with a member of the opposite gender. In the case of Oscar Wilde, he then went on and had affairs with men while at the same time maintaining the status of parent, husband, and lover simultaneously. As we all know, there was hell to pay for it in the end. Let's call this the Victorian Method.

People tired of the Victorian Method for obvious reasons: it involves many unpleasant things, including lying to oneself and to others, ruining lives, extremely hurt feelings among the parties concerned, and a serious potential for considerable embarrassment. In a maturing homosexual society, where gay people have begun to lead more visible lives, the need for a duplicitous situation of living with a spouse and child and a secret lover of one's own sex has generally fallen out of favor. Many people, therefore, after marriage to a person of the opposite sex, step out of the closet for marriage with a person of their own sex. But because there were children in the first marriage, the person stepping out of the closet now becomes a gay parent. We can call this the Liberation Method.

However liberating this might be, this method of having children is far from ideal from a number of perspectives – namely the spouse's, the children's, and most certainly, the judge's. One of the biggest problems with this method is that, during the ensuing divorce – and there would most likely be one – the newly recognized homosexuality can be used as a weapon against the declaring partner to the marriage. In other words, by virtue of coming out of the closet, a gay or lesbian parent can seriously compromise his or her rights to be with their children in any capacity. It should not surprise anyone to know that gay or lesbian parents can be and often are severely curtailed in their custodial arrangements in the wake of a divorce involving children. During the HIV epidemic, there was an added excuse to discriminate against gay men – the fear of HIV contagion or even of saddling a child with the burden of watching a gay parent lose health and eventually die. Often it was, and many times still is, a matter of a judge interpreting the parent's emergence from the closet as a choice of sexual desire and gratification over the desire to be a parent.

Lesbian Baby Boom

Today, there are a number of ways to have children – ways that fall under the category of the Direct Method, meaning having children biologically or adopting them while self-identifying as gay or lesbian. Lesbians have largely spearheaded this. During the 1970s and especially in the 1980s there was a growing number of women, both straight and gay, who were becoming single parents, something that was often regarded by mainstream society as scandalous – the term "out of wedlock" really meant something bad. Today the term "bastard" is more likely used to describe someone who just cut you off in your lane change on the freeway or refused to commit to a relationship, rather than to describe a baby born to a single parent.

Not only did lesbian women begin having children in larger numbers, unlike other methods (Victorian and Liberation), they were having them *after* coming out of the closet. They accomplished this either through donation of sperm by a friend or through an unknown donor. Later, gay men, also in growing numbers, began having children. This was mainly by adoption, due to the obvious lack of equipment to whip up their own, or through surrogacy. Either way, gays and lesbians have two ways to go when considering children – either your DNA or someone else's, meaning either biologically giving birth or adopting.

Still, for any gay, lesbian, bisexual, or transgender parent, there is the looming threat that another person – your former spouse, his or her parents, your parents, or even your former lover – could seek to limit your custody or visitation rights with your children. The law, while getting better, has not always been a friend to such a parent.

Are You a Fit Parent?

There was a time when the custody or adoption of children by singles, and certainly by gay or lesbian couples, would have been nearly impossible. However, with the increasing divorce rate, courts have had to make decisions over the custody of children born into marriages in which one partner is gay or lesbian. Once, homosexuality was grounds for cutting off or severely restricting visitation or custody rights. However, with society's evolutionary feelings about gays and lesbians progressing rapidly over the past thirty years, the courts have not lagged that far behind, and today the standard by which custody issues are resolved has likewise evolved in both divorce and adoption, though this is not universally true. These matters are not regulated by the federal government, but by the states. Therefore, your status as a homosexual parent is going to be largely dictated by your geography.

Today, the guiding light by which most courts decide whether a child or children belong with a parent, either biological or adoptive, is a legal standard known as the "best interests of the child." In short, what that means is that the law will take in all of the factors regarding a child and judge whether placement, or in the case of divorce, visitation or custody situations are being undertaken with the best interests of the child at heart. This is supposed to have the effect of eliminating a categorical analysis of a situation – i.e., you are gay and so therefore you are being ruled out as a parent. Rather, if in fact it can be shown to be in a child's best interests to be placed in a particular home or situation, then your sexual identity is not the deciding factor. Unfortunately, the interpretation of what exactly is in a child's best interests can be a highly subjective, rather than objective, exercise. This means that a judge or legislature, looking at a matter through a lens that is smudged with prejudice and ignorance, may see fit to enforce or create policies that are not, in fact, in the bests interests of the child in question, or for that matter, of any children. Some states, for example, despite the fact that there are children in need of good homes, will deny an adoptive parent who is gay. Others may not allow a gay to become a foster parent to a child, even though there is a shortage of foster parents available, particularly for HIV positive children. But the trend is toward more open acceptance of the notion that a parent's sexual orientation alone is not a factor in determining best interest. Rather, it is the ability to provide a loving, caring, healthy, safe, and nurturing environment that is being placed on a higher level than prejudice.

Why You Need Legal Help in Having Kids

As stated early in this chapter, an increasing number of gays and lesbians are becoming parents and are forging new kinds of families. There are several ways of having children that are open to you. The decision to have a child is not a legal one – no one has the right to tell you that you are unfit to be a parent based solely on your orientation. You have to get a license to do many other things in our society, but you do not have to get a license to be a parent. Whatever method you choose to have a child, artificial insemination, surrogacy, adoption, or even by sexual relations with a member of the opposite sex, it is your decision.

You may not always be able to readily find someone to assist you in any of these methods, but that doesn't make it impossible or even improbable for you to become a parent, whether you are single or in a relationship. In the end, the decision is up to you – weighing the factors that all potential parents must weigh when considering such a step. Do you have the resources – financial, emotional, psychological and even spiritual – to provide a good and fitting home for a new life? For you it is a matter of reflection and perhaps consultation with your family, friends, therapists, and even religious counselors. The only real legal role in this decision is that the law provides some of the "how to" but is not a factor in your "what if." In short, no one has the right to decide that you would not be a good parent, except yourself.

For lesbians and gays, having children is not a casual happenstance. It is not as easy as finding someone you like or who is attractive and getting them to donate their sperm for your child or, conversely, to have them carry a child for you. The donor parent (womb or sperm) may have rights, too. It is not so easy as finding a child who needs a home and saying that you want to take care of him or her, even though you may be the most appropriate person to do that. It is also not enough to be living with your lover and his or her biological child and knowing that everything will turn out fine should anything happen to your partner or in the event of a break up. There is no system to protect you or your rights regarding children during a break-up. There is only the system that you design – the steps that you take to ensure the stability and happiness of your relationship with your children, whether they are born to you or become your family by other means. The notion of family in the lesbian and gay community is being stretched every day in every way, and the legal system does not always stretch to catch up with it. It is up to you to build the protections you may need. You need to be legally aware because you must be extraordinarily careful in how you proceed when it comes to parenting decisions. The legal system by itself will not protect you, nor will it protect your children.

Current Events – Creating a Family

You've signed the documents that mark your status as an "official" couple. You've registered at Bloomingdale's, received lots of presents, and have settled down after a celebration at your church that is called anything other than a "wedding." You buy a house, maybe indulge in the picket fence to keep in that faithful child substitute, your dog, from roaming the streets and inside your beautifully self-landscaped lawn. It can't get much better than this, can it? But then you figure it can. Hey, we've done really well with the dog, why not take the next ultimate step? Why not have a baby?

Being gay or lesbian is no longer the obstacle to being a parent that it used to be, and increasing numbers of lesbians and gays are deciding to become parents. Today, there is every reason that you can have a baby, but you will have to sit down and do some serious planning. For example, if you are half of a lesbian couple in which your other half elects to become pregnant by artificial insemination, in order for you to become a legal parent, you will have to adopt the child, an option that may or may not be open to you. It is complicated, and therefore important that, before you take the plunge, you know what you are getting into. You will need to consider a number of circumstances and plan carefully a series of steps that, in the end, will mean that your child will know that you really wanted him or her, because so much planning went into it. Children of heterosexual couples don't always have that distinction. In other words, in only the rarest of circumstances do gays or lesbians refer to their children as "accidents." It is one of the many things that set us apart.

The question boils down to this: by what methods? Because the traditional method of having offspring is not particularly relevant for lesbians and gays, when they decide to have kids – they must explore non-traditional methods more fully than their heterosexual counterparts. By their very nature, children growing up in gay or lesbian households challenge traditional notions of family. Obviously, these kids will have two moms or two dads. Some lawyers have set up arrangements so that a child actually has four parents: a biological set who provided sperm and egg, and a set who provide love and attention. Is the law ready to handle a child with four parents? Gays and lesbian pioneers are stretching the definition of family to cover a range of experiences. With new families come new laws and new court challenges.

This chapter will look at all the ways that you may become a parent. Discussed will be

- adoption, both in the U.S. and foreign countries
- second-parent adoption
- parenting agreements
- sperm donation
- fertilized egg implantation to a third party (surrogate motherhood)
- impregnation by a friend

By the chapter's end, you will know some of the many obstacles to adoption as a gay couple or single gay parent and have an understanding of the legal ramifications of parenting a child with another individual.

Types of Adoption

For those who don't mind borrowing someone else's DNA, adoption is a worthy consideration. For a gay or lesbian couple, though, it will depend on where you live. In considering adoption, you will have to consider a number of variables: where you live, where the adoptive child lives, and, of course, whether you want a domestic or import.

Adoption is just what you think it is: becoming a parent by assuming all of the legal, ethical and moral responsibilities to a child, who, in turn, gains rights as a result of becoming your child (such as inheritance) and whose biological parents terminate their legal relationship with the child. It is not to be confused with foster care, which is often a stepping stone to eventual adoption. Foster care does not involve all of the rights and responsibilities inherent in adoption. Foster care is not permanent; adoption is. In addition, while foster care does come with a great many responsibilities, it does not create a "legal" family.

There is no shortage of kids in need of loving homes. The most recent available data shows that there are approximately 500,000 children in foster care, with 100,000 of them seeking permanent homes as adoptees. Sadly, it is estimated that for every five of these kids, there is only one set of qualified parents (or singles) who are seeking to adopt them. For those who have decided it is time to have a family, whether single or in a couple, there is a good chance that the loving home could be yours, though your success and frustration level may largely depend on the state where you live.

Adoption and foster care, like marriage and wills and estates, are largely products of state, not federal law. That means that what follows is information that is designed to give you an outline of what is generally the procedure for adoption and foster care, the details of which will vary from state to state. In some states, your adoptive efforts will be treated like anyone else's. However, while adoption is legal in every state, in some you may find that you are going against the law as a parent simply by virtue of who you are.

There are a few different ways to adopt a child. There are independent or private adoptions, and there are adoptions that are done through agencies. For couples in which both want to become a legal parent to a child, there is a procedure called second-parent adoptions that allows both individuals to adopt the same child.

Usually people use an agency, but it is not always necessary and there are both public and private options.

Independent or Private Adoptions. Most states allow for a procedure called Independent or Private Adoptions. An independent adoption occurs when a child's biological parents have identified adoptive parents for their child. For example, a single mother facing a fatal illness may wish to see her child placed with an identified friend or partner prior to her death, or a child born to a woman who did not wish to abort but cannot keep the child may have identified a relative. Sometimes this is done directly, sometimes through a third party such as a clergyman, doctor, or lawyer, and regulations that guide this sort of adoption will vary greatly – from highly detailed to largely open regulation – among the states. In Connecticut, Delaware and Massachusetts, there is no allowance for this type of adoption, and use of a third party without an agency is not legal.

Adopting through a Licensed Agency. The other way to adopt is through an adoption agency – either a public agency run by the state or a private agency that is licensed by the state. In approaching an adoption agency, you will want to know if it is licensed according to your state's regulations. You will also want to know whether it is open to dealing with lesbian and gay adoptions, or single-parent adoptions if that is your case. Resources for finding the answers to these important questions are located at the end of this chapter.

The conditions of adoption, as stated, will vary from state to state. Some states require there to be a set age difference between the adoptive parent and child. Others may require the consent of the child if the child is of a particular age. You will be required to pay the fees that represent the expenses of the adoption, e.g., the cost of a home evaluation by a social worker, court fees, etc. However, payment for anything beyond the actual fees connected with the adoption, such as a finder's fee, could be construed as baby selling. It is important that you seek out the assistance of an agency with a solid reputation and licensure. You can check on licensure by contacting your state licensing specialists (see resources at the end of this book). In 2001, an international adoption incident occurred in which parents who had adopted twin girls via the Internet had the children removed from their home because of questions regarding the authenticity of the adoption.

List of Prerequisites for Adoption

For the actual adoption, there are some prerequisites that you need in order to initiate adoption procedures.

- You need at least one child, preferably located in the same state in which you reside. Though this is not absolutely necessary, it will make matters less complicated.
- The child's consent to the adoption, if applicable. (Depending on the state, the child's consent may be important if he or she is not an infant. Age for consent may range from 12–14 years.)
- The birth parents' consent. If you cannot find the birth parents, they have presumably signed over the custody of the child to an agency.
- You may be either single or married; however, in some states there is a strong preference towards couples.
- You must be an adult.

If you have these prerequisites in order, then you will be ready to file a petition with the court.

Making a Petition for Adoption

The petition is a legal document and requests to the court to apoint you to become the legal parent of a designated child. The way the form is filed, where it is filed, and the contents of your petition will vary by state. The purpose of the petition is to demonstrate that everyone consents to this adoption and that birth parents have legally relinquished their rights with respect to the child.

A petition tells the court the following:

- That everyone that should have been notified about the adoption has in fact been notified. This could be the birth parents, a court appointed guardian, or anyone else who has legal authority over the child. No one wants a surprise here – meaning, for example, a wife cannot punish her husband by putting the kids up for adoption without his consent or knowledge.
- The history of the child and how he or she came to be up for adoption.
- The race and religion into which the child had been born. Depending on the state, this can be very important, with some states holding fast to a policy of matching up children with parents of compatible race and religion.
- The circumstances of the prospective adoptive parent or parents, meaning where they live, what they do, why they want to adopt a child.
- That you are in a financial position to support a child. You will need to demonstrate financial means, so organize your financial records – your wage statements, past tax returns, retirement plans, benefit explanations, bank records, and investment portfolio.

How the Court Gets to Know You

As the process for adoption unfolds, the court will have to get to know you and know you well. That will occur through several means: visiting your home, interviewing relatives, and talking to you. The result of this assessment is a report issued from an agency advising the court about these circumstances and making a recommendation that the court will consider when it makes its own determination. The report will be very persuasive with the court.

The process by which this information is gathered will inevitably include a home visit or "home study." This is required in every state (unless the child you are adopting is already related to you, in which case it may be unnecessary) and may consist of several interviews with you and your partner, either separately, together, or both. The precise way in which the home assessment is conducted is set by the state in which you are adopting, and the process can usually take from three to six months of time.

In addition, the court will examine financial information, religious outlooks, and overall fitness and suitability to being a parent. The court may want to interview witnesses in pursuit of its decision. Once reviewing the materials, the court will make a decision based on the best interests of the child. The court will be in the same jurisdiction where you and the child will live, but if the child is from another state, it will be more complicated. Every state has requirements under the Interstate Compact on Placement of Children that ensures that a child's welfare is protected throughout the adoption process.

This process necessarily involves a large number of questions regarding a broad range of topics. The nature of these questions and the impact of their answers are going to be very different, depending on where you live, the adoption agency being used, and the experience and outlook of the individual who is evaluating you, your home, and, if applicable, your partner. Both New York and California protect lesbian and gays from discrimination in this regard, but it is important to go into this with eyes open – society is still basically prejudiced toward lesbians and gays. The removal of legal barriers does not mean that you will not face bias. On the other hand, the nature of the questions you will face, intrusive as you may regard them, are attempts to define the environment that the child will face and your ability to provide support that will be in the best interest of the child.

Think also about what the people in your life who are close to you will say about your ability to be a parent, because it will be important. You will need to be free of a serious criminal record – the kind beyond your propensity for parking tickets, so if you have a habit of committing felonies, you need to consider something other than adoption. This is beginning to sound like a pledge for the girl or boy scouts, but you will also have to demonstrate that you are physically fit, so that you will be around for a long time to care and provide support for the child. If you are single and have already had a few heart attacks by age forty, you may find that the agency reviewing your fitness is not anxious to provide an infant for your care. Having HIV or TB may compromise your ability to adopt, not because of discrimination or fear of transmission, but because you will be considered to have a serious, life-threatening illness that could make it difficult for you to provide for the child. Even high blood pressure, if not responding to medication, could provide medical grounds for being unfit.

You need to be realistic and patient about the process. Adoption is not cheap, nor is the process a breeze. Unlike giving birth, you need to convince strangers that you are fit and able to act as a parent. These strangers will ideally be evaluating you based on your ability to care for the child, not on your sexual orientation – meaning that the questions they ask you will probably be the same questions they ask of any other adoption applicants. But that doesn't mean that the social worker evaluating you won't have concerns and questions about how you may handle sensitive issues with the child, such as:

- How will you explain to the child what it means to have two mommies or two daddies?
- How will you advise the child if he comes home from school having been teased about having gay or lesbian parents?

- How will you help the child with his or her own sexuality during adolescence, and how will you explain to a straight child why he or she has a different sexual orientation from yours?

Another part of the process that may intimidate you at first, but which you will eventually really get into is that you may have to draft an autobiography. It may come through a series of questions or points for you to address in narrative form that will probe, very comprehensively, your life, how you got to be where you are, where you want to go, what it is like where you live, and what it is like just to be you. It is the most important report along the lines of "What I Did on My Summer Vacation" you will ever have to write.

Special Issues for Couples

In addition to all of the considerations above, if you are a couple, you will have to face questions about the strength of your relationship. These questions are not discriminatory; they are also the type of questions that would also be asked of a heterosexual unmarried couple. But because you are legally barred from expressing your commitment to one another through marriage, an investigating social worker may want to know other facts about your relationship, such as:

- How long have you been together?
- Do you own real estate or other property jointly? Do you have joint checking accounts?
- Have you had mutual wills and powers of attorney drawn up (see chapter 4)?
- Are you in a secure financial position? In other words, the stability of your relationship is important. If you met just six months ago on a cruise ship, you should probably consider waiting a bit before trying to adopt. You need to get the infrastructure of your lives and your relationship built up a bit more before considering having a child.

Foreign Adoptions

For those interested in imports, foreign adoption is a practice that is up sharply in the United States over the past several years. In fact, this has provoked some reaction from some countries – embarrassment that Americans are coming in and removing a generation of babies. If you follow the List of Prerequisites for Adoption earlier in this chapter, please note that you must add several more steps to this already complicated process in order to apply for an international adoption.

Like any other method, there are advantages and disadvantages to this type of adoption. With foreign adoption, you can bypass some of the inconveniences you may face domestically. As well, you can chose a child compatible to your own ethnic heritage and possibly provide a lifestyle that he or she might not otherwise enjoy.

Foreign adoption also has its risks and obstacles. Adopting parents of children from Romania often had no way of knowing that their child already had HIV or suffered from fetal alcohol syndrome. With foreign adoption, you have to negotiate the laws not just of your state and federal government, but those of a foreign government as well. Those laws may not allow a single or a gay or lesbian couple to adopt a child. They may also require a requisite age range for adoptive parents. Lastly, there are considerable travel costs associated with adopting a foreign child, over and above the already considerable costs associated with adoption. As with any situation in which a child comes into a family, either by birth or adoption, there are no guarantees.

First, you need to decide from where you wish to adopt your child and then choose an adoption agency *in* the United States that *also* operates in the foreign country you have designated. You also need to contact an agency that is licensed in your state to conduct the home study that is described above for domestic adoption. By working with an agency that is located both in this country and doing business in the country of your adoptee, you will have the benefit of knowledge regarding requirements for your home study by the foreign government. An agency that is able to work in both countries will also be able to enumerate for you the types of documentation you will need to carry out the adoption. Additionally, they will direct you to the proper forms you will need from the United States Immigration and Naturalization Service. If all goes smoothly and you bring a child home, you may need to consider a formal adoption process in the United States in order to ensure the legal status of the adoption.

As reported by the National Adoption Information Clearinghouse (NAIC), half of all states recognize foreign adoptions fully, as follows.

States Recognizing Foreign Adoptions

Alaska	Kansas	Oklahoma
Arkansas	Massachusetts	Oregon
Delaware	Minnesota	Pennsylvania
Florida	Missouri	South Carolina
Georgia	Montana	Tennessee
Hawaii	New Hampshire	Vermont
Idaho	New Mexico	Wisconsin
Illinois	North Dakota	
Indiana	Ohio	

In addition, the following states have statutes that allow parents to petition a court for domestic re-adoption of children adopted in foreign countries.

States Allowing Domestic Re-Adoption

California	Kansas	Ohio
Colorado	Maine	Oklahoma
Connecticut	Maryland	Pennsylvania
Georgia	Minnesota	Tennessee
Hawaii	New Hampshire	Virginia
Idaho	North Carolina	Wisconsin

States Without Laws on Re-Adoption

Alabama	Nebraska	Texas
Arizona	Nevada	Utah
Kentucky	New Jersey	Washington
Louisiana	New York	West Virginia
Michigan[7]	Rhode Island	Wyoming
Mississippi	South Dakota	

Second Parent Adoption

Let's say you already have a child – meaning that either you or your partner has a child by a previous marriage, or that one of you has adopted a child through the means just described, or that your partner has given birth via artificial insemination. While you act and care for each other as a family, you want to be a family in the legal sense. Your desire to do so isn't merely based on sentiment. For legal reasons you both want to parent the child so that you both have rights when it comes to the child's needs, such as making medical decisions or even having the child inherit from you should you die without a will. For example, if the adoptive partner leaves town on a business trip and the child has an accident, without adoption you would have no legal right to sign permission forms at hospitals. For a host of reasons – emotional, psychological and legal – you want to become the child's actual legal. Would any state allow that?

Believe it or not, the answer is yes. "Second parent adoption has been around since 1985 and is now available at various court levels in twenty states," says Kate Kendell – a mom, lesbian, and executive director of the National Center for Lesbian Rights (NCLR). "It would be fair to say that tens of thousands

7. Though there is not statutory law, there are judicial procedures in place.

of second parent adoptions have been granted and have perhaps been the single greatest achievement in terms of protecting our families that we have been able to secure on a wide scale." If, however, your partner has a child by reason of custody from a previous heterosexual marriage, you will not be able to effect a second parent adoption unless that former spouse is willing to relinquish parental rights entirely or unless your partner is widowed. Second parent adoption would also not be allowed when a woman has had a child by insemination but the donor father has not relinquished his parental rights.

Second parent adoption is a legal mechanism with an established track record. These adoptions have been granted for hundreds of lesbian and gay couples, if not thousands, and they enjoy widespread judicial acceptance.

However, it is worth noting that second parent adoption is not a less cumbersome process than any other adoption. You will still have to file a petition for the adoption and undergo interviews, a home study, and an inspection. You will have to pay fees to cover the costs associated with this process, and it will not be an overnight event. Still, once accomplished, you will have a child who is legally joined with both of you, with all of the rights and responsibilities associated with that.

The process can be long and arduous, but the result is that you and your partner can legally become a family. If you happen to live in Vermont (see chapter 1) and you and your partner engage in a civil union, you will, in every sense of the legal word, be a family. You will be on nearly the same footing as every other family – for as long as you stay in Vermont, that is.

States Laws Recognizing Second Parent Adoption

(This listing was obtained from the National Center for Lesbian Rights)

Connecticut	New York
District of Columbia	New Jersey
Illinois	Vermont
Massachusetts	

Connecticut and Vermont recognize second parent adoption because of state statute signed into law. The District of Columbia, Illinois, Massachusetts, New York and New Jersey recognize second parent adoptions by virtue of state appellate court decisions. However, in 2002, the Ohio Supreme Court ruled against allowing second parent adoptions in that state.

Trial court judges have also supported second parent adoption in the following states, in select, but not all counties.

States with Court Decisions Allowing Second Parent Adoption

Alabama
Alaska (Juneau)
California (several counties)
Delaware
Hawaii
Indiana (White County)
Iowa
Louisiana (Orleans Parrish)
Maryland
Michigan
Minnesota (Aitkin & Hennepin Counties)
Nevada
New Mexico
Oregon (Multnomah County)
Pennsylvania
Rhode Island
Texas (Austin, San Antonio, and other select counties)
Washington (King, Spokane, Thurston, and other select counties)

Legal Status of Adoption for Gays and Lesbians

Adoption might not be a legal option for you. There are states that, in addition to outlawing marriage between gays and sex between gays, have also seen fit to outlaw adoption by gays. (Sometimes you have to wonder – if they could outlaw your very existence, would they do it?) In the recent past, several states have made or attempted to make gay adoption illegal. As recently as 2001, a court in Florida affirmed that state's ban on gay and lesbian adoptions. In the past, Massachusetts has had a history of legal problems regarding gays as foster parents, as has Arkansas. In addition to legislation that is either enacted or repealed, the courts can sometimes complicate legal matters by issuing rulings that are based more on an individual judge's prejudice than on what is in the best interests of the child.

Right now, states that outlaw gay adoptions by statute include Florida, Mississippi, and Utah. Several other states have seen legislation introduced that would affect gay and lesbian adoption.

In December 1997, however, a case brought in the state of New Jersey made clear that adoption sought by an unmarried couple should be treated with the same respect as adoption sought by married couples. In effect, New Jersey became the first state to say that gay couples on the same footing as married heterosexual couples seeking to adopt. This ruling was significant. If a couple wished to adopt a child, one partner would have to apply and gain adoption of the child and then his or her partner would then have to apply separately for joint rights. However even getting that far can be not only expensive but difficult, with less than half of the states allowing such an effort, known as second parent adoptions (see page 71).

If the child you want to adopt lives in another state, you may be able to use the laws of your state to effect the adoption. However, each state will take care to ensure that the children in its care will be placed in a setting that is in the best interest of the child. If the child you want to adopt is coming from a state where gay adoption is illegal, you may have a problem. Adopting an out-of-state child who is not already related to you can be more cumbersome than adopting one who is located in the same state in which you reside.

After you have adopted in a state that allows it, should you move to another state where adoption by lesbians and gays is not accepted, you should not have a problem according to Kate Kendell. She says that there has never been a case where an adoption that occurred in another state is not recognized. Adoption, she says, is a lot like marriage; states have to recognize one another's laws in this regard.

If you are living in a state that makes gay and lesbian adoption illegal but recognizes foreign adoption decrees, you may feel you can get around your state's law by using the foreign adoption decree as a basis for your adoption. Of the states that outlaw gay adoption (Florida and Utah), both recognize the validity of foreign adoption decrees, therefore it would seem that all would be in order. However, to effect your foreign adoption, you will have to have an agency in the state where you reside submit a home study report, and they will be make a recommendation. If the agency considers homosexuality a reason to declare a parent unfit, you will have a serious obstacle to getting your foreign adoption. The state of Mississippi recently passed legislation that not only outlaws gay adoptions, but also refuses to recognize such adoptions if they occur in other states – a policy that will inevitably face constitutional challenge.

Adoption Substitutes

Adoption may not be for everyone. For those who choose not to adopt, there are alternatives to adoption that may be possible for you. Again, their availability will depend on where you live, but they are viable alternatives that offer varying degrees of parental rights.

Parentage Decrees. Parentage decrees are a potential alternative to second parent adoption. These decrees bestow the rights of a legal parent on a person who is a non-biological parent under circumstances where it can be demonstrated that the child was brought into the world by the biological parent for the purpose of being a family together. For example, let's say Roberta and Toni – a lesbian couple who have been living together – decide that they want to have a baby. Roberta opts to get pregnant, because her job offers better maternity benefits, and Toni earns more money than Roberta does. Roberta becomes pregnant through means of artificial insemination performed at a physician's office using sperm from an unknown donor. Suppose that either second-parent adoption is not recognized in their state, or they have decided that they do not care to go through the process that is required with the adoption option. They may make this decision because they do not like the invasive nature of the home study or would rather avoid some of the cost of adoption, such as paying fees to cover the costs of the home study, so they decide to petition the court for a parentage decree.

It is important to bear in mind that parentage decrees are a relatively new legal mechanism and, as such, they are far more untested than second parent adoptions. In addition, according to Kate Kendell, the availability of parentage decrees to gay and lesbian couples is far more limited: "I only know of a handful of cases in the entire country, which occurred in Colorado and Massachusetts. At NCLR, we have been successful with them in California in the Bay Area."

Still, the parentage decree once it exists in a state, may offer a more streamlined and less stressful method of having a child or creating a family than does second parent adoption. "Such decrees hold great promise," says Kate Kendell, "and they will continue to be pursued in states where there is case law that talks about the intention to parent being almost as important or as important as a biological connection." If this is an option you think you would like to pursue, you should only try it with an attorney who has already had experience in it, or with the assistance of an organization like NCLR.

Parenting Agreements. What can a couple do if they live in a state that does not allow second parent adoptions and, as is most probably the case, live where they cannot seek a parenting decree? They may have the option of writing their own parenting agreement. Just as you can create a live-together agreement that defines your rights and responsibilities in your relationship, agreements can be drafted that can consider the roles of parenting.

Essentially, this is a contract, not unlike a live together agreement (see chapter 3) and a parenting agreement can even become part of such a contract. The existence of such an agreement will confer on the non-biological or non-legal parent rights while at the same time respecting the biological or legal parent's understanding of who they are to the child. The document doesn't affect the relationships legally, in the sense that school systems would acknowledge it or the IRS or Social Security or even hospitals delivering medical care. For those kinds of institutions, the non-biological or non-legal parent is a "legal stranger" to the child. Then why bother to do one at all? For one thing, it does set up some, though not all, of the rights that you might get in second-parent adoption. But for another reason, it will preserve the notion that the non-biological parent at one time was considered to be a co-parent by the biological parent. That can be essential after a break up.

In any relationship, there is always the possibility of a break-up, which can be a source of tremendous hurt not only to the couple, but especially to the children involved, as anyone who is the child of parents who divorced can attest. In the event of a break-up, the agreement may well be all that a court needs in order to preserve some visitation between the child and the co-parent. The agreement then, while not changing the entire structure of legal relationships between any children and the non-biological or non-legal parent, may be a tool that later provides assurance that those relationships do not suddenly stop at a whim.

This same reasoning applies if the biological parent dies. In that event, the non-legal co-parent may be left facing a difficult situation if there are family members of the deceased who want to assume custody of the child and perhaps sever the visitation rights of the surviving co-parent. Since that person lacks a relationship with the child that is recognized in the eyes of the law, the parenting agreement may well offer protection to a co-parent from losing custody. But would a state honor such a document?

The law may be in a state of evolution on this point. At one time, contracts that tried to delegate parenting rights in this manner were routinely invalidated, because the general legal thinking was that parental rights were too intimate of an authority to delegate away, and it was simply considered to be a violation of public policy. However, courts have become more sophisticated and have begun to understand that couples who don't have marriage as an option, or adoption as an alternative, can create an agreement with respect to parental rights and responsibilities that may need to be enforced in order to ensure that children are protected.

Not only might the agreement be in the best interest of the child, it may be in the best interest of your relationship. NCLR encourages lesbian and gay couples to enter into parenting agreements and to make very clear in those agreements what their respective rights and responsibilities will be in the event that they break up or something in the relationship changes. They find that the process for going through the agreement can be extremely helpful in highlighting issues of contention and enabling the couple to work them out in a time of peace when they like each other and are living under the same roof. It is in the child's best interest to have his or her parents work out their differences when they are happy with each other, rather than slugging it out in a big court battle when and if they split up. Kate Kendell encourages people to think of this kind of agreement as "a gift to each other and to the relationship."

As to the enforceability of the contract, NCLR acknowledges that, while there are increasing numbers of courts that are willing to enforce them, there will continue to be courts that invalidate the agreements. But just having an agreement may be enough to head off problems. "You never know," says Kate Kendell, "my view is that if the couple thinks that they are bound by the agreement, then they are very likely not to ever challenge it."

While not conferring the full rights that a second parent adoption offers, a parenting agreement is an alternative for a gay and lesbian couple in which one has the legal custody of a child and the other would like to maintain that relationship.

Foster Care. It is not uncommon that gay adoptive parents begin with a fostering situation, in which an individual or couple is acting as a foster parent to a child or children. Many times, given the needs of today, the child is HIV-positive. There are states that have restrictions about gay fostering, even though, in the case of HIV children, it is difficult to imagine a better foster parent than someone with an intrinsic knowledge of the epidemic and the needs of people with HIV. Still, as you may have already guessed, state legislatures do not operate on a level of logic as often as they do political expediency and even – dare it be said – stupidity and bigotry. Arkansas and Mississippi have placed or attempted to place restrictions on foster care and gays and lesbians – taking the matter so far as to disallow the placement of a foster child with anyone who is a homosexual – or who lives with a homosexual. In other words, if heterosexual parents have a gay son or lesbian daughter living with them and they seek foster parenthood, their application could be denied on the basis that they are living with a homosexual.

There are nearly a half a million children in need of foster care in the United States. Somehow these states believe it is preferable to place them in a group home rather than risk these kids ever meeting a homosexual.

If you are interested in foster care, check with the foster care specialist in your state to see if your circumstances would permit you to be a foster parent.

Childbirth

Overview of Options. Medical arts in helping people to conceive children have advanced dramatically. Women taking fertility drugs are having absurdly large numbers of multiple births. Women who are grandmothers are made pregnant through in vitro fertilization. It is not inconceivable that your neighbor might come over one day and, rather than ask for a cup of borrowed sugar, ask to borrow a cup of sperm. Well, *OK*, not a cup, but perhaps just enough for a sperm donation. Or instead, how about a few eggs?

In fact, the basis of the question itself is very real. More and more people are creating new kinds of families. The decision for a same-sex couple to have a child often involves considerations beyond the fact that they want to extend their love to a larger family, but there may be very strong feelings that that family should, as much as possible, be biological and not just legal. In that case, for a gay couple, it may involve asking a third party (in this case, definitely a woman) to bear the child using the sperm of one of the men in the relationship. Or a lesbian couple may decide that one woman in the relationship should become pregnant by using the sperm of the brother or other relative of the non-child-bearing partner, or you may go to a stranger and pay them for the use of their sperm or womb. Any way you look at it, the desire to forge new kinds of families is going to test everyone involved, including the law. And it goes beyond a legal considerations or tests, because society at large is not going to be accustomed to you. It is going to question you at every turn – socially, psychologically, and religiously. You will be a square peg trying to fit into a round hole. And for that reason, it will be an on-going test for you and your partner that goes way beyond the legal considerations. Everything, from what your child calls you and your partner, to how your in-laws regard the offspring, to the PTA meeting where you and your partner show up and want to list the biological donor as a parent, will be a test.

On the other hand, some gays and lesbians have found that, once they are a parent, the heterosexual world relates to them on a different level than before. They are identified first as a parent, second as a gay or lesbian. The dynamic of relationships with co-workers and friends opens up in a new way. For our purposes in this chapter, we'll stick to the legal stuff, which is complicated enough. But know that the legal considerations are always going to be colored by the majority's perceptions, and those perceptions, are going to be mightily tested by the fact that you are a parent and by the way in which you do your parenting.

Some of the benefits of this method over adoption seem obvious. You don't have strangers poking around in your life, questioning how you live in exhaustive detail and wanting to make sure that you will be a fit parent. When you go biological, the state does not involve itself in your character. "If you can reproduce, you can have it" is their unofficial motto. In addition, your child will be aware of his or her medical history, whereas an adoptive child may not. By having your own biological child, you will also have the ability to raise him or her from birth yourself – always a factor in the environmental aspects that shape a child's adult character.

However, there is a cost to these benefits. Consider what people face when a lesbian asks a man for a sperm donation for the purpose of having her own child, or when a gay man asks a woman for a far greater favor, i.e., to please carry and then give up a baby for him. There is always the reality that a third party must enter your relationship in order to make this birth possible. And, what happens if the child whose birth you arrange is born with serious mental or physical disabilities? What if instead of one child, there are twins or triplets? There are no guarantees, and while there are a lot of emotional, social, and psychological issues to deal with in your considerations, the law is not the least of them. However, without paving the way for circumstances legally, you can certainly complicate the other aspects (emotional and psychological) considerably. So it is best to know what you are doing legally and otherwise.

Surrogacy. Surrogacy involves a woman agreeing by contract to carry a child for you and then giving it up to you so that you may raise it as your own. It became a household word when in 1988, when the New Jersey Supreme Court issued a decision regarding a surrogacy that drew national attention. In the case, a couple named Stern hired a New Jersey woman to have a child for them and drew up a contract whereby the surrogate agreed to carry the child of the couple after using the sperm of Mr. Stern to become pregnant. Once she gave birth, she decided not to release custody, and a highly publicized court battle ensued. The child, known as "Baby M," made headlines in nearly every newspaper in the world. While the Sterns had won custody in a lower court, and Mrs. Stern was given the right to adopt the child of her husband and the surrogate, the New Jersey Supreme Court reinstated the parental rights of the surrogate and dissolved the adoption by Mrs. Stern. The surrogate was given rights of visitation and Mr. Stern was awarded custody.

Even though there had been a contract for the surrogacy, things went wrong. The contract was made between the sperm donor father, the husband of the surrogate, and the surrogate herself, and allowed for a payment of $10,000. The way the contract was worded with respect to payment – the money was payable only if a live child were delivered to the Sterns – caused the court to construe that payment was being made in exchange for the termination of parental rights by the surrogate and her husband, not in exchange for her expenses related to the pregnancy.

The Baby M case, in turn, gave birth to a number of laws among the various states regarding the practice of surrogacy and generally outlawing payment to a woman for the purpose of having a baby. In other words, payment could not be for the baby itself; rather only the expenses of the surrogate are covered. As well, states moved to protect the interests of surrogates to ensure that they are not being exploited.

Surrogacy laws, like marriage, estate, and family laws of all kinds, are regulated by the state, not the federal government. Each state can decide for itself if and under what conditions surrogacy is permitted. Laws may vary considerably. Each will require that the biological parents be of majority age. But the rest of the circumstances can be different. It is possible that the state will require that the biological mother be incapable of carrying her own child. Therefore, if it is something that you are considering, you will need to know how your state regulates the matter. You will also need the expert counsel of an attorney, as will the surrogate. In other words, *DO NOT TRY THIS ALONE AT HOME.*

There are two types of surrogacy, one in which the child is biologically related to the surrogate, and another in which it is not. In the first kind, a couple may ask a surrogate to carry their child for them, because while the biological mother can conceive, she cannot carry the child to term herself. In that case, the couple has eggs removed from the woman, which are then fertilized by the sperm of the man and placed into the surrogate for the gestation. For example, in the case of a gay or lesbian couple, it is conceivable that Alice and Jane who may want to have a child that is biologically connected to them both. They could provide one of their eggs with the sperm of a close relative of the other. So Alice provides the egg, but Jane's brother Zack provides the sperm used by a physician to fertilize the egg that will then be placed in a surrogate. This, of course, assumes that Alice cannot carry the child to term herself. Naturally, the child that is born to the surrogate is in no way biologically related to her. Only the sperm donor and the egg donor are biologically related to the child.

In the second type of surrogacy, the sperm of the biological father is used to fertilize the surrogate by means of artificial insemination. In the surrogacy described above, you are literally borrowing the body of someone to carry a child to term. In this case, you are borrowing not only the body, but the DNA as well. In other words, the surrogate will be biologically related to the child, though she will still relinquish her parental rights to the child, with the biological father covering her expenses, both legal and medical. Many of the rights and obligations explained above are inherent in this situation as well, though of course there is, legally, a relationship between the biological father and the surrogate mother. The psychological screening in these circumstances is perhaps even more important, because the child she will be giving up is her own.

While there is a great deal of risk for both parties involved, legal experts who work in this field are able to anticipate many of the circumstances that can cause that risk to turn into serious injury. It is therefore essential that both parties are represented by legal counsel, who will draw up an agreement to try and cover those circumstances. What considerations need to go into a surrogacy agreement?

The couples who are hiring the surrogate are probably going to have to agree to:

- Cover the medical expenses of the surrogate;
- Compensate the surrogate for her services;
- Compensate the surrogate for her incidental expenses, such as maternity clothing, uninsured medical expenses, the cost of caring for her own pre-existing children, etc.;
- Place funds in an escrow account at various periods throughout the pregnancy to assure that the surrogate's needs are met;
- Carry possible insurance policies on her behalf; and
- Cover other needs, which could include the type of hospital care the surrogate mother will receive.

In short, the process is going to be expensive for the prospective parents. The surrogate is undertaking a task of enormous consequence, and therefore, the costs that are normally associated with having a baby are going to multiply (no pun intended) when using a surrogate, just so that her risks are minimized. For example, the pregnancy may not be viable full term and she might miscarry – a contract will have to protect her interests in that event and will afford her some compensation, depending on the length of the pregnancy. It is also extremely important that any surrogate is screened psychologically as well as medically before beginning the pregnancy. Screening can determine whether a Surrogate is in fact at a place in her life and development in which she can actually carry, give birth to, and then give up a child to be raised by others.

The Surrogate will also have to agree to:

- Relinquish all custody rights to the child and to yield any such rights to the biological parents;
- Abstain from sexual intercourse with her own partner, because they would otherwise risk that she could become pregnant by him;
- Protect the health of the fetus by refraing from activities such as smoking, drinking, or drug use;
- Have the biological parents named on the birth certificate;
- Permit medical examinations of herself and the fetus; and
- Agree to other contingencies providing for the termination of the pregnancy if a problem is detected with either the fetus or because of a medical problem experienced by the surrogate, or if there are multiple fertilized eggs.

For any type of surrogacy, it is imperative to get good legal help, and this is especially true for lesbian and gay parents. If for no other reason than that it is non-traditional and involves people who are perhaps not legally considered "family," there is more risk inherent for gay and lesbian couples than for anyone else who attempts to have a child in this manner. Still, there are great rewards. However, it is important that any couple wanting to begin their family ensure that they are entering into their contract so that the best interests of all parties are protected. What that means is finding attorneys who are expert in this field and following their advice. While the use of any expert will increase cost, it is not exactly a place where you want to cut corners. Because there are so many contingencies – things you would never consider that are too numerous to tick off here – it is vital that you enter into this arrangement with eyes open.

A plot line in the popular sit-com *Friends* depicts a character, Phoebe Buffay, agreeing to be the surrogate for her brother, Frank, and his wife. The eggs are placed into Phoebe and, to everyone's surprise, three of them take hold and she gives birth to triplets. That was not a planned-for event. In the episode, as she is getting ready to deliver the babies, she decides she wants to keep one. All works out well in the end, even though they did not have any kind of written agreement. That is why these are called sit-coms and not "Life." Again, *DO NOT TRY THIS AT HOME.*

Though that example is fictional, those kinds of things happen in real life. In June 2002, a gay couple in Kentucky found that their surrogate was expecting quadruplets. Fortunately, while that was a surprise, it wasn't a problem for anyone because their contract addressed the possibility of multiple births, but is a real-life example of how necessary it is to be involved in detailed planning when considering surrogacy.

At least one organization has formed for the purpose of assisting gays and lesbians who want to have families through surrogacy. Located in California, the firm matches surrogates with prospective parents throughout the country. The firm oversees the process for parent wannabees, coordinating medical screenings and providing referrals for legal services. It is an added expense to the surrogacy process, but you may feel that it benefits you to have a voice of experience guiding you in your efforts to achieve parenthood through surrogacy.

Even with the many protections for both the surrogate and the biological parent or parents, there is always the possibility that something can go terribly wrong. Don't let that discourage you – just try to plan for it. After all, that is true for every person who takes action to be a parent.

Sperm Donation. The term "sperm bank" is perhaps a misnomer. You can only make a deposit to a sperm bank if you are a man, obviously. If you go to a sperm bank and make a deposit, it is not considered to be an "interest-bearing" account. In other words, they have sort of a "no deposit, no return" philosophy.

You will terminate any parental rights you have with regard to the use of that sperm in the insemination of a woman. If a child is born from the use of that sperm, your legal right as a parent is non-existent.

If, however, you use the sperm of a friend or you donate sperm that is specifically intended for a known individual to have a baby, then the matter may not be so black and white and you may have both rights and responsibilities as a consequence of your deposit. On the rights side of that equation, there may be custodial rights or visitation rights, given various circumstances. On the responsibilities side, there is the fact that any child biologically born to you and known to be yours may have rights to your estate or for child-care up until the time he or she reaches majority. Giving your sperm to a friend so that she can have a baby opens you up to these possibilities. Sperm donation with a sperm bank is more like Parent-Lite – you don't have all of those added rights and responsibilities.

If you are a man and someone asks you, or you are a woman who is about to ask for the favor of a cup of sperm to be used to have a child, keep in mind that there are serious consequences. You should talk it out carefully before proceeding. By no means do it unaided on your own. You should both still seek medical and legal assistance – medical for health screenings and legal so that your agreement is recorded and future circumstances, as far as possible, are anticipated and considered.

If you are a woman wanting to make a withdrawal from the sperm bank, do you really need to go to the bank? Why make a withdrawal when you have plenty of friends with sperm on hand, so to speak?

There are three advantages to using the bank and the unknown donor. *First of all*, you have the benefit of a medically screened donation. You don't get this if you "try it at home" without outside help, and it is a key health consideration. Going private without any medical screening involves risks to you and your child, including HIV, hepatitis C and other sexually transmitted diseases. *Secondly*, by going to the bank, you also have the benefit of privacy, meaning that the donor's role in your child's future can be non-existent. The rules will vary with the state in which you live and the sperm bank with which you are dealing. *Thirdly*, by going to a bank you generally are taking control of your child's future. You will not know the father and he will not know you. When your child grows up, his or her ability to find out who the father is will depend on what the law is at the time the child reaches her or his majority. But if you do this at home with a friend (either through intercourse or with any other means you may devise), as mentioned above, then the child does have an identified father, you do know who it is, and he will have legal rights and responsibilities.

If you use a known donor, it is legally riskier if the lesbian parent intends that he not be a parent to the child. The law either regards you as a parent or not, and there is no in between. A biological father is the legal parent unless he has signed a consent to termination of his parental rights, in which case, he is not a parent. This necessarily complicates the matter for both the mother and the known donor. If he does not sign a termination, he may be liable. If he does, he is no longer a parent. This can involve a complicated mix of legal and emotional issues.

That set of circumstances may make the decision to have a baby by a known donor one that carries more legal risk. Many couples feel that they want their child to reflect their mutual families, so that Roberta may get pregnant using the sperm of a male relative of Toni's. If that were the case, a written agreement would be a wise thing to have before any efforts to have the baby. Be aware that a known donor may well be considered a legal parent if there is a dispute. The donor is perfectly entitled to fall in love with the child and thereafter change his mind about the level of his involvement. In that case the courts may support him in that change of heart.

Even with an agreement there is some risk involved. Some of the agreements are not upheld, according to Kate Kendell. If a father changes his mind and asserts a paternity action, she says, "There are cases that have invalidated the agreement that he signed saying that he, in fact, would not pursue such an action. Case law on this point is mixed and the best advice is that all parties involved have absolute clarity about their respective roles, desires, intentions and that this be codified in a contract."

The contract, even though cases decided in courts are mixed on this point, is absolutely essential. This is true even in circumstances where the donor is well known to the lesbian couple who want to have the baby.

NCLR has seen cases in which a lesbian and a gay man who have been friends for a long time decide that he will be the donor for her baby, with the understanding that he will be the "uncle" and not the parent. Because the couple knows one another so well, they do not write up an agreement. But when the child is born, the "uncle" is no longer talking about a concept, he is talking about a baby that he is holding in his arms and becoming attached to. Suddenly, he yearns to watch him grow up, to spend weekends with him, to be the father to this little baby and make up for all the places he feels like his own father failed. Suddenly, he doesn't want to be an "uncle." As the lesbian couple moves to a second parent adoption, the father may seek legal advice. However, if he had signed an agreement beforehand that terminated his parental rights, then most states would honor the agreement and allow him to be excluded from the child's life.

Without the agreement beforehand, when the time for the second parent adoption comes about, he may refuse to terminate his rights. "The situation," says Kate Kendell, "is fraught with emotional trauma and huge legal bills as both sides fight for what they each think is their relationship with the child. In those situations, it is difficult to find a party to blame. It is the fault of the legal system for being so inflexible in its notions of who is a parent and how to negotiate complicated familial relationships."

For every case that has this kind of breakdown and failure, however, Kendell states that there are dozens in which all parties are in agreement and accepting of their agreed upon rights and responsibilities, in which everyone acts with honor and everything flows. But it is important to remember that if you are considering this, your agreement with the donor father should be reflected in a written document and not by a handshake or verbal agreement. It is not simply the matter of having the contract, it is the process – the lengthy discussions that take place and the planning that will contribute to the stability of the relationship.

In the past, it was sometimes difficult for single women to use fertility services for artificial insemination at a medical facility. However, there is an increasing willingness on the part of these institutions to help. The best way to determine the rules and availability of services to you is to check with one of the many parenting resources available to you. The growing trend of gay and lesbian parenthood means that there are also growing resources from which you can draw.

Future Directions – Cloning Around

Send in the clones. Not long ago, that would have sounded silly, but not very many years ago, test-tube babies were only theoretically possible. In other words, to fertilize an egg outside of a women's body and then place it into a woman and have it grow was something that smacked faintly of science fiction. Then, it sounded silly too. When it became feasible, the children born through such a process were even referred to as "test tube" babies. Yet when surrogacy began, and hence legal and ethical problems that were inherent in its practice, there were no laws that regulated it. The controversy raised by the case of Baby M created an enormous demand for law, and state legislatures got busy and passed them, either regulating the practice or outlawing it.

Now theoretically at least, human beings can be cloned. During 2001, an international team of scientists announced their intention to clone a human being. Like "test tube" babies, this seems like science fiction, but within the very foreseeable future it will become science fact. However, unlike surrogacy, the law has wind of this scientific development. The mere specter of cloning caused some state legislatures to respond by outlawing the practice. Like laws passed to ban sodomy, that will not stop it from happening. It is perhaps inevitable that very soon, the first human being will be cloned. If you haven't kept up on scientific advances in the last ten years, what that means is that, shortly, there may be an added option for a gay or lesbian person seeking to have a child. That option would mean taking your own DNA and making a new you. You can recreate yourself – entirely.

By December 2002, a group known as Clonaid announced the first cloning of a human being, though did not offer evidence of their claim. In January, 2003, they announced a second birth to a lesbian couple and revealed that a cloning effort was underway for a gay couple in Nevada.

One can debate the desirability of this from now until the cloned cows come home, but the fact is that someone will attempt the cloning of a human being, and it is possible that it may be commercially available for people, if not in the United States, then in foreign countries. In such an event, it could certainly add a new facet to the on-going debate about whether homosexuality is genetic or learned behavior. That aside, there are no laws that account for such a possibility at the present time. That makes sense – right? There were no driver's licenses until there were cars.

However, it stands to reason that the scientific ability to clone human beings will result in a torrent of laws in the United States and many, if not all of those laws, may be hostile to the practice, perhaps outlawing it. But it will be fascinating if U.S. law forbids the practice, yet U.S. citizens can travel to foreign countries to have themselves cloned. How will U.S. law treat those children? Despite the fact that cloning may be illegal, once the child is born, it is a little difficult to ignore it legally.

In the spring of 2001, Congress held its first hearings on cloning, hearing from ethicists as well as scientists who asserted their intention to attempt human cloning. Clearly Congress is concerned enough to hold hearings. Cloning may at present be the least possible option offered by the science of genetics and medicine, but it is nevertheless getting a great deal of attention in the legal arena. By 2002, there were proposals before Congress to ban cloning entirely. This would possibly shut down scientific research into the cloning of human stem cells which hold promise for curing several diseases. More moderate proposals call for a ban on any cloning for the purpose of human reproduction.

The point is raised in this chapter because, though not imminent this year or next, clearly the advent of cloning will present serious, if not bizarre, new sets of circumstances for gays, lesbians, and those who regulate the institution of the family. The definition of family, as it has over the past thirty years, will continue to evolve, even in ways we cannot foresee.

OK, enough cloning around.

CHAPTER 3

Family Feuds—Fighting and Breaking Up

History and Perspective – Breakups and the Law

NOT ONLY DOES the dog need fencing in, but your partner has begun roaming, and you've had it. The spankings and electronic collar have only worked on the dog. Besides, you are getting kind of tired of waking up next to the same face every day. There isn't any romance in your lives anymore. The other day, someone half your age put a hand on your arm while you were chatting at the gym. You think perhaps you've been cheated on – or you *know* you've been cheated on, because your partner isn't even trying to hide it. Your fortieth birthday came and went, and all you got was a card and even then, it was late. You've had it and you are going to get out. Whatever the reason, this is the messy part of relationships.

And it happens in any kind of relationship, gay or straight. The degree to which the law is involved in your breakup may depend on the degree to which it was involved in your getting together. What that means is that if you are legally married to a member of the opposite sex, the law will go a long way toward handling your breakup. But if you are gay, then the involvement of the law is a little more unpredictable, and just as your gay marriage was "self help" so may be your gay divorce.

For gays and lesbians who are married, it can be particularly complicated. Many people leave a heterosexual legal marriage to enter into a gay or lesbian relationship, and if there are children involved in the legal marriage, the situation can become drastically complicated.

Even in the absence of a legal marriage, homosexual relationships are becoming more complicated and consequently so are gay and lesbian breakups.

You can't live together with someone for twenty years and not be facing some difficult circumstances when it comes to dividing up property. And, as seen in previous chapters, it is not just about property anymore, it can be about children – who supports them, who doesn't, and who gets to see or visit them.

Needless to say, with the growing number of gay and lesbian households in America coupled with the gay baby boom, there are going to be a lot more breakups. As gay and lesbianfamilies grow in complexity and nature, there are going to be many different kinds of legal issues between couples that sound just like the issues your parents may have faced. Palimony or galimony (heterosexuals call this alimony), child support, custody of children or of pets, or selling jointly owned homes are all the trappings of a legally recognized divorce. Gay or straight, it isn't fun, and it isn't easy. But when a legally married couple busts up, they can turn to the courts to help them make a decision. Your path won't be as assured.

Current Events – The Nasty Side of Relationships

If you are single, this is the one time that the grass does not look so green on the couple's side of the fence. Relationships, after all, are swell in the beginning, but when it comes to the ending that is not "happily-ever-after" things are not so much fun.

Many times a breakup is amicable. Though the sizzle is gone, that doesn't mean you have to hate each other. Couples often decide that, despite the good time they've had, they need to stop being lovers and start being friends. They can maturely and fairly divide their home and move on with their lives. If that is happening for you, then you probably don't need to read this section.

But many times that isn't what is happening. Emotions get piled on emotions and hurt fuels anger, and before you know it, the good times are bad – really, really bad. The way that manifests itself may be in abuse, or it may be in a refusal to leave, or just a plain and simple property or custody dispute.

If Things Are Falling Apart – Abuse

Unfortunately, there are often unpleasant events leading up to a split that can involve violence. In that case, you need to understand that there may be protections in place for you as well as places to which you can turn in a time of need.

Domestic violence among gay couples is not uncommon. The National Coalition of Anti-violence Programs issues annual information on domestic violence. They find that not only does domestic abuse occur in as many as one-third of all lesbian and gay relationships, it appears to be on the rise. Many gay and lesbian victims do not feel comfortable in contacting the authorities or seeking help from domestic-violence counselors. Others who do seek the help of the law may find that help simply unavailable to them solely because of who they are.

Recognizing Abuse. A little slap and tickle is one thing. But when it gets beyond the play stage, you may be in danger. Sometimes the onset of abuse is so gradual, a person may not notice it until it reaches a level that is obvious. Or just because you've never been physically hit, you don't consider that you are in an abusive situation. What are the bad behaviors that constitute abuse?

People tend to consider abuse as physical bashing. It can and often is physical, resulting in bruises and broken bones. That's the most obvious form that abuse takes, but it can also be emotional, psychological, or even financial. Abuse comes in as many forms as there are people to perform it and can encompass a range or combination of behaviors. Name calling, belittling, and stalking is all part of abuse.

Abuse can be emotional. Hollering at a person to intimidate them into doing or not doing something can be a form of abuse. If there are actions being taken that are causing you to feel threatened or intimidated, you may be suffering from abuse even though no one has lifted a hand to strike you.

Abuse is an act of coercion to cause you to either do or not do something. Say, for example, that you are in a relationship that you have decided to end. Your partner is desperate to keep the relationship. To keep you from going, your partner actually threatens to drag you out of the closet where you work or with your family. Or one partner in a relationship may be considered the responsible one when it comes to money and takes care of all of the finances, but uses money to control his or her partner.

When do arguments constitute abuse? A mere fight is not abuse – a fight is a fight. But don't let that lull you into a false sense that repeated fighting which is meant to intimidate and control you is not abuse. Fighting is an event, abuse is a process. Abuse is a pattern of behavior, not an isolated incident.

The crossover telling you when abuse is considered abusive isn't really a legal question. You have to decide. Whether some actions are abusive can be highly subjective. One person may consider an action to be very threatening and intimidating that another person might not. There is not always a clear trip wire lets you know when something in your relationship has crossed a line. Naturally, if you have been beaten or are being stalked, the abuse is obvious, but other actions may be subtler.

You may have seen abuse in your past, perhaps even with your parents – but you never thought it would happen to you because you're a gay man or lesbian woman. People often tend to consider domestic abuse as something heterosexual couples do, but around the country, there is a growing awareness that spousal abuse is a gay and lesbian problem, too.

In fact, when it comes to domestic violence, there seems to be little statistical difference between the straight household and the gay household. Where there are differences, however, are in the resources that are available to heterosexuals, because they far outnumber those that are dedicated to gay/lesbian domestic violence.

Abuse Protection. Fortunately for people who suffer abuse, there are a good number of resources and laws that protect and aid a person who is in such a situation. In short, there is no problem in the law with doing something about domestic abuse. What you may find you need is to get the person as far away from you as possible. If that is the case, then there are legal mechanisms available to do just that.

In fact, every single state and the District of Columbia provides protections against domestic abuse. If a husband is beating his wife, or vice versa, he or she can walk into any court in the land and get protection in the form of a protective or restraining order.[8]

Unlike other court actions, such as suing another individual, the process of getting some sort of protective order does not take forever – it can be accomplished in a relatively short amount of time and at low cost. A person can file the necessary paperwork to get a protective order with the assistance offered by one of the many domestic violence organizations that exist in every state.

Domestic violence organizations run shelters and support groups and provide advice and assistance to the battered victim in gaining refuge. The nature of the protection for a victim can cover a broad range – from getting a restraining order that keeps the person away from the victim, to evicting the offending party from the shared living premises, to limiting contact in just about any way you can imagine. And that is the good news.

There is, sadly, bad news. Just as heterosexual lawmakers want marriage to only pertain to heterosexuals, some of them also only want protections against abuse to be limited to heterosexuals. In six states, there is no protection offered to lesbian and gay couples, because the laws that guide the provision of protective orders against domestic violence apply only to persons in heterosexual relationships. In other words, some state statutes deem that heterosexuals are the only ones who can get married, and they are therefore the only ones who deserve to get protection from one another when the going gets tough. As for the rest of us, since we are not legally able to get married, and in fact, not legally able to have sexual

8. Depending on where you are, this may be called a temporary restraining order, protective order, stay-away order or no-contact order – you get the idea though. It means stay away.

relations in many states, we are left out – at least in some states. Those states are Delaware, Louisiana, Montana, New York, South Carolina and Virginia.

This would actually be funny if it did not have such serious ramifications. Several of the states have, either by law or practice, specifically excluded gays and lesbians from the protection of domestic abuse laws. That is discrimination, with a punch. On the other hand, a small handful of states – Hawaii, Illinois, Kentucky, Ohio and, recently, Arizona – have specifically included gays and lesbians. Arizona used to be one of the states that did not include gays and lesbians. The vast majority in-between includes language in their statutes that is gender neutral, so that it could be perceived that the statutes cover people other than heterosexual couples. You would think, then, that for the most part, lesbian and gay households are protected under those laws. You would think.

But it is important to keep in mind that in order to avail yourself of the law's protections, you will naturally have to reveal the nature of your relationship to legal authorities – i.e., that you have a lover who is of the same gender as you. When that happens in a state where there are sodomy laws forbidding sex between persons of the same gender, you are telling the representatives of the law that you are a sexual outlaw. This is just one of the many public health harms caused by sodomy laws. The end effect is that a gay man or lesbian woman who is suffering abuse at the hands of a partner often has to face a decision between staying with the abusive partner or trying to get help from an abusive system. Either way, they end up abused.

Stalker Protection. There are other laws that protect people aside from domestic-abuse laws. For example, all fifty states and the District of Columbia offer remedy or protection for persons who are being stalked. Stalking is defined broadly in most of the statutes to be any course or pattern of behavior that is designed to intimidate or harass another person – something that would cause the reasonable person to feel threatened or terrorized bodily or sexually. By definition, some states require only two acts that could be deemed to be harassing in nature to constitute stalking. Some statutes refer to telephone calls or electronic means. We have all seen enough movies and bad television shows to come up with a definition of what stalking is. States tend to classify this as a felony, though some put it in the misdemeanor category. If a stalker is a repeat stalker, the seriousness of the crime escalates, particularly if the stalker is violating a court order. Something interesting to note: in many states, stalking not only includes a pattern of behavior directed toward you, it can include members of your family. In those states with such a provision, "family" is defined beyond the traditional sense, allowing members of your household who are not blood relatives, such as a lover, to be counted as family. What this means is that, should your ex be trying to harass you by following your new partner, you may be able to file charges for stalking against your ex. Once again, however, you might consider whether or not your state is one that outlaws sodomy, because in calling on the law to protect you, you will have to admit that you are also a lawbreaker.

Where to Turn for Help. Naturally, if a person is beating the crap out of you, you would expect that if you pick up the telephone and dial 911, you will get a helpful response from the police. That may not be the case. While some police departments have formal outreach programs to the lesbian and gay community, the vast majority do not. It is not impossible that an officer responding to the call will arrest both parties.

If you are a victim of domestic abuse, the natural action for you to consider is to seek help from one of the many domestic abuse resources that are probably available in your locale. That, however, may not be your best option. You may find that, while many such organizations are very helpful to heterosexuals, when it comes to gays, lesbians, bisexuals, and especially transgenders, they are at best, flummoxed, or at worst, too prejudiced to be of help.

So what can you do? Fortunately, there are a number of gay and lesbian organizations you can contact, even if they are not in your immediate locality. Many gay and lesbian service organizations have anti-violence programs and may be able to tell you what the law is in your state and whether or not there are any available counseling programs that are either gay and lesbian oriented or sympathetic.

If you have access to the Internet, you may be able to determine whether or not there are resources available to you in your area. It may also pay to check the website of your municipality to see if your local police department has any outreach program to the gay, lesbian, bisexual, and transgender community.

If you have had a series of problems, then the time may have come to end the relationship. Pack up your dancing shoes and begin your journey as The Gay Divorcee. We'll begin by looking at how legal marriages dissolve and then move on to looking at gay and lesbian breakups specifically.

When Married Couples End It

There are just three ways for a marriage to end. The first and most obvious is through death. The second is by annulment, and the last is by divorce. For issues associated with death and dying, see chapter 4. For our purposes here, annulment and divorce issues will only be examined insofar as they relate to the fact that you are a homosexual.

Annulment. Remember that a marriage is a contract. In order for any contract to be valid, a basic staple is that both parties entered into the agreement in good faith and that there was a "meeting of the minds." If there is a condition that exists that negates that meeting of the minds, then the contract becomes null and void and never existed in the first place.

If you enter into a contract with Sarah to have her remodel your bathroom, and you then find out that Sarah is not a plumber and has never remodeled a bathroom, you can have the contract declared null and void. That is because if you had known that Sarah, was in fact, not a plumber or contractor, but a decorator, you never would have entered into the contract in the first place. In other words, there is a condition that exists that prevents there having ever been a "meeting of the minds" about what the contract was about.

Annulment is the same thing. It is a court decree that states that the marriage never existed in the first place, because when the parties entered into the contract of marriage, there was a condition that existed that made the marriage null and void. Grounds for annulment are based in fraud, meaning that the person you were married to failed to mention to you that they were already legally married or were actually a close blood relative of yours. Other grounds include a refusal to engage in sexual intercourse, mental incompetence, or underage status. In some respects, you could say that one party to the marriage being homosexual would actually undermine the marriage contract, but if there was sexual intercourse and the marriage lasted for a reasonable period of time, then it is not likely that an annulment is the appropriate course of action.

Some people might prefer an annulment, particularly for religious reasons, because an annulment states that the marriage never existed in the first place, and they are therefore free to remarry in their faith. If they get divorced, then marriage is forbidden to them. But the challenge for you is that you are going to have to prove that the marriage never existed in the first place, which actually may not be that easy. The type of proof that you may be called upon to produce is going to be much more far-reaching than your testimony. You may have to produce witnesses to support a particular point of view. You will be trying to prove state of mind, which is daunting. Actually the grounds for annulment are far fewer than for divorce. More importantly, grounds for divorce are far easier to prove than are those for annulment, so if you are looking to end a marriage and don't care how it ends, then divorce is probably your best option.

Divorce. There are a lot of people who found that coming out of the closet was so difficult that they barricaded themselves in it with a marriage. Then one day, they either find that they can't stand their confinement and need to leave, or are motivated to leave by the formation of a new attachment – someone of their own gender. Whatever the reason, when a person in a marriage recognizes that they are homosexual, the heterosexual marriage often ends in divorce.

When you look at the laws that surround marriage, what you'll find is that most of them are actually about the dissolution of marriage. That said, it is important that any gay or lesbian understand the divorce process for heterosexual marriage, because there can potentially be some issues associated with the notion of "fault" in divorce that may affect you. In other words, if it is your "fault" that the divorce is ending because you are homosexual, then some states may attach more importance to that than others may when it comes to the division of property, alimony, and, most importantly, children.

While annulment decrees that a marriage never existed in the first place, divorce is a decree that states that the marriage existed, but has officially ended. You can obtain a divorce by applying to the court where you live.

The nature of divorce has changed significantly over the past forty years. It used to be that you had to show that someone was at fault for the end of the marriage, and you had to prove grounds for the divorce. Grounds could include a number of things, including abandonment, abuse, adultery, and addiction. However, there has been a transition to allowing divorce where there is no fault for the marriage falling apart. In fact, some states only have "no-fault" divorce, leaving others to still provide both no-fault as well as divorce based on fault.

It is the most usual circumstance that people enter into an agreement to divorce. That agreement outlines the division of property and the custody of children. While that is true of most couples, for a gay or lesbian person, there may be hurt feelings on the part of a legal spouse that will stand in the way of any agreement. While there are no statistics available in this regard, it stands to reason that a gay or lesbian person involved in a divorce may be more likely to face a contentious divorce rather than one where mutual agreement results in a judge issuing a divorce decree.

In dividing property, fault used to be considered a factor. But it is a difficult thing for a court to get tied up in the emotions that brought down a marriage, therefore making it much more likely now that only economic factors are considered when deciding on a property division. But if you are involved in a contentious divorce, you will want to find out from your divorce lawyer whether or not fault is going to be a factor that the court in your state will consider when dividing property.

If you have moved out of the domestic arrangement you had with your legal spouse and live in a new state, you will need to find out what the residency requirement is in the state in which you are living for obtaining a divorce. Some states have no residency requirement.

States Without a Residency Requirement for Divorce

Alaska	Massachusetts
Iowa	South Dakota
Louisiana	

Alimony and Support. While fault is usually not an issue in property division, it may come into play when considering alimony payments. In nearly twenty states, fault can be an issue. That means that if you are gay, lesbian, bisexual, or transgendered, and your marriage is ending because of this, it may be a factor that weighs on the amount of alimony that you end up having to pay, because the divorce may be perceived as your fault. It is not unheard of for a judge to characterize a formerly heterosexual person who emerges from the closet as someone who is making a choice, and even perhaps a depraved one.

On the other hand, if you are a spouse seeking alimony and the marriage dissolution is considered to be your fault, you may be barred from it. In other words, if Sue came out of the closet and her husband wanted a divorce, if she sought alimony from him then she might be barred from it if her lesbianism is considered the fault of the divorce.

States Where Fault Counts in Making Alimony Determinations

Alabama	Maryland	Pennsylvania
Connecticut	Massachusetts	South Carolina
District of Columbia	Michigan	South Dakota
Florida	Mississippi	Tennessee
Georgia	Missouri	Virginia
Idaho	Nevada	West Virginia
Louisiana	New Hampshire	Wyoming
Maine	North Dakota	

Child Custody Issues During Divorce

The custody of children in a divorce is perhaps the most painful part of the process. A child sees his or her parents at war and will likely perceive that his or her future is at stake. Where will we live? Where will I go to school? What will my friends think? The simple act of splitting up can have profound effects on the well being of a child. That is true when a child is going through an every day heterosexual divorce. But when one of the parents is gay or lesbian, the child has additional issues to face. The child must deal with accepting or rejecting the identity of his or her parent, or dealing with the question of his homosexual parent's "friend." Then the child will have to deal with how this information is shared within his or her own circle of friends.

The stress can be compounded when splitting up goes beyond the simple act – when parents begin using children and access to those children as a bargaining chip or as a way to "get back" at a spouse. Then the stress felt by a child naturally multiplies to the point that an already painful experience can become excruciating.

The breakup of a traditional heterosexual marriage because one partner has decided to enter a homosexual union can take the hurt feelings that accompany any divorce and multiply them. With this kind of situation, the spouse who is being left may feel particularly hurt, and there may be an even greater temptation to exact a payment from the departing spouse through use of the children.

Homosexuality as a Grounds for Denying Custody. Where matters of custody are concerned, a parent may seize onto anything he or she can in order to be chosen as the parent who gets custody. A weakness in the character can be opened up in court to demonstrate the unfit nature of a departing parent. A determined parent can easily exploit any "defect," either real or perceived.

For example, in 1984, a man sought custody of his daughter from his divorced wife, who had entered into an interracial relationship with another man. Determined to gain custody of their child, he said that it would be in the child's best interests to remove her from her mother's custody because of the social stigma that the child was facing as a result of her white mother's choice of a black man as a husband. While that stigma might in fact be a reality, when the issue went all the way to the Supremes, the Court made it clear that they would not "give effect" to such bias. In other words, though prejudice exists, they were not going to dignify a racially prejudicial outlook by ruling that the mother could not have custody of her child solely based on the racial identity of her new partner.

Still homosexuality can be perceived as a weakness by the weak-minded and, just as it can be a factor in alimony, it can even more readily come into play when you are engaged in a divorce and there is a question of child custody. There was a time, not very long ago, when, in any divorce case, if either the husband or the wife was accused of homosexuality in the course of the divorce proceedings, it was the death knell for any hope for custody, and perhaps even visitation rights for the lesbian or gay parent. Age-long stereotypes of gays and lesbians as predators upon children resonated, and resonate still, with many judges. Because homosexuality was long regarded as an illness, there was concern that a child should not be exposed to it. There was fear that the child would grow up gay. And while the court in the 1980s would not indulge the prejudice inherent in the stigma that a child might bear because her mother's partner was of a different race, the prejudice that engenders stigma that a child would face with a lesbian or gay parent was and still may be very much indulged. Custody could be out of the question, and visitation might be allowed only under heavily restricted circumstances.

However, nothing stays the same forever, and the way that gays and lesbians are perceived by the larger society has been changing. Even divorce courts have been swept along with greater social evolution regarding lesbian and gay legal and political status in the United States. It is part of a bigger social metamorphosis regarding the rearing of children. In the time of June Cleaver, circa 1950s, the idealized image of a child's life involved daily on-going support from a Mom. She baked chocolate-chip cookies and stayed at home during the day. This was coupled with the occasional appearance of a tired stranger in the evenings and on weekends who was called "Dad." Deviation from that norm had been seen as damaging to the child. This was despite the fact that a mere decade before, the image of women heading to factories to support the war effort was highly encouraged as a matter of (short-term) social policy. Still, with the advent of a societal liberation of sexual mores, of women and of the work place during the 1960s and 1970s, the configuration of family began to change and the status of children changed as well.

But when it comes to the breakup of a marriage in which one of the parents is gay or lesbian, then it is quite likely that a judge will impose a structured- visitation situation. That structure means that when the child is visiting with the gay parent, the court may direct that there be no other non-related person of the same sex present in the household while the child is there. While this is not the case universally, it is the case in more places than not. If the situation involves a contentious divorce, the attorney for the non-gay parent is very likely to use every possible advantage in representing his or her client's interests. That means the fact that you are gay or lesbian will most likely be used to limit your rights.

That is especially true if you are not only leaving your spouse but are doing so for a new homosexual partnership. In that circumstance, you could be in for a difficult time, especially if you are planning on having a household with your new partner. The idea that a gay or lesbian person can be a good parent is one thing, but if they are engaged in a new domestic partnership, that may tilt the scales of justice altogether. You may be surprised to find out that this is not only true if you are gay, but also if you are straight.

Many courts will do more than frown if a parent is leaving a marriage to reside with a new partner without the sacrament of marriage, gay or straight. In some states there are laws that say that any kind of co-habitation, heterosexual or gay, without the benefit of marriage is a factor for a court to consider in awarding custody. Of course, while that may sound equitable, the fact remains that it is heterosexuals who can remedy the situation by marrying their new partner. Gays and lesbians obviously don't have that option.

So if you are gay and you want to live with your new partner, what should you do – hide it? Lying won't help, and it might even hurt you. That is particularly true if you are under oath or in a deposition. Engaging in a lie about the situation could result in its discovery later. That, in and of itself, could justify a switch in custody. You may not like the answer to the question in this case.

If you are in a state that takes a dim view of co-habitation, then your custody interests may best be served by putting off any habitation with your new partner as the custody proceeding moves forward.

While the standard has seen progress and some states now take other matters into account when awarding custody, there are still more places in the United States where the gay or lesbian status of the parent will be the predominant factor in whether or not you can have custody. And it may guide your visitation rights. Some of the more progressive states focus on the standard known as the "best interests of the child," but that can be a very subjective standard.

The Best Interests of the Child Standard. Divorce courts used to decide matters of child custody by traditionally awarding it to the mother, with weekend and holiday visits with the father, who also had to pay child support. Slowly, this old formula for custody – give the kids to the mother and make the father pay support – began to change. Many times, the woman was the top earner in a family. The concept of stay-at-home dads became less and less of a startling exception. Courts had to decide cases less by a knee-jerk categorization than by engaging in an analysis of what, in fact, is in the best interests of the child or children in question in settling a custody question. As in matters of adoption (See chapter 2, Are You a Fit Parent?), this standard, "best interests of the child," began to be applied more and more widely.

Couple this new standard with an increasing body of evidence demonstrating that children of homosexuals are not at any higher risk of turning out damaged than they are if brought up by heterosexual parents. Add in the growing realization that homosexuality is perhaps not a learned trait but genetic in nature (hence the "sexual orientation" phrase as opposed to "sexual preference"), and you get a situation in which some courts began to find it acceptable, and at times even preferable, to award visitation and/or custody to gay or lesbian parents. It would appear, at least in certain geographies and court systems, that a corner has been turned on the matter of a gay parent and the custody of his or her child, in that it is no longer a *fait accompli* that gay = no custody. Decisions regarding custody and visitation arrangements were less categorical and began to be decided on a standard of what situation would in fact be in the best interest of the child.

What that means today is that the best-interest-of-the-child standard requires a court to look at the situation objectively and consider a wide range of circumstances to determine the best course for the child. "No gay no way" has fallen, at least to a limited extent, opening the door to the finding that a lesbian or gay parent may in fact be the best parent for a child. With that door open, the custody landscape for gay and lesbian parents brightened considerably. Many courts have a more open mind towards lesbian and gay parents and have come to realize that sexual orientation alone does not impact one's fitness to be a parent. That does not mean, however, that the standard is applied in all cases, or that lesbian and gay parents facing custody battles still aren't going to face homophobia or the inability of a court to apply the best interests of the child standard.

How the Standard Is Applied. There are some states that are definitely less inclined to view homosexuality as a basis for denying custody or curtailing visitation, but it is not as if there are clear lines of demarcation on this issue. It is still possible even if your state has case law saying that lesbian or gay status is not enough of a reason to deny custody, that there can be an unfavorable ruling. Even where such denials are not the knee-jerk reaction, you will have to be careful, in that some judges may harbor prejudices that will color their analysis of what is in the best interests of the child. If you are in this situation, it is advisable that you and your attorney get counsel and advice from one of the national organizations experienced in this area.

And in fact, there is a geographical factor that needs to be considered, because it may victimize you. While there is a new "best interests" standard to guide courts, it may vary a great deal, depending on where you are. To determine what is in the best interests of the child, it is up to a judge, who may include in that analysis the detrimental exposure of a child to his or her parent's homosexuality. In other words, a homophobic judge could still determine that exposure is not, under any circumstances, in the best interests of the child. While legal circumstances have been evolving away from that sort of extreme, the attitude still does exist among many individual judges around the nation. Acceptance of new standards is not universal, especially where issues are charged with emotions evoked by religious conviction – as with both evolution and homosexuality. How the standard is applied and what factors are considered by the judge can vary from jurisdiction to jurisdiction.

For example, if you are a lesbian in Mississippi coming out of a heterosexual marriage, the court may construe what is in your children's best interest far differently from a court in California that is examining the very same set of facts. It is highly possible that homophobia will play a huge role in the determination by the court in Mississippi. But in California, the judge is more likely to have a perspective that is much more understanding of gay and lesbian parents, and their sexual orientation will be irrelevant in determining whether or not one is the best parent to assume custody.

There are real-life consequences for divorcing parents who are gay or lesbian. Florida is one of the states where sexual orientation is not by itself supposed to be sufficient reason to deny a parent custody. Yet a lesbian parent, Mary Ward, lost custody of her child solely because she was a lesbian. That in and of itself could be called an outrageous outcome, but it is made more so by the fact that the child's father was convicted of murder. Apparently, there was less stigma and less risk to a child, in the court's wisdom, to be raised in the household of a murderer than of a lesbian.

"Mary Ward would never have lost custody of her child if it had not been for her sexual orientation," says Kate Kendell, who assisted in the argument on the appeal of the case. "In some jurisdictions, the best-interests-of-the-child standard is a bit of an empty promise." She points out that the places where that promise tends to be more empty are places where there are smaller gay and lesbian populations and which are more conservative in their political and social outlooks – and this may not only vary from state to state, but within a state. For example, in southern Florida, you might be treated equitably by a court. Whereas in the more conservative sections of northern Florida, you would find that if you were leaving a heterosexual marriage and it is known that you are lesbian or gay, then "the possibility of retaining custody would be troubling," says Kendell.

An Extreme Case. Your spouse is not the only person you may have to deal with in the matter of custody. It is not impossible that you may face a battle with grandparents, your spouse's parents, or even your own. If you are living with your homosexual partner, then you may have a particularly difficult time; if you are not living together, your chances of success will be enhanced.

No one, perhaps, knows that better than Sharon Bottoms. She did not have to face off against a spouse who was trying to gain custody; she had to square off against her own mother. This case was as difficult as can be imagined.

Once again we find ourselves in Virginia – home of the anti-miscegenation laws struck down in chapter 1 and, of course, one of the bastions of sodomy laws, as you will see in chapter 8. While living in Virginia, Sharon Bottoms gave birth to her son Tyler in July 1991. In 1993, her mother, Pamela Kay Bottoms, brought suit in court seeking custody of the baby, alleging that her daughter Sharon was unfit to be a mother based on her homosexuality. Despite the fact that a court-appointed specialist testified that there was no basis for assuming that a lesbian mother would be harmful to the child, the court awarded custody of the two-year-old to his grandmother. The court said a lesbian was an unfit mother.

On appeal the following year, that decision was reversed.

Then, in 1995, the grandmother took her case to the Virginia Supremes. That court found that, while custody could not be denied solely on the basis of the sexual orientation of a parent, there could be stigma attached to a child growing up in a lesbian household that would be harmful. And though the judges were divided in their opinion, they reinstated the custody award to Sharon's mother. This is a prime example of how the best-interests-of-the-child standard can be twisted by minds with political goals.

By 1996, Sharon had decided that she could no longer put herself and, more importantly, her son through the rigors of the court actions.

The Bottoms case was highly publicized and was a terrible loss for gay and lesbian parents.

There is a ray of hope. In 1998, the same court that denied custody of her son to Sharon Bottoms awarded custody of two children to a woman with a same-sex partner, meaning that, in Virginia, the knee-jerk reaction to deny custody based solely on sexual orientation was no longer jerking.

How to Minimize Trouble. How can you determine your chances? How do you know if you are getting divorced in a jurisdiction that is going to judge you fairly or knee-jerk custody away from you because of your sexual orientation? The most helpful thing you can do if you are in such a situation is to get help before you act. Where there is negative case law, or where you are in a hostile geographic region it is important to have an attorney conversant with the role homophobia might play in the proceedings. You should immediately seek assistance from one of the national organizations. They can aid you in getting credible and authoritative experts who can speak to the court and educate the judge out of socialized bias against lesbian or gay parents. It is important to seek this kind of help, because according to Kate Kendell, unless a judge has shown that he is "affirming, tolerant and accepting, a lawyer in a hostile region should assume that he is otherwise and should proceed accordingly. It is never a lost cause," she notes, "but it will require a significant extra effort to protect a lesbian or gay parent from enduring significant injustice."

If you are concerned or have questions about your area of the country, check with a national organization before you begin your divorce proceedings and, perhaps, even before you seek representation. The question of geography is one of the first asked when an intake call is received at the National Center for Lesbian Rights, because your answer will clue them in to the biases you are going to face in your legal situation.

Gay and Lesbian Breakups

When gays and lesbians break up, there are fewer rules than when your mom and dad got divorced. There are also fewer certainties. And that can create a number of legal complications in what is usually an already emotionally complicated circumstance. Because of that, the law has developed some of its own unique responses to gay and lesbian breakups that could impact you if you are in this situation.

How Breakups Differ from Divorce. Frederick Hertz is a lawyer who practices gay and lesbian family law in Oakland, California, and the author of *the* book on gay divorce. Literally – he wrote the book. He has a clear understanding of how gay and lesbian relationships are affected by their lack of legal recognition when it comes to breaking up. He says that one of the fundamental distinctions between heterosexual and gay relationships is that when a heterosexual couple gets married, there is a defined starting point at which the couple will jointly begin to acquire and own property. But for gay and lesbian couples, the lack of a "starting date" means that the notion of joint property or deciding on how property even comes into being in the relationship is far less certain. At breakup time, that can be extraordinarily inconvenient as you are try to decide what property goes to who.

In fact, marriage law is there to provide straight people with a roadmap on how to breakup; they don't have to feel their way around it.

You may feel relieved by that. You might think that you are better off not having the law involved in gay relationships, and, in fact, the law up until now hasn't been involved in the bond between you and your lover. You aren't in a legally recognized relationship. Some states even outlaw your sexual relations. How then, can the law be involved in your breakup?

You are of course, right to ask. After all, you don't have to go to court to divide the property; you can do it yourselves. It was understood when you got into this relationship that you each would walk away from it with what you brought into it, right? And hey, they aren't your kids; you don't need to support them. Or hey, they're your kids; you can keep them away from her forever. Why should you have the law involved? Divorce is a problem for straight people, isn't it?

To think that the law isn't involved is off the mark – it is just the *way* the law is involved that is different. If you are in a heterosexual marriage and getting divorced, the law is going to help you figure it out in a place called family court. But if you are in a long-term gay or lesbian relationship, the family court doesn't care what the hell you do or don't do, because you are not legally recognized as a family. That doesn't mean, however, that you won't end up in a court. Some unmarried people have gone to court already in cases that began to establish rights for unmarried partners. This makes it very possible for a homosexual couple to end up in court, fighting as they might in a divorce court for property, but without the benefit of all the rules laid out in marriage law. Rather, if you and your partner get into a property dispute because of the breakup of your relationship, you will find yourself in a place called civil court, which in many cases, is anything but civil.

What difference does the name of the court make, you may ask, court is court. If straight people go to family court and we go to civil court, who cares? But Frederick Hertz points out that the fact that marriage laws are almost all about the dissolution of the marriage makes a big difference when you get to that court. In family court, he notes, the judges have been specifically trained for their job, and the system is designed for this purpose. "There are pre-printed forms you can use, the schedule is relatively quick, and there can be mediation involved, Hertz says. "In many cases, you don't even have to have a lawyer. And in family court, if one of the parties behaves in an unreasonable fashion, then the judges have the ability to punish them." In fact, Hertz notes the system of marital law is so geared to break-up that it takes on a paternalistic role, one that assumes couples cannot make decisions for themselves. For example, he says, in California, if the husband and wife are economically disparate, the court will require the wealthy one to pay for the attorneys for both sides to ensure that they are equitably represented and that "the rich one doesn't oppress the poor one."

But for gay couples, who end up in civil court, the picture can be quite different. "You have no specifically trained judge," says Hertz, "and you are in there doing battle with the shopping-center developers who are disputing a contract." In civil court, he notes, the kind of irrational behavior that would not be tolerated in family court can go on unabated. "The kind of emotional drama that most couples face is really less in the marital world than it is in the non-marital."

The Development of Palimony. There were no rights for unmarried couples before the 1970s. There had been some attempts, and a few cases here and there involving a claim for support, but there was no standard. All that was about to change, however. As increasing numbers of unmarried heterosexual couples began living together, the law began to deal with their issues. The legitimate and landmark birth of "palimony" was something right out of Hollywood – literally.

It is perhaps safe to say that most actors would like to be remembered for their fine portrayals in film or on the stage – for that performance that won them the Tony or the Oscar. Actor Lee Marvin had many memorable moments on film. He even won an Oscar for his role in *Cat Ballou*. However, in the legal world, he will be remembered less for his artistry on celluloid than for the precedent he and his female companion established in the courts of California in a case that would have far-reaching effects for unmarried couples everywhere – straight and gay. In their case, the couple had lived together for an extended period of time. Mr. Marvin's partner had even adopted his last name as her own, even though they never got married. When the co-habital tectonic plates shifted and the big split came along, the female Marvin felt summarily dismissed without prospects by the male Marvin.

To address this imbalance, she went to court and asserted that the couple had entered into an oral understanding that outlined their relationship – that they would live together, combine their incomes, and share their property. In other words, she said, though they had no written agreement, they had mutually understood that she was living with him as his companion and supporting him in his career, and his career was being pursued to support the two of them. The court thought about it and agreed that if a person is found to be making sacrifices to benefit another in an unmarried living situation, and the parties understood their roles, then a contract could be understood to have existed. The case made headlines, and even though there had been such cases in the past, they were stillborn compared to the Marvin case which established a legal right of action popularly known as palimony.

Afterwards, there were bound to be gay versions. In 1981 Billie Jean King, the famed tennis player, was the subject of such a suit. She was in a legal marriage and held fast to claims of her heterosexuality. But she was sued by a former employee, Marilyn Barnett, who claimed that she was entitled to support because of a relationship in what was to be referred to as "galimony." The following year, another employee of another celebrity, Liberace, also filed a suit for support in California. In a case with a twist, the former lover of Rock Hudson filed a palimony suit that included claims for compensation for having unwittingly been exposed to HIV.

What Palimony Is and Is Not. Hey – if we can't have the rights of marriage, how is it that we have to deal with the rights allowed in divorce? How can we be held responsible for paying alimony by a legal system that doesn't even recognize our existence?

Technically, you are right – the law will not hold anyone in a gay couple responsible for paying alimony, because alimony is something that only comes with marriage. When a heterosexual couple gets married and then, as half of them do, gets divorced, the law allows one to apply for alimony. That is a right of marriage and is part of all those collections of hundreds of laws that make up the marriage contract. In fact, because alimony is a marriage right, it can safely be assumed that one of the reasons some avoid marriage is to avoid the need to pay alimony upon divorce. Palimony is not on such sure-footed ground.

The fact that it is a right makes alimony different from its poor cousin, palimony – which is not a right. But in terms of being held responsible financially, it is possible that you may have to pay out, or have a right to receive, something very similar – either galimony or palimony – whatever reflects the nature of your relationship.

Palimony must be proven. All marriage involves the possibility of alimony, but all living together situations do not necessarily mean that there is a right to galimony or palimony. You don't get palimony just based on the fact that for a couple of years you played house. Palimony is only available where you can make a case for it. That case has to do with contracts.

One who wants palimony from a partner will have to prove that he or she is entitled to it. To do that, one must prove that there was an agreement made between the two unmarried lovers that property would be shared, particularly, where one party is financially dependent on the other.

For example, giving up a career to move cross-country to be with a lover may necessarily involve one partner giving up something very substantial for the sake of the other. In the absence of a written agreement that anticipates these circumstances (See chapter 1, Live-Together Agreements) there may be a basis for one partner to claim support from another in the event of a breakup. The dependency or lack of balance can also be the result of a couple's decision to have children and designate one parent as the primary caretaker while the other is the primary breadwinner. If the decisions a couple makes have caused a financial dependency of one on the other, that may have to be recognized as they split.

Economic Gaps between Couples. Frederick Hertz recently handled a case that he says is increasingly common, involving a lesbian couple who were similarly situated when they got together but later developed a very traditional relationship as one of them began to assume the role of breadwinner while the other became a stay-at-home mom. One of the women gave birth to a child, while the other became a legal parent to the child through a second parent adoption (see chapter 2).

The breadwinning partner became very successful in business, and the couple became increasingly affluent. They had done some initial planning when they began their relationship, but their circumstances changed so rapidly and meteorically that, Hertz says, "It became woefully out of date." The breadwinning partner, as a function of her position in her company, was awarded large sums in stock options, but the stay-at-home mom was left out of that because she was not a legal spouse. "What happened with this couple," says Hertz, "is what happens with so many others. Over time, two things happen: you have a state of actual dependency, where one partner hasn't worked in several years and the other has eighty-five percent of the assets in their name." Then, because the stay-at-home mom hasn't worked in many years, after the break-up it is going to be hard for her to go back to work. In the case Hertz was describing, the stay at home mom had never finished her degree. And there, says Hertz, is another note of caution.

"It is always going to be the lower-earning person who stops work to take care of the kids and therefore, as a result, gets poorer over time." The partner with the higher-paying profession will consequently emerge as the breadwinner – which makes economic sense. "If someone needs to go half-time in order to take care of a kid, is it going to be the lawyer or the social worker?"

And it isn't just about having kids; it is also about who lives where or who takes advantage of what opportunity. Why would someone turn down a job transfer for a big job in order to save a little job?

While economic disparity is not inevitable, the possibility of a disparity developing is an important issue for unmarried couples. And because the law does not recognize the relationship, those issues become more complex than they are for married couples. Married couples buy things jointly and file taxes jointly. Unmarried couples, however, often develop a "paper gap," because their life together is not reflected in the papers that document their lives. People begin creating two lives – the life on paper and the life that is real. The life on paper, says Hertz, can be "mind-boggling," because people act in a way that is inconsistent with their reality. One partner may be earning more, so the poorer partner will have less reason to collect the tax deductions, e.g., the mortgage payment. And therefore, the interest deduction that goes along with it for tax purposes goes to the higher-earning partner. "If you put all the property in one name because he has the good credit, then the one with bad credit can suffer. If you put 100 percent of the tax deductions into the pocket of the wealthy partner and the poorer partner just buys the groceries, and they break up . . ." well, then the grocery buying partner is left holding the bag.

This is exactly the kind of thing that happened in the case that Hertz described. "There was an increase in the gap, with a discrepancy in their paper life as opposed to their real life. And when there is a breakup in a circumstance like that, the wealthy one doesn't want to pay the poor one and uses the paper reality to justify his or her point of view. And because we don't have marital property or community property laws, the dependent one has to show that there is an actual agreement there, and it is just one person's word against another person's word." All of this is because a gay relationship evolves over time while a straight relationship is born on the date the couple says, "I do."

Hertz notes that gay and lesbian couples are more likely to be financially equal than their heterosexual counterparts who have more children. For those gay couples who are financially uneven, "the poorer partner is much worse off than in a heterosexual relationship." With the greater affluence in the gay community and the increasing number of relationships, it only stands to reason that the need for written contracts will rise, as will palimony cases.

With regard to children under these circumstances, the family court has jurisdiction over matters involving custody and visitation, and nothing can change that. However, the financial issues and settlement would have to be heard civil court. If the couple were straight and married, it would all be handled in family court.

Proving a Case. Remedying a situation involving an inequity in the relationship may, as in custody issues, depend on where you live and what the courts have done with the matter. If you live in California or New York there is a legal history to draw upon. If, however, you live in a state where there is no solid legal precedent for honoring palimony claims, then the matter may not be a simple one. You might have to assert your suit in a different way – one that is more related to property rights.

Palimony suits rely on a matter of fact – i.e., that there was an understanding between the parties that it was their aim to create this sort of union. This is where palimony suits can be tricky, in that the alleged agreement may be a matter of one party's word against another's. A court may see the agreement between the parties as one that was implied by their actions, rather than being a written expression of their intention such as a live together agreement. The contract may be implied, as in the Marvin case, from a string of circumstances, so that the agreement is derived from the behavior and actions of the couple during their relationship.

There are only about a half dozen states today that deviate from this norm, and some states, such as Illinois and Mississippi, refuse to honor any sort of contract between unmarried couples, because the relationship is viewed as immoral. Some states ban claims by unmarried straight couples on the grounds that it is a "back door" to common-law marriage.

In proving a contract exists, here is a note of caution. The basis of your contract cannot have anything to do with sex. That means that a person can't claim that they gave up their career to be the sexual partner of a well-to-do individual in exchange for being kept in a comfortable lifestyle. That would likely be construed as payment for sex, which, as you might guess, is prostitution – and a court isn't likely to endorse a contract on that basis.

A Note on Blackmail. There is another complication you may face, one that reveals the darker side of divorce, particularly between a gay or lesbian couple that does not have the benefit of laws guiding a breakup – and that is blackmail. One party may threaten the other with the a palimony/galimony lawsuit, not because of a financial inequity in the relationship, but because they know that the action will embarrass the other by bringing him or her out of the closet in a public way.

Frederick Hertz has seen it. Blackmail, he says, is "alive and well." He has seen situations in which a former partner has threatened to bring a palimony suit against a person of prominence – the kind of situation that could become national news. In such cases, many people settle. However, Hertz has also seen people who refuse to settle. In one such case, his client was hit with a suit that described a range of activities, including sexual and drug abuse, and a copy of the claims was mailed out to the employer of his ex-partner. Your options may be extremely limited here. The only sure protection against an effort to blackmail you because you are in the closet is to be out of the closet. Does anyone have a better argument for better planning between couples?

Child Custody between Two Mommies/Two Daddies

OK, you've divorced your straight wife to marry your gay lover, and now you can't stand the sight of him. You want a divorce. Some might call you fickle. Your lover might call you something else. But you don't care – you know what you want and you want out. There's just one little problem. The problem has a name – her name is Courtney and she's the little girl you and your lover both adopted after you read the last chapter. Now what? Who is going to get custody and who is going to get visitation?

Children Adopted by Both Partners. Where a gay or lesbian couple has adopted a child together, there is no reason to believe that the standards used for heterosexual custody cases would be applied any differently. In other words, the standard is still the same – what is in the best interests of the child? The court will have to look at the relationship the child has had with both parents and will look to the needs of the child and the abilities of the adoptive parents. Visitation will have to be handled in family court. The problem is that judges in family court may be somewhat inexperienced at making that kind of assessment where the couple are of the same sex and unmarried, yet both are the legal parent of the child.

If you are not in a geographical region where that experience is more common, then your legal representation should be consulting with one of the national gay and lesbian legal organizations, such as the National Center for Lesbian Rights or Lambda Legal Defense and Education Fund. They are in a position to help determine how best to educate and work with the court under these unique circumstances. But in the end, the assessment should be no different than it is for a heterosexual couple who is splitting up, and the best interests of the child should be the driving force.

Keep in mind, however, that one of the factors that can be persuasive is the living arrangement of each of the parents following the breakup. If you are planning on leaving your lover to move in with a new lover, that may be a factor in the court's decision regarding custody and visitation and might result in your having visitation supervised or restricted. As in heterosexual divorces, courts may not be eager to embrace your new situation unless you marry your new partner. Now since you don't have the legal option of marrying your new partner, you are somewhat disadvantaged compared with your straight counterparts, unless you are in Vermont and can enter into a civil union. However, bear in mind that if you are leaving your current living arrangement, you will need to demonstrate stability in your new one. Jumping from one domestic partnership to a new one might be construed as something less than stable.

Legal Parent vs. Non-Related "Parent." What are the standards in the gay and lesbian community when lovers get "divorced" from each other? Judy Moats, a gay and lesbian family attorney in Fairfax, Virginia, says that many woes can be overcome if people just plan for this contingency from day one. She counsels couples that they need to consider the possibility of a breakup even before they consider having a child.

"I think problems arise from not absolutely sitting down and being honest with one another about the relationship, and what it means to bring a child into the world, and the couple's commitment to raise that child," she says. "If there is a breakup, they still have the same commitment that they wanted to have at the outset of their relationship." Moats does everything she can to ensure such planning takes place with her clients. She is especially sensitive to situations involving a parent and a biological child with a non-biological partner, and to attempts by one to withhold custody or visitation or even support as a result of the non-biological relationship. "I do lectures, and don't pretend that they are not, that you cannot say later on that 'it is my child, you can't see it,' or vice versa – 'it is your kid and I won't support it,'" she says.

Relationships among gay and lesbian families are complex, and not every couple will have been so fortunate as to have both partners able to adopt a child. But children can still be in your family unit. It may be that you or your lover has custody of a child from a previous heterosexual marriage that you left, making one of you the "bio-parent." Or, one of you may have adopted a child, while the other was unable to do so by law, making one parent related to the child legally and the other a legal stranger.

When there is a child at issue in a break-up in which one of the parents is the bio-parent or legally recognized parent, and one is the long-time partner of the bio-parent, the law is in a state of flux. Is a bio-parent automatically guaranteed an ability to get his or her way in a custody battle? Because this situation is more and more common, courts are more often having to face the question of whether a non-bio-parent has some sort of legal right to visitation and even joint custody of children involved in gay and lesbian breakups.

Until recently, a bio-parent who brought a case to deny rights to a non-bio parent had an easy time of it and would almost be guaranteed success. But that is no longer a certainty. Courts are becoming a bit more aware of the existence of lesbian-and gay-headed households, and are approaching the cases with a sense of responsibility to fairly and genuinely deal with these kinds of disputes. Even where a bio-parent is concerned, then, there is hope for the non-bio parent if the argument on behalf of the non-bio parent is framed in terms of what is, in fact, in the best interests of the child. In other words, there is reason for hope for the non-bio-parent if the case can be clearly made that depriving the child or children of the company of the non-bioparent would not be in the child's best interests.

By way of example, in 2000 the New Jersey Supreme Court heard a case involving a woman who was the non-biological parent of twins born to her partner. She and her lover had gone through what is covered in the first few chapters of this book: they dated, bought a home together, and had a religious commitment ceremony. They had twin children. By 1996, their lives had reached the subject of this chapter, and they broke up. When that happened, the non-biological parent had to sue for visitation. An appellate court granted the non-biological mother her right to visitation, which was unanimously affirmed by the New Jersey Supremes. In their decision the court carved out the rights of "psychological" parents, i.e., non-biological partners.

What happened in this case is important in two respects. In the first place, a very high court gave recognition to a non-biological parent who was not only unrelated to the child, but who was a lesbian. Either one by itself is important, together they are extraordinary. The concept of psychological parent means that a court recognizes that a parent who is non-biological can be extremely important to the child and therefore can have an important bond – and that the disruption of that bond would not be in the best interests of the child. To prove yourself a psychological parent, you will have to prove the relationship existed and was fostered and encouraged by the bio-parent.

Is that all there is to it? Not quite. You will also have to be in a jurisdiction that recognizes the legal status of psychological parents because it is not universal.

In the second place, the New Jersey case is also an example of what can happen as gay and lesbian relationships spawn children in increasing numbers. It also reveals the types of problems that can arise during the dissolution of a relationship, particularly one that is outside of the law. People who were once loving may grab onto any defense to make their former partners miserable or to get them out of their lives. The intense love that was once a relationship can turn to intense hate in a breakup. And the legal tools that some have been known to seize in the heat of dispute can involve some very homophobic arguments.

But along with the rights of non-biological parents are new responsibilities. In December 2002, a Pennsylvania court ruled in a case between two lesbians regarding not only on a matter of custody, but also child-support. During a relationship that lasted several years, the couple decided to have children and one of them bore them. However, during a breakup, the non-biological parent sought custody while the biological parent sought child support. The court provided shared custody, but ruled that the non-biological parent was responsible for support of the children. As the gay and lesbian baby boom continues, there may be an increased willingness of courts to forge both rights and responsibilities for couples, even where there is no statutory law that recognizes the situation.

Future Directions – "New Clear Families"

Indeed, there is a growing and almost grassroots concern among some gay and lesbian attorneys that in the course of gay divorces, use of the homophobia that may exist in the courts should not be used against one another.

"It is alarming to me where lesbian and gay couples are breaking up and the non-biological mother is totally disenfranchised, because the courts will not recognize our legitimacy as parents," says Lorri Jean, former executive director of the National Gay and Lesbian Task Force (NGLTF). "Sometimes lesbian mothers and donor gay fathers are fighting. We seem to be able to replicate the worst behavior of heterosexual dissolutions, where kids are used as pawns and people in our own community take advantage of homophobia in the law to punish their former partners and to get what they want. There are a lot more people having kids now and a lot more instances of bad dissolutions."

This brings some in the gay and lesbian legal community to a conflict in their loyalties – are they loyal first to their clients, and willing to grab onto any legal tool in their grasp, even if it means undermining broader gay and lesbian rights?

With cases like the one in New Jersey, homophobic arguments against a lover over custody issues may meet with less and less success, though it will largely depend on matters of judicial education and geography. There is greater judicial understanding and sensitivity to the claims brought by lesbian and gay parents today. That means that with the growth of gay and lesbian families, there will be a corresponding growth in legal protections for lesbian and gay family structures. That isn't going to decrease these kinds of disputes, but there is a growing trend that will result in better treatment of non-biological parents.

There are an unprecedented number of gay and lesbian families who either have children by former heterosexual marriages or in which gay and lesbians have begun forming their own families and, like their heterosexual counterparts, find that things are not working out. While the law has begun moving, as seen in chapter 1 with the Vermont Civil Union and in chapter 2 with second parent adoption, to form a legal recognition of at least some aspects of gay and lesbian familyhood, it is still largely unprepared to deal with the break-up of those families.

Slowly, the rights of lesbians and gays in forming family units different from the traditional nuclear family are being granted recognition by the courts. From a time when just the mere fact that a person was not heterosexual was enough to deny them their parenthood, it is becoming increasingly clear that courts are taking the position that a person's sexual orientation is not enough, in and of itself, to deny parenthood. With that new understanding, perhaps one day in the not-too-distant future we will arrive at a widely held understanding that not only are we clearly not unfit parents, but we are, in fact, extraordinarily fit. As Judy Moats put it, we have to work and plan so hard to have children – which means these kids are really, really wanted.

In the meantime, just as there are ways to emulate marriage rights by doing wills, powers of attorney, and living wills, there are also ways to reinforce your family – ways that require good planning and an experienced lawyer. As we have seen in this chapter, as we evolve the law evolves with us – though only through our persistent prodding, patience, and the winning legal skills of the individuals mentioned in this chapter, their colleagues and organizations such as the National

Center for Lesbian Rights, Lambda Legal Defense and Education Fund, and the American Civil Liberties Union.

Any hard-won rights arrive combined the other half of the rights equation – responsibilities. Those responsibilities include how we treat one another when our own relationships dissolve. One day, palimony/galimony may be unnecessary, because like gays and lesbians who live in Vermont, we will have to go through the courts to dissolve those relationships. Laws will guide the process, not a big shoot-out in the Wild West of courtroom drama and law. Instead of palimony or galimony, it will just be called alimony for everyone. One day, we may get what we have been asking for and we will have to judge for ourselves whether or not we are ready.

Frederick Hertz offers a perspective that is both unique and poignant as we witness the growth of the gay and lesbian family culture. "For much of the past 50 years," he says, "we have been focused as a community on protecting lesbians and gay men from injustices brought on by straight people. But what I see in my work is gays and lesbians who are oppressed by other gays or lesbians – others who they have loved. We don't really need state legislatures to tell us how to treat people better, whether we are talking about fights over kids or over money." In a final ironic comment, Hertz notes, "If you were to do a survey in the San Francisco Bay area and asked the question, 'who has caused more pain in your life, straight people or gay people?' I think gays and lesbians would acknowledge that it is gay people."

Based on that experience and belief, "I hope," he says, "that we can take on these intracommunity issues with the same fervor that we have our battles in civil rights." It will be a wonderful change of pace to shift from the fight for our rights to the struggle we will have in choosing how we exercise them.

Be kind to one another.

CHAPTER 4

Till Death Do You Part

History and Perspective – Discrimination in Death

IT MAY BE HARD for you to believe, but even in death, heterosexual society has found ways to discriminate against gays and lesbians. That sounds funny, but the real life (real death) effects are actually serious enough to have tragic consequences. Individual gays and lesbians have experienced this time and time again, as one partner dies and the other is left trying to take care of a relationship when the law recognizes no such relationship. But it really became apparent when the AIDS epidemic resulted in so many tragic deaths so quickly in the 1980s. That experience was echoed during September 2001, when many gay and lesbian partners found that, despite the death of their life partner, they were perhaps not eligible for some of the hundreds of millions of dollars being donated to help families of the victims of September 11.

In chapter 1, you learned all about what it takes to get married and a little bit about some of the rights and responsibilities involved in marriage. One of those rights is a right to inheritance. For people who get married, the law recognizes their relationship as a family unit, and as such, when one of them dies, a whole lot of rights fall to the survivor. The same is not true for gays and lesbians. It may strike you as somewhat odd that in a chapter about death and dying we are going to talk more about marriage, but that is exactly what we are going to do. You probably didn't think that inheritance laws could be so romantic.

The Power of the "I Do" Factor with Inheritance

To appreciate fully the power of the "I Do" factor in a heterosexual married couple's lives, consider the following scenario involving a couple we will call Tony and Roberta. After a whirlwind courtship lasting all of two months, they decide to make it "official" and get married. She gets to wear a fancy bridal dress and he a tuxedo. There is a church, some music, guests, and of course gifts, catered food, and annoying relatives, a cheesy band. There are a train of attendants wearing rented suits and dresses they wouldn't otherwise be caught dead in, with shoes that have been dyed the same unbelievable color as the horrid dresses. The climax comes after they march down an aisle. They say the magic words "I Do," and at that moment, the law recognizes their relationship and they will get all of the many benefits offered by marriage. One of those benefits is the right to inherit property, even if your spouse did not have a will – don't worry, the law wrote it for them.

This brings us to a sad twist to the tale of Tony and Roberta. After the big "I Do," they have their reception, tuck away the expensive gifts (many from gay and lesbian friends for whom they will never have to buy a gift), and take off to the airport to catch their honeymoon flight to the Caribbean. On the way, however, a drunken cab driver runs a light and broadsides the car the newlyweds are driving. Miraculously, the bride is unhurt, but the groom has been thrown from the car. Tony is literally in pieces.

An ambulance arrives and takes him away, and he is placed in the intensive care unit. Roberta rides in the ambulance with Tony, and when she gets to the hospital, the doctor consults with her about the course of medical treatment, keeping her apprised of their options and allowing her to make medical decisions for Tony. She tells the doctor that on one of their (few) dates, Tony had told her that he would always want the most heroic measures taken to save his life. Tony's parents doubt this, but Roberta, as Tony's wife, is his next of kin, and so heroic measures are taken. Still, despite everyone's best efforts, Tony dies with Roberta at his side. She makes the funeral arrangements and arranges for his bodily remains to be taken care of in a way that was special to them – scattering his ashes in the Caribbean, even though Tony's parents had already bought the couple burial plots. When Roberta comes home from scattering Tony, she is frightened about her future. But her groom was not a struggling waiter – he was a successful owner of a chain of auto parts stores (what could be more heterosexual than that?). Despite the fact that he did not have time to write a will between the time of their marriage and the time of his death – a mere two hours later – the law will take care of the young bride. Even though there is no will, there are laws that provide for inheritance under these circumstances, called the laws of intestacy. These laws will come to her rescue and allow her to inherit his entire estate. She will be financially secure and, in fact, his house – the one in which they were both going to live – is hers now. Everything is hers.

And further, angry that she was unjustly robbed of her future happiness by the drunken cabby, she can sue the cab company for her pain and suffering at being deprived of her husband and for negligence in allowing a drunken cab driver behind the wheel.

To recap, Roberta got to visit Tony in the hospital, make medical decisions, funeral arrangements, inherit the estate, and sue on behalf of her husband and then reap the benefits of that lawsuit. She got all of this solely by virtue of the fact, that for two hours, she was legally married. Had her spouse lived, this couple could have owned property together, she would get the benefit of any retirement plans and social security, and they could jointly file taxes. If they had children, they could have both made decisions in the upbringing of that child. And, if they had ever divorced (remember, as nearly one in two do), then the law would have provided some game rules for protecting everyone's rights, including those of the children, and for trying to make the process somewhat fair. That is the power of "I Do."

Minus the "I Do" Factor – Gay and Lesbian Reality

Now let's change this scenario a bit to allow us to see the consequences when a relationship is not legally recognized as valid. Let's consider the story of Tony and Robert. Tony and Robert are struggling actors (a.k.a. waiters) who have lived together in a committed monogamous relationship in New York for the past five years. They consider themselves spouses. One day, Tony's agent calls with the big news that he has landed a part as a regular in a new television series. It is a breakthrough for them, but requires that they relocate to Los Angeles. Tony, with his new salary, has been able to buy a home in the Hollywood Hills for the both of them. They pack up their belongings and send them ahead. They had always wanted to drive cross-country, so they set out to make the trip by car. They make vacation stops, and make some purchases for the house along the way, always on Tony's credit card, since he is now the one with income. But while driving somewhere in the Midwest, there is a terrible car accident. A drunken truck driver runs a light and rams the car. Robert passes out, and when he comes to, he is in a hospital room. Tony is not there. When he makes inquiries, a nurse tells him that Tony has been transported to another hospital, where he is in the intensive care unit. She says that his parents have been notified. Robert is upset, because Tony has for years been estranged from his parents, who had kicked him out of the house when he told them he was gay. Robert spends part of the little bit of money he has left when he is discharged that day to get to the hospital where Tony has been taken. When he asks at the desk where he can find Tony, he is asked if he is a family member. Robert doesn't know what to say at first, caught off guard by the question, and he says no. The hospital, he is told, has a policy that only family members can visit people in the intensive care ward, and then only at particular hours. Robert goes to a waiting room, and there he discovers Tony's parents talking with a doctor. He overhears that Tony's condition is gravely serious and that Tony has sustained brain damage – he is having trouble breathing on his own. Tony's parents explain to the doctor that their religion demands that everything that can possibly be done to keep Tony alive – respirators, feeding tubes, anything – must be done.

Tony and Robert had lost a lot of friends to AIDS, and they had often talked over the past five years of their mutual desire to never be hooked up to needless life support that would prolong pain and suffering. Robert interrupts to say that Tony's wishes, expressed many times to him, were that extraordinary measures never be taken on his behalf.

Tony's parents and Tony's doctor give Robert a "Who Are You?" look and proceed with their conversation. Tony is placed on a respirator, where he remains for several days, in painful, prolonged, and steady decline. Finally, Tony dies. His parents remove his body back to the southern home town where Tony grew up, and there they hold a large funeral and have him buried. This is in spite of the fact that, while he was alive, he had always expressed his secret fear of burial and instead talked only about cremation. Robert tried to tell this to Tony's parents, but they warned him with legal action if he kept trying to interfere during their bereavement. Robert was barred from Tony's funeral.

Tony had been an only child, and because he died without a will, his parents inherited his new home in Los Angeles. Even the things that had been bought by Tony and Robert on the road, purchased on Tony's credit card, became the property of his parents. Tony and Robert had given up their apartment in New York, and Tony's parents now had the house in Los Angeles and all of Tony's money. Robert did not get to visit Tony, make medical decisions or funeral arrangements. Robert didn't even have a home by the end of the ordeal. Tony's father had become the administrator of Tony's estate and, on behalf of the estate, he sued the trucking company and the driver and reaped that settlement, which ended up paying for the Hollywood house. They even put in a pool. They did not invite Robert.

While the circumstances you face may never be as dire as that of Robert and Tony, the truth is, they could be. Some of these situations you will face if you want children or if you get sick or, as will inevitably happen, if one of you dies before the other. It is not necessarily because of a disaster such as was faced by

Tony and Robert that a couple finds themselves facing the bitter disadvantages of not having a legal married status. As Winnie Stachelberg, policy director at the Human Rights Campaign, points out, it also comes at tax time. In fact, it comes in a thousand unexpected ways. The "I Do" marriage contract really covers life very universally.

Current Events – Creating the "I Do" Factor

What follows are a number of options that are open for consideration by gay and lesbian couples who want to "commit" to one another in a way that affords their relationship some degree of legal legitimacy. These are the pieces of tape that you can use to patch together your relationship – wills, powers of attorney, living wills, live-together agreements, and domestic partnerships (as seen in chapter 1). For the couple wanting greater legal rights and responsibilities for their relationship, any one or combination of these options offers greater legal security and gets you some of the "I Do"-factor rights.

Any self-respecting gay or lesbian couple who yearn for a legally binding commitment can easily recreate many of the rights and responsibilities that make up the marriage contract. The ability to live together, own joint property, make medical decisions, and inherit property is all within your grasp. All that is required is that you go out and get those legal rights in a very proactive way. While church ceremonies are increasingly popular for gay and lesbian couples, no matter how loudly you exchange promises during that ceremony, you aren't going to get a single legal right. It may give spiritual satisfaction; it will not give you a contract. For the latter, you have to go to a lawyer. But try not to think of her as a lawyer – think of her as a justice of the peace.

In estate planning, there are a few instruments that a gay couple can have an attorney draw up that will recreate, to a large degree, pieces of the institution of marriage in your own image. By signing a will, medical directives and powers of attorney, a gay or lesbian couple can walk out of a lawyer's office with many of the rights grabbed by the "I Do" couple, with some notable exceptions. In fact, your bundle will so much resemble their bundle of rights, you won't believe it's not marriage. Perhaps even better, the opt-out divorce clause may be much simpler and of your own design.

Remember Tony and Robert? Things could have been much different for them. Had those boys signed mutual wills that left one another as both the beneficiary and the executor of the estate, then when Tony died, Robert would have inherited Tony's estate and managed the process as well. In fact, because he was appointed by Tony to be the executor of the estate, he would have been under a duty to sue the negligent truck driver on behalf of the estate, rather than Tony's parents getting that privilege. And as the sole beneficiary, he also would have reaped the benefit of that lawsuit, rather than Tony's parents. If they had signed mutual medical powers of attorney, or designated one another as their medical decision maker, then (depending on the state), Robert would have gotten to make medical decisions for Tony – even when Tony's parents showed up and began to assert their own ways. If Tony had signed a living will or a directive to his physician, he would not have had to suffer the extreme life saving measures that were ultimately futile. Robert and Tony would have been in control – together – just as if they had been married.

Wills as a Way

A will. It doesn't sound like a way to say "I love you" does it? It is hard trying to imagine that one day you will take your partner's hand, get down on bended knee and say "Honey, will you write a mutual will with me?" You open up a small gift box from a jewelry store and inside is a new Marc Cross pen.

Not only is it not romantic, it is so non-romantic that it makes writing a live-together agreement look like a trip to Niagara Falls. Mixing the notion of death and dying with romance is a tough stretch, particularly since our society generally finds death and dying an entirely avoidable topic. But it is a not-so-obvious document that will bring you and your partner many of the benefits married couples already get – rights beyond inheritance. If you can overcome your notions about it, estate planning is definitely a very powerful tool for couples to gain legal rights and to protect their interests, not only financially, but also emotionally.

Therefore, the writing of a will accomplishes the following. A person (the testator) can write a will leaving all or part of his or her estate to a non-family member (lover, domestic partner, significant other). In addition, he or she can name that person as the executor of their estate. The rights of inheritance given married couples by operation of law are now a gay or lesbian couple's by operation of a few well-crafted instruments of law.

To understand how wills work, it is important to understand what happens when they don't work – meaning what happens when a person dies without a will. When a person dies before having had the chance to sign a valid last will and testament, then he or she is said to have died *intestate*. This vaguely nasty sounding word means nothing more than that: dying without a will. The other side of the coin, as you may guess, is dying with a will, and that is called dying *testate*. They both sound nasty.

Dying Without a Will – The Laws of Intestacy. For now, let's concentrate on intestacy. When you die without a will, the state in which you reside will pass out the property to your blood or adoptive relatives according the its own laws. Guess what they are called? They are the laws of intestacy. The way they work would generally look like this. There is a person who goes to the court and gets himself declared the administrator, otherwise known as the person in charge of the estate. This is quite often, though not necessarily, a relative. Once so declared by the court, he or she will look for a legal spouse and/or children. If any of those people are found, the hunt ends. Generally speaking, a state will give all the property to a living spouse or to living children, or, if there are both, will split your estate between the two. However, where there is no spouse or children, then the administrator will look to parents. Without parents, then he will look for brothers, sisters, aunts, uncles, cousins, and grandparents. These next of kin survivors are called legatees – people who get your legacy. If none of these legatees can be found to exist, then the state does everyone a real big favor, steps up to the plate and inherits the estate.

For a gay or lesbian or any other single person, when death knocks at the door, the laws of intestacy would dictate that the worldly goods of that individual would be inherited by only his or her next of kin. Under no circumstance is the next of kin considered to be anyone other than a blood or adoptive relative, or a legal spouse. In fact, in some states, there is so much respect for the surviving spouse that it is impossible for a legally married individual to write a will that disinherits a spouse – she or he will always have a right to elect against an estate where a will says otherwise. So, in homosexual case A, in all likelihood parents or siblings inherit despite the presence of a live-in domestic partner; in heterosexual case B, the spouse inherits automatically, with or without a will. There is no case C for a homosexual partner, except in the state of Vermont, for couples who have entered a civil union (see chapter 1).

Administrators of Estates. The transfer of property cannot happen by legal magic alone. Before property can be transferred to anyone, someone has to be in charge of the whole process, because when you die, your estate takes on its own identity and becomes like a minor child in need of a guardian. That guardian, where there is no written will, is the administrator under the laws of intestacy. The person who elects to become the administrator has a big and unpleasant job ahead. The administrator, as guardian of this estate, must treat it much in the way he or she would a child. He must apply for a tax identification (akin to a social security number) for the estate, pay all the debts and expenses of the estate, file for and pay for all taxes, and manage the assets of the estate to their best advantage. Once the administrator does all that, then he can distribute the property according to the laws of intestacy of the state in which the deceased person resided.

One of the many duties of the administrator is to collect any debts owed to the deceased. If the deceased had a cause of action (a lawsuit) against someone, then the administrator is honor bound to carry out that lawsuit on behalf the estate and collect any judgement on behalf of the deceased.

A non-family member can become an administrator, but it is important to realize that if there is a non-family member who wants to become the administrator and that position is challenged by a family member, it is altogether likely that the family member will wind up being top dog.

What does any of this have to do with being married? A lot. Because the laws of intestacy will first look for a spouse and then stop, the spouse of a person who dies without a will can step forward, become the administrator of the estate, and then actually also be the person who inherits the estate. For a gay or lesbian couple, the gay spouse can step forward and become the administrator if he or she wants, but can forget about inheriting a dime. The estate will go to any blood relative of the deceased, but it will not go to the gay spouse. (Vermont civil unioners excepted – see chapter 1.)

Changing Intestacy Laws By Writing Your Will. That is, unless there's a will. Because when a person writes a will, what they are doing is necessarily taking the laws of intestacy and rewriting them their own way. When a gay or lesbian couple write mutual wills, then the rights and responsibilities remarkably resemble a big chunk of the "I Do" contract. How does that happen?

When a person writes a will, they can distribute their property any way they see fit. They can split it among all family members or give all the property to one family member, or they can give it to the cat. Property includes personal property as well as real estate. They can name specific properties to go to specific family members. Or, most importantly, they can write a will that leaves some or all of their property to a non-family member. In essence, the will allows a person to embrace a non-family member as a family member, something that isn't possible under the laws of intestacy.

A will begins by picking out specific property that one wants to leave to individuals. When you leave something to someone in a will, it is called a "bequest." When all is said and done, there is something called a "residuary clause" which leaves the balance of any property to an individual. That individual can be someone who has already gotten a bequest in the body of the will. This person is called the "residuary beneficiary."

Will Challenges by Nasty Relatives. For many gay and lesbian couples, the fact is that they have embarked on a life that may be frowned upon by their families – and there may be a significantly high level of estrangement. In such a case, it may be that a person may want to write their will and omit any mention of their family, leaving everything to their life-partner. However, in doing so, they may be fearful of provoking a will challenge from their disapproving family. In that case, there is a handy feature available to someone writing a will called an "inter rorem" clause. It is the "let's make a deal" clause because it forces a bet. In effect, an inter rorem clause allows the person writing the will to pose a dare to relatives who he or she might suspect will be a problem and may challenge the validity of the will. To write an inter rorem clause, it is necessary that you leave a bequest to the individual you suspect could be a troublemaker. Then, the clause states that if any person named in the will as a beneficiary challenges the will and loses, then they also lose any bequest made to them in the will. So if Aunt Delia is left a bequest of $5,000, in order to challenge the will, she will be gambling that entire amount. If she loses the challenge, she loses the $5,000. You can have the money in your hand or what is sitting behind Door Number One. Aw, look you chose the canned ham. Shucks.

That may not sound like much of a buy-off, but mounting a challenge to a will can be a daunting, lengthy, and expensive process. To overturn a will, a challenger must present at least one of three circumstances, all of which are somewhat difficult to prove. The first is that the will is a forgery. The second is that the testator was simply out of his or her mind – really out of it, not just eccentric or slightly goofy. The third is that the will was signed under duress, meaning that some type of undue influence was brought to bear on the testator that made him or her take leave of his senses and sign a will that left everything to non-family members. This third one is the most dangerous in that it has been successfully argued that a person was persuaded by the passion of a shameless sexual liaison to the point of senselessness, and that is why family were disinherited in favor of a non-family party.

Keep in mind that, first of all, will challenges are only mounted by those who would have inherited had there been no will, i.e., your legatees, or by those named in a will previously written by you that has not been effectively revoked. Will contests are expensive and are a difficult burden of proof, which means that, statistically, very few wills are challenged and even fewer challenges are successful. If you take care when writing your will and work with a good lawyer, it is highly doubtful that a will challenge will be successful, though the aggravation of one could be highly inconvenient.

Naming Your Executor. One of the most important aspects of writing a will is the naming of the executor. That is the person who is in charge, (the administrator under the laws of intestacy). A person can write a will and name a non-family member as the executor of the will. The Executor, like the administrator, is responsible for paying all debts and expenses and recovering and distributing all property. And he or she is similarly charged with executing any lawsuits. Your executor can also be named as a beneficiary or even the sole beneficiary in your will.

However, even if your main object is to give your estate to your partner and to have him or her to be in charge, you may want to consider contingencies. You may have a wonderful partner, but he or she may not really be a whiz kid when it comes to getting things done in official channels. Let's say your partner just hasn't gotten around to filing his income taxes in the last ten years – that kind of attention to official bureaucratic functioning doesn't bode well. You may, in such a case, wish to name a co-executor to serve with him. Maybe that isn't the case. Maybe he is a C.P.A. and you have utter faith in his ability to do this, but you still can't discount the fact that you could both be involved in a common accident, meaning that Mr. or Ms. Math may not be able to act as executor. In that case, you should name a back up – someone who is going to serve as an alternate executor should your chosen executor not be able to serve.

Needless to say, the person you choose to act as executor needs to be someone you can trust. Your executor will take all of your assets, have access to bank accounts, check cards, checks, income tax filings and refunds and virtually get to be acting as if he or she were you. If you are choosing someone not your partner, be sure it is someone you trust absolutely. Being an executor requires a lot of investment of time and trouble, meaning that the person you choose will have to up to the job. There is some incentive for the executor, because under most circumstances, they are permitted to elect a fee from the estate for their trouble, though many waive that right.

Some people choose their lawyer to be their executor. That can be fine, because presumably he or she should know what he's doing. One thing that your executor gets to do is hire a lawyer (with money from your estate) to tend to matters after you die. If you choose your lawyer, they may actually be able to double dip into the estate – one fee for their legal expenses and one fee for acting as executor. Even if it is legal, it is not always the most advisable thing to do – your executor is someone whose first consideration should be the estate. Your lawyer is a functionary in that process, but it is conceivable that there could be a conflict of interest between the two, and it might be best to keep them apart.

Who Gets What – Writing Your Will. There are some considerations in writing your will, however, that merit serious consideration. Wills and estates are guided by state law, not federal, so the variations on what you can and cannot do may vary from state to state, and when you go to a lawyer he or she will be able to describe them to you.

For the most part, however, it is your will, and you can do whatever you want to in it. However, bear in mind that the more complex you make it, the greater opportunity you give to a potential will challenger. You may have elaborate arrangements to make – there may be trusts or complicated property transactions.

It is possible to write a will that makes a gift conditional – meaning that within the will, you are exerting your will upon a beneficiary. For example, you can state that the gift is only valid if someone survives you by a certain time period. In that way, you ensure that you don't leave your entire estate to someone who just happens to pass away a few days later. Putting such a condition on a gift is quite common, but your condition does not have to be that practical. The gift may only be valid if the beneficiary fulfills a need that you state in the will. You may say that the person named as a beneficiary will only get the gift if they wear a feather boa to your funeral. However, you should be careful in this regard. A condition laid out in your will that is considered too extreme will not be honored and one that is too glib may seriously call your sanity into question. For example, you cannot force a person to change their faith or to give up religion entirely as a condition of a gift. Do what you need to do in your will, but avoid being flamboyant and try not to be too elaborate. Get the job done, but leave the window dressing at home and resist the temptation to use the will as a soapbox to scold from beyond the grave the people who have done you wrong. There is no dramatic reading of the will, such as you often see on television.[9]

Essentially, the tasks you have to accomplish in your will are the recitation of what goes to whom as well as who is in charge. Beyond that, there really aren't many requirements. You can make conditional bequests, you can insert an inter rorem clause, you can divide property between relatives, you can include or exclude whomever you want (though if you are legally married or have children, your right to fully exclude them may be inhibited by state law).

---

9. Though it goes without saying that some people cannot live without this (pun intended) and will make a will reading a condition. Some have even recorded their last will and testament on videotape. If you feel compelled to try this, be sure it is legal in your state.

On the other hand, the will, in fact, can be very, very simple. Many people wonder whether they can just name their partner as their sole beneficiary as well as the executor. Actually, that is the point – you can, and in doing so, you are managing to empower your partner with several of the rights that married people get automatically with the "I Do" factor. The will most certainly can name your partner as your executor and your sole beneficiary. That can be the extent of it and that makes your intent pretty clear. You absolutely do not want to be foggy about the expression of your intent in your will. The clarity of your intentions is going to be very important when the will is reviewed after your death.

To add some shelf life to your will, just as you may have considered alternative executors, you may want to consider alternative beneficiaries. You may know perfectly well who you feel should have what, but consider the fact that the beneficiary you have in mind for a $10,000 bequest may not be alive when you die. Or maybe they don't want the bequest you have made for them. Perhaps you think your cousin Timmy loves your vintage denim upholstered 1976 Pinto, but in fact, he loathes it. He was just being nice to you when he nodded after you told him that you were leaving it to him in your will. For that reason, you may want to name alternative beneficiaries. If you do not, then the bequest that didn't make it goes to the person who has been named in your will as the residuary beneficiary, – i.e., the guy who gets anything and everything that hasn't already been given away.

There is an important thing to remember about giving your property away in your will. You cannot give away more than you have. In other words, you may want to leave everyone $10,000, but if that's all you have and you die with any debt, your debts and expenses must first be paid off before any bequest is made. So if you leave five people $10,000 in your will, but you only have $10,000 and you happen to owe $8,000 to MasterCard, you are leaving those five people to split the $2,000 that is left over.

Some people want to state their preferences for their funeral in their wills. You can do that, and it doesn't hurt, but there is no legal effect to a will for many weeks after death. Stating your funereal and body disposition wishes in your will merely serves as witnessed evidence of your desire, but does not have any direct legal bearing.

One last thing to bear in mind, when you sign your will, the signing must be done in accordance with the laws in the state in which you live, that includes the types of notarized statements that may be necessary to accompany the will and the number of witnesses. However, some general guidelines may be of assistance. For example, never, ever, ever, under any circumstances have anyone you have named in the will as a beneficiary or executor act as one of the witnesses to your will. If they do act as a witness, they may have to forfeit their bequest. If you leave your estate to your partner and your partner is a witness, it could even be construed that your partner was trying to influence your decisions. In fact, unless you are involved in doing mutual wills at the same time, the process by which you both do your wills should ideally be as separate as possible to avoid any appearance that there was undue influence bearing down on your decision-making process. If you break any of the rules prescribed by your state law, you could inadvertently endanger your whole purpose in writing the will in the first place.

You may ask yourself, if a will is as simple as writing down who gets what and who is in charge, why do I need a lawyer? While you can write your own will in some states, not all allow it and even those that do sometimes only allow them under dire circumstances (e.g., you are a dying soldier on a field of battle). In some places, you can go to stationery stores and purchase will kits and you can get them on the Internet. But I can't imagine that you'd go to a stationery store to purchase a kit on how to perform your own surgery, and you are about as well advised to avoid will kits. You may not like paying a lawyer to write a will, but remember, that is what she went to school to learn – three years of it – and probably she wouldn't have gone if writing a will were as simple as going to a shop, or looking on the Internet for a form. Lawyers know pitfalls and red flags that will be there for the court when your will goes to probate, and you can avoid a lot of headache and cost down the road by seeing a good lawyer – more than you will save by writing it yourself. For that reason, among others, it is very important that you consult with an attorney in planning your estate.

Getting Yourself Organized for the Will. Naturally getting all this done requires a little organization on your part. There are a list of things you should do in order to get this done and get it done right. Remember, it is not only important what you put into your documents, it is important that you do it all correctly so as not to raise any question when those documents actually come into use. You don't want a judge saying, "Gee, it doesn't look like he knew what he was doing." So that you go prepared, here is a checklist to run through that will make the going easier:

Take Your Address Book. When you go to your lawyer's office to write your will, the address book will come in handy, because you will need the correct addresses of all the parties mentioned in your will.

Construct a Family Tree. Even if you are not mentioning your family in your will, you and your lawyer will need to put together a family tree, and you should go back at least as far as your grandparents, showing who was married to whom, who is alive, and for those who aren't, when and where they died. The family tree makes it much easier to contact your legatees when your will heads to probate.

Construct a List of Your Bounty. This is not about paper towels. It is about making a list of the property that you have that you want to talk about in your will. It is also about making a list of the property you don't want to mention in the will, so that your executor will have something to go by that is organized. In all likelihood, your lawyer will produce a questionnaire that asks you about your property. Go through it thoroughly and leave nothing out. You should gather your thoughts together so that you list all of your property that will pass through your estate, as well as all testamentary substitutes (see next section) that you have. And remember; do not try to give away property in your will that you do not, in fact, own. Do not try to give away property you anticipate owning. Nothing makes a person look battier to a probate court than when a will is giving away property that does not exist. It sort of makes it look like you don't know what you are doing.

Talk to Your Executor. Believe it or not, the person you name as executor in your will may not want the job. After all, this job is no small task. The person named as executor has a great deal of responsibility. They basically have to close down your life. One perk of the job is that they may be allowed to take a fee from the estate for the task of acting as executor. So sit down and ask your executor if they want to do this, before you appoint them in your will. The last thing you want is someone to say, "I had no idea – I don't want to do this." At that point, you will be in no position to appoint a new one.

Transferring Property Without a Will

Maybe you don't feel like writing a will, or feel that you don't have enough assets to consider doing one. If you are in a relationship where you want to protect a partner in case of your death, there are still things that you can do together that will help ensure that. Writing a will is not the only way to give property to another person after you die. There are ways for property to pass to another person without a will and the subsequent probate, sidestepping the laws of intestacy. These are called testamentary substitutes.

Even though the name is funny and sounds a little off, testamentary substitutes are very useful for same-sex couples. They allow a couple to own property with one another and convey it to one another without having to wait for the wheels of probate to grind. The primary advantage of testamentary substitutes is that they are light years faster than waiting for courts to convey property after your demise.

When a person writes a will, they create what is called their "testamentary estate," which consists of all of their property that they talk about in the will. However, they may own property that is considered to be outside of that estate, because it passes to another individual by operation of law upon the death of the owner.

To understand why testamentary substitutes are so great, you first have to understand a little about probate. Probate is the process undertaken by your Executor in taking your will to court and getting it declared valid (see page 40). As we all know, courts are not in a hurry.

But if you have at least some testamentary substitutes, this entire operation can be bypassed. There are lots of testamentary substitutes and here are a few:

- Ownership of real estate under joint tenancy;
- Joint checking or savings accounts;
- Any type of account or instrument with beneficiary statements attached to them, such as
  —life insurance policies
  —retirement accounts such as 401(k)s or IRAs
  —certificates of deposit.

Basically any kind of property that you have that can have a beneficiary statement attached to it where you fill in a name of someone can be a testamentary substitute. When you die, rather than go through the estate considered by your will, they pass to the named individual when a *certified copy* of your death certificate is presented. Photocopies of death certificates are not acceptable.

For example, one of the ways in which a couple can purchase real estate is through joint tenancy, though in some states joint tenancy may be restricted to legally married couples. This is the way that it works. When a deed is made, you indicate at the time of your purchase that you are making the purchase as joint tenants. In that way, when one of you dies, the other will be able to have the property transferred automatically upon proving death with a death certificate. With joint tenancy, even if a person makes a mistake in writing his will and leaves that property to another individual, it would not be effective. Though such a circumstance would probably cause the court to hesitate before issuing letters testamentary, wondering if the testator knew what he or she was doing.

Be mindful of what you may have that could potentially become testamentary substitutes. If you have a checking account, you could make it joint. If you have a life insurance policy, you could ensure it passes automatically by indicating a beneficiary. In fact, if you don't have a beneficiary named with your policy, the money would pass to your testamentary estate. In that case, it will not only be tied up through the probate process, but it can also fall subject to attack by creditors. You may not have those kinds of creditors now, but you never know what will happen by the time you leave us. After a long illness, many people incur unexpected debt. Leaving your life insurance to your estate rather than a designated beneficiary runs some risk.

If you have a question as to whether something you own could potentially be a testamentary substitute, call the bank, agent, or broker with whom you dealt with when making the purchase and ask them if you can attach a beneficiary statement to the property. If you do, be sure you do not leave conflicting instructions for that property in your will, because that will make it appear to the court that you didn't know what you were doing. It will also create a bad situation between the people benefiting from the conflicting instructions. Keep copies on file of every beneficiary instruction you make. And, if you break up, be sure you rearrange all of these beneficiary statements, because your break-up won't affect them until you send specific instructions.

Powers of Attorney

By writing a will and making your partner your beneficiary and executor, and by making some of your property jointly owned with a right of survivorship, you've succeeded in gaining many of the rights that married people have when they die. In terms of your death, you have successfully made your partner very nearly your spouse. But what about while you are living? As an inherent part of estate planning between a couple who are not legally married, there are some other instruments that your attorney may offer you that will also protect your interests while you are alive but perhaps incapacitated by accident or illness. The first of these is a power of attorney.

The phrase "power of attorney" is a very lofty sounding name for something that is pretty mundane and ordinary. It simply means this: If there is something that you have the legal capacity and ability to do, then you can appoint someone else do to it in your place. Over time, there have been various types of powers of attorney developed in order to respond to people's needs. While some of these listed below may be offered to you by your attorney at the time you do a will, not all of them necessarily would be or are applicable, but they are included here so that you get an idea of how powers of attorney work.

Business Powers of Attorney. This is an example of a power of attorney you probably won't need. Powers of attorney have traditionally been used in a business capacity. For example, you have an ability to sign a contract and by signing a power of attorney instrument, you can hand over that authority to allow another person to sign on your behalf. Let's say you have a real-estate closing and you can't attend because it happens to conflict with your trip to the Cannes Film Festival. You can sign a document that says that all of the documents you were going to sign at the real-estate closing can now be signed by your friend (actually, probably your attorney) John Doe. It is doubtful that you would need to sign one of these, nor would your lawyer be inclined to include it as an option when you go to do your will.

If you do need to draw up a business power of attorney, you best do it with your attorney, because you want to ensure that you have covered all contingencies to guard against abuse.

Financial Powers of Attorney. One of the most common uses for a power of attorney is in finance. You can designate another person to sign a check or a series of checks for you in your place, and your bank will honor the check.

Powers of attorney could be written up very broadly, but for the protection of people, they are usually constructed more narrowly. For example, you can say that your friend Joe can sign your checks for you and that allows Joe to sign any and all checks in any and all amounts. Or, you might be more wise to say that Joe can sign only checks numbered 101-103 in amounts not to exceed $1,000 and your liability for any of Joe's temptations to excess would be limited.

Financial powers of attorney are not always necessary between couples, whether married or not, because of the ease provided by a joint checking account. However, there are powers of attorney that can be important for the non-legally married couple. These became particularly useful and necessary with the emergence of the HIV epidemic, but can and do serve in a broader capacity.

Anyone can draw one of these up, but banks usually prefer to use their own forms and may even state that they won't accept anything else.

Medical Power of Attorney. The epidemic broadened gay and lesbian rights on a number of fronts, many unexpectedly. One of the most unforeseen ways was the approach physicians would take when administering serious medical care to a gay or lesbian person and his or her partners.

As stated, traditional powers of attorney tended to deal with financial or business matters. In fact, the law fashioned them that way, because there were some aspects of life that were deemed simply too personal to delegate to another individual, the best such example being the right to vote, a right that cannot be legally delegated by a power of attorney or any other legal document. Another such example might be medical decision making. Prior to the AIDS epidemic, the law did not explicitly permit the delegation of such authority. But the epidemic brought doctors face to face with young gay male couples who were often far away from their nearest relatives, either geographically, emotionally, or both. Vital medical decisions had to be made, often under circumstances where the patient was incapable of making such a decision. AIDS service organizations and gay and lesbian bar associations began supplying couples with "medical powers of attorney," stating that, in the event that one was unable to make medical decisions on one's own, then he or she elected another to make those decisions in his/her place. Even though there was no statute permitting this at the time, the physicians often accepted them, because it was easier to confer with someone rather than no one. It happened so often, that physicians who were located in the epicenters of the epidemic grew accustomed to talking to significant others – lovers and domestic partners – when considering life-threatening decisions on behalf of a patient.

Eventually, the law caught up to reality. Today, several states accept medical powers of attorney, though they aren't always called by that term. There are many different rules about signing these that vary by state, so don't run to the stationery store on this one either. If you are involved in an emergency that brings you into a hospital, you may find that the hospital's social work department will know about them and be able to produce the forms, or organizations serving the gay, lesbian, bisexual, and transgendered community can do so, as can AIDS/HIV service organizations. However, that won't be true when it comes to "living wills," so it is best to try to attend to this ahead of time. Don't wait for a medical crisis to try to get your legal affairs straightened out.

Springing Power of Attorney. That sounds happy, doesn't it? This is not really a particular type of power of attorney – you aren't giving someone else the ability to spring for you, but rather it affects how a Power of Attorney goes into effect, and can be included in any of the powers of attorney talked about here. A springing power of attorney literally means that the validity to act under a power of attorney springs from a future event, such as one's incapacity. That means that you can sign a power of attorney to be effective only upon your medical incapacity. However, the person you appoint under the power of attorney to act in your place and stead must then demonstrate and prove that medical incapacity in order to act.

Durable Power of Attorney. If a springing power of attorney sounds happy, this one sounds sturdy. Unfortunately, the name tends to make people think that it is so durable that it cannot be revoked. But actually, when a power of attorney is characterized as durable, it simply means that in the event you are disabled after you have signed the instrument, then it is still valid. Naturally, a medical power of attorney has to be durable or else it would have no point.

When the Going Gets Tough – Living Wills

We don't like to consider it, but it is highly possible that one day we may be sick and in the hospital. In fact, that sickness may be so serious that extraordinary means, sometimes referred to as heroic measures, must be taken in order to sustain life. It is safe to say that virtually no one in the lesbian and gay community who was of adult age during the period of 1981–1997 was untouched by the experience of watching a friend or relative undergo unwanted medical procedures merely to prolong their pain and suffering. Since the advent of protease inhibitors, the mortality rate for HIV has dramatically fallen, but it is important to remember that it has not gone away. And lest the fall in mortality make people complacent, lesbians get breast cancer, men get prostate cancer, and, oh yeah – there is that occasional car or skiing accident. Anything can bring about a serious condition that is unforeseen and that has you or your partner facing decisions regarding treatments that may save your life or prolong your pain and suffering.

In that circumstance, another instrument that is important to consider is called a "living will," though it also has different names depending on the state where you live. The concept was popularized by the case of Karen Anne Quinlan, who as a teenager ingested a drug and alcohol combination that caused her to enter a deep coma. She lay in a vegetative state while the courts and the nation engaged in a great debate about the morality of "pulling the plug" or removing life support systems.

The removal of life support, and its timing, is a very personal issue and often depends on the circumstances surrounding the illness or malady that has resulted in a coma or extreme state. Some people may not want life support withdrawn under any circumstances; others would prefer it be withdrawn when the capacity to lead a normal life is compromised. Many others fall somewhere in between. To the extent that you feel you know what your directions might be in this regard, many states allow you to express them in a written document that you keep on file with your physician. States such as California have passed statutes that allow people to be fairly specific about the conditions in which they want life support and those in which they do not. Still, it is not an exact science, and the signing of this type of document is not a 100 percent locked-up deal. There can be circumstances at the time of an accident or illness that complicate the situation so that your instructions are not followed, as you might like. In an accident, your living will (or "directive to your physician" as it is sometimes called) may not be readily available. Remember that it is often easier to keep someone off life support or from extraordinary measures to keep them alive than it is to remove the life support once it is begun.

Living wills are not the same as do not resuscitate orders (DNRs). DNRs may be taken into the patient record when a person is entering the hospital and placed into a file. They forego the use of life saving means should one's heart stop beating.

Living wills are also not the equivalent of assisted suicide. The state of Oregon is the only state in the United States that permits assisted suicide for the terminally ill.

Any document of this type you sign you should then file with your doctors and maintain copies for yourself. If you haven't drawn up these documents and face a medical emergency, hospital social workers will sometimes be able to supply them. However, filling out a living will while in the midst of a medical emergency is not the best way to go about it. It could be argued that you were signing forms and giving directions under the duress of your illness or accident, making decisions that you otherwise would not have made in a healthy state. For that reason and many others, it is best to be proactive about getting the job done.

In executing a living will, or whatever it is called in your jurisdiction, you are free to state what you want as well as what you don't want in the way of care. You may want every single extraordinary and heroic measure taken to save your life. In that case, you can state that.

Living will forms are sometimes available from organizations that specialize in the rights of individuals to make their own care decisions, particularly regarding extraordinary means. However, some of the forms can be lengthy and may include terminology with which you are not familiar. The best thing to do is to visit an attorney and write mutual wills, execute powers of attorney, and take care of your living wills all at once. Not only will this help you understand the documents better, but the fact that you went to a lawyer's office and executed this entire package of documents gives the appearance to any future court that may be involved that you conscientiously sought to reinforce your relationship and forge your rights with respect to it. In other words, by going to a lawyer and going through the process in his or her office, it will, in many ways, look like you went and got yourself married.

Widowhood

As you saw earlier in this chapter, how your partner's estate is being handled when he or she dies depends on whether there was a will. If there was not a will, you will pretty much be left out of the picture, unless you held joint property with a right of survivorship or have entered into a Vermont Civil Union. If there was a will, then the property should pass to you after the will goes through the process called probate. In either case, the first thing you will need is your partner's death certificate.

Death Certificates. You have a birth certificate. It has probably been useful to you, to get a passport for example. It certifies the fact that you were born. An instrument you will never see is your death certificate, which, as you can guess, certifies the fact that you have died. It is the legal proof, and it is issued by the jurisdiction where you live. That legal proof will be required by a lot of people and your executor, if you had a will, your administrator, if you did not, or people with whom you share property, checking accounts, savings accounts, or for whom you have left money in an insurance policy or retirement plan. They are going to need to have that proof. Each copy costs money, because they are certified, usually meaning that there is a little raised seal from your city or county. Taking a certified copy and making a copy on a copy machine isn't going to work. This is the first thing that you have to face, and it is upsetting, but you will need to order several copies of the certificate and it is best to order more than you think you will need. Ordering the certificates is usually done by the person who is going to be the executor or the administrator of the estate. If you are not that person, you will need to talk to them about your needs in this respect.

Estate Administration – If Your Partner Had No Will. As we saw earlier in this chapter under the section entitled "Dying Without a Will – The Laws of Intestacy," when a person dies without a will, their property is passed to their next of kin through a process called estate administration. In that circumstance, non-relatives do not inherit.

Someone, presumably a relative, will step forward and file a death certificate with the court that handles this matter. All next of kin will be identified and notified, as well as all property that the deceased had. When the court is satisfied that this has been done, it will issue the person who filed the petition documents called Letters of Administration. These letters empower the person, now called the administrator, to act on behalf of the estate, paying expenses and collecting sums owed to the deceased and identifying and collecting all property owned by the deceased. Once that is done, the administrator will be allowed to distribute the property to the next of kin. For example, if your partner died without a will and had no legal spouse or children, his or her parents were deceased, but had two brothers who survived him, those brothers would share equally of the estate. People who inherit the estate by way of intestacy are called legatees.

If no one steps forward to become an administrator, then there are public administrators who can be appointed by the court. This is the least desirable way to have your estate tended to, because the administrator is someone who does not know the deceased, the family or you.

If your partner has died and left family who are geographically distant, there is no reason that you cannot become the administrator, but you will have to have their cooperation in doing so. While you will not inherit anything by doing so, you will be able to charge a fee for your effort – the amount of which is dependent on the jurisdiction where you live.

The forms you will need are with the court. If the estate is large, you would be well advised to hire an attorney to help you. The hiring of help is an expense of the estate, and before any property is distributed, the expenses of the estate will be repaid. Therefore, any expenses, such as hiring a lawyer or an accountant to file the income taxes of the deceased, will be reimbursed or paid before property is distributed.

Probate – If Your Partner Died with a Valid Will. Many people misunderstand how wills work. They think that they go into effect just because they are signed. But that isn't the case. Your last will and testament does not even go into effect when you die. It only goes into effect when a court says that it does, and not before then. The process by which that occurs and your estate is disseminated is called probate, and to get through it, there is a lot to tend to. Unfortunately, all of that work comes at a time in your life when you don't feel like doing anything but sitting and grieving. That is why it will be important to find good help.

Probate is the process by which the court examines the will and ensures that it was written up and signed in accordance with the laws of the state in which you live. The person who is named as the executor of the estate will file a petition with the court that is accompanied by the will.

As a part of probate, the court requires notification to those people who would have inherited the estate had their been no will (the legatees), as well as the people who are named to inherit under the terms of the will (the beneficiaries). In addition, the court will want statements from the people who witnessed you sign your will, attesting to the fact that you signed it, you were who you said you were and that you appeared to know what you were doing and were doing it of your own free will.

Once the court has ensured that the will was signed and that there are no challenges being made to the validity of the will, then Letters Testamentary will be issued to the executor. Grounds for a will contest are based only on three aspects of the matter:

- Was the person who signed the will sane when it was signed? (A relative, but nevertheless important question.)

- Was the person who signed the will in fact the person he said he was – in other words, was it a forgery?
- Was the person who signed the will acting under duress of some kind, i.e., was someone holding a gun to the head of the testator?

Whenever there is an estate to transfer, large or small, it is important to find good legal representation. If your partner died having a will and you are the executor, you can go hire a lawyer to manage the process for you. Often people hire the attorney who drafted the will.

One important factor to consider with respect to the value of your estate is whether your executor has to go through probate at all. There is often an abbreviated process that is undertaken for estates that are of small value.

Letters Testamentary and the Executor. In either case, through probate or the shorter version, once the court is satisfied that your will was validly signed and that there is no reason to believe that it represents anything other than your true intentions, the court will issue Letters Testamentary to your executor. If your partner died without a will, and someone has filed papers to become the administrator of the estate, then these are called Letters of Administration.

This begins the actual work and means that the executor or administrator must take care of all of the unfinished business of the testator – e.g., paying all debts and expenses, and filing the federal income tax on behalf of the person in the year in which he or she died. In fact, if the business of the estate takes long enough and the estate begins to get income through bank interest, for example, the estate itself may have to file a tax return. There are a tremendous number of tasks involved in closing out someone's life. The executor will sell those things that the deceased may have directed be sold, create bank accounts in which to deposit estate funds and manage a complex set of circumstances. The checklist of issues faced by an executor differs greatly given the circumstances of the estate and the state in which the will is being probated. Entire books can be and have been written about all that an executor must consider.

There can be many other aspects to probate, depending on the value of your estate and the circumstances surrounding your will. Estate taxes may be a factor, but only if your estate is large enough. In order for your estate to owe federal estate taxes, it must be of several hundred thousand dollars' worth (the ceiling has changed frequently over the past twenty years) and, in fact, there is popular public sentiment to remove the "death tax" entirely. However it may be lower for your state estate taxes, and you should consult with your attorney regarding this matter, particularly if you own real estate that could be valued highly enough to put you over the mark.

The process is not an overnight one. By the time a person dies; the executor gets his act together and gets the will to court; the court gets its act together and sees that there are no problems with the will, then issues Letters Testamentary; and the executor then gets his act together again and pays all debts and expenses and gets the many hundreds of things he must do checked off his to do list, a lot of time can go by. Years in fact. And that assumes that there has been no challenge to the validity of the will.

Once all the money owed to the estate has been received, and all the debts and expenses paid, the executor may distribute the property as directed by the will. Needless to say, especially if an estate has any complications to it, it is best to seek legal counsel. Most lawyers are retained under these circumstances by receiving a percentage of the estate, though some may charge hourly rates.

All of this Love and Death stuff has probably gotten you to wondering if there is any way in hell the writing of a will could be construed as "getting married." Well, it does lack the pomp and circumstance of a wedding, but even in that over-rated ceremony, the words "till death do us part" are invariably uttered. The macabre is never far away from the romance.

Future Directions – Teachings of the Past

First during the AIDS epidemic and again in the wake of the events of September 11, gays and lesbians learned that the fundamental lack of respect that the law has for their relationships can mean more than inconvenience when it comes to death and dying.

One need only look at the developments of the past twenty-five years to see that there is increasing recognition for legal mechanisms that will support lesbian and gay families. From the simple mechanism of domestic partnerships to the institution of civil unions in Vermont, gay and lesbian families are finding support in the law and removing many of the barriers to equality that exist in our society. But until such time as gay and lesbian relationships are recognized on an equal footing with those of the heterosexual world, it is important that for now and the foreseeable future, gay and lesbian couples look to see how they can shape the law for themselves, examining their options to effect their own marriages, both through the means discussed in chapter 1, as well as through those described in this chapter. Getting involved with your partner to make provision through estate planning may be the difference between being considered married by the law, for all intents and purposes, and being a victim.

CHAPTER 5

Discriminating Tastes

History and Perspective – A Crash Course on Rights

WHILE THE OTHER AREAS of law that we have looked at in the four previous chapters involved state law, discrimination is covered under both federal and state laws. That means that, in some cases, you may have a choice about what law you seek to enforce to protect you against discrimination. In other circumstances, you may find that there is no law to protect you at all. This chapter will help you sort through the maze of laws that exist as well as to define whether you have a case and, if you do, whether you can prove it.

Where Rights Come From

Rights come to you from the constitutions of both the state and the federal government under which you live. Enforcement of those rights comes from laws passed by your city council, your county government, your state legislature and the United States Congress. Usually, these are laws designed to guarantee you those rights. Sometimes, however, as you will see in the next section, laws are passed to interfere with rights guaranteed you by one of the constitutions mentioned above.

There is an almost knee-jerk reaction by people who have been discriminated against: They believe that their constitutional rights have been violated. But nowhere in the Constitution does it state that "Thou shalt not discriminate against . . ." nor does it say that all men are created equal – that was the Declaration of Independence.

In fact, ironically, you could say that the first instance of discrimination in the United States began at the very moment the Constitution was written. To begin with, only white, straight men were allowed to write it and vote on it. That in and of itself evidences some systemic discrimination. For the longest time, only white men were allowed to have any sort of political power in the country. At the time the U.S. Constitution was granted, women were considered chattel of men – something that was not quite property, but not far from it. And then there were slaves, who were considered property.

After the Civil War, amendments were made to the Constitution that guaranteed the former male slaves the right to vote. Nearly another half century would pass before women of color got that right, and they would get it at the same time as all other women. Naturally, the right to vote did not translate into a status of equality – and of this, there are endless examples.

What does any of this have to do with your rights? It means that interpretations of the U.S. Constitution regarding your rights have been somewhat slow in developing. After all, it was only just after the Civil War that the term "homosexual" came into being, and it was many, many more years before there was any discussion of equal rights for gays and lesbians.

Under the Fourteenth Amendment to the U.S. Constitution, all people are supposed to have equal access to the protection of the laws. That is, by the way, as near as the document gets to saying that we are all, in fact, created equal. The Fourteenth Amendment is an example of the way that the Constitution, without mentioning anyone in particular, guarantees rights to all. If one group were to be denied equal access to the laws of the United States, then that would be discriminatory. But there is no part of the Constitution that otherwise guarantees that you won't be discriminated against.

What Makes Gay and Lesbian Rights Different

Because lesbian and gay protections are relatively new to the scene, coming behind those for other minorities, gays and lesbians face particular problems in trying to protect their rights. For gays and lesbians, the road to discriminatory protection has been fraught with disadvantages distinct to homosexuals. Let's call them the three stigmas.

To begin with, for many years, gays and lesbians were regarded as mentally ill – a status that carries a stigma not associated with other minorities. It is a blot that has stood in the way of real progress for lesbians and gays for many years, and though recently lessened, it is still an influential factor. It was not until 1970 that the American Psychiatric Association declared their own emancipation on that count by removing homosexuality from the list of mental illnesses.

Aside from the stigma of mental illness, there is another taint that has dogged lesbian and gay individuals. The second stigma would be the matter of moral choice. Other minorities do not choose to be who they are, but in the public mind, there is the widely held perception that lesbians and gays choose to engage in their "lifestyle" and, further, that the choice to do so is an immoral one.

Lastly, a third obstacle in the quest for equal rights is the widely held view that gays and lesbians are more prone to being sexual predators on children, a stigma that has, by itself, resulted in the recall and repeal of anti-discriminatory protections that were passed in some cities and counties to protect lesbian and gay rights.

In addition to the three stigmas, there are other differences between gays and lesbians and other minorities that affect the ability of the community to achieve rights equal to the majority.

First, there is no closet for other minorities. Targets of racial and gender discrimination have their identities out there for the world to see. Skin color and gender appearance give it away for racial minorities and women. However, gays and lesbians could have stayed in the closet forever.

Second, progress for African Americans and women has largely occurred from the top down – meaning that legislative advancements have been won on the national stage. Progress for gays and lesbians has been more piecemeal and local, making these advancements vulnerable to local attack and repeal. There are no federal laws that broadly protect gays and lesbians from discrimination.

These differences have resulted in another difference between gay and lesbian rights and those of other minorities. The victories and advances by other minorities have been achieved and built into the permanent infrastructure of our legal system. No one campaigns for the repeal of their rights, and no one tries to pass laws to forbid other minorities from trying to achieve their rights. But advances in rights protections for the lesbian and gay community have often been a matter of two steps forward, one step backward.

Trial and Terror – Repeals of Rights Laws

Progress has almost always met with resistance – as seen with the kinds of efforts led to repeal such protections where they occur. If a legislature votes for protections, citizens may petition for a state-wide ballot to repeal them, causing precious resources to be poured into emotional and costly political battles. Ballot initiatives – an absurd form of democracy that puts emotionally charged, polarizing, and complex issues on a ballot for everyone to vote on following an advertising blitz in which the loudest and richest side wins after distorting every conceivable truth about the initiative – are a particular bane to those involved in the struggle for recognition of lesbian and gay rights.

One of the most famous of these occurred in 1977 when Dade County, Florida, passed a county ordinance protecting gays and lesbians from discrimination. An orange juice spokeswoman and pop singer led a public campaign for its repeal. The campaign was couched in terms of saving children and borrowed heavily on the three stigmas mentioned above. The battle was the focus of national attention whereby the very nature of gays and lesbians was maligned and distorted. The effort was ultimately successful, and the Dade County protection law was repealed. In 1998, the Dade County board again voted into law anti-discrimination protections for lesbians and gays. On September 12, 2002, it again faced a ballot initiative to recall it. (People in Florida must have had a profound sense of deja vu.) Fortunately, the outcome of the second election revealed that this time, the voters of Dade County were not so bigoted and the repeal failed.

Some efforts targeting gay and lesbian rights go beyond mere repeal of laws. One such initiative was proposed and passed by voters in the state or Colorado in 1992. Known as Amendment 2, this handy piece of legislation differed from ballot initiatives that repealed laws passed by legislatures – it went one step further. Amendment 2 actually forbade any laws passed by anyone in the state that would protect gays and lesbians from discrimination. In other words, it made equal rights illegal. The measure passed with 53 percent of the voters in the state favoring it. This wasn't a law, it was a hate crime. Before the law could take effect, however, it was taken to court by the Lambda Legal Defense and Education Fund and the American Civil Liberties Union. A judge, believing that the measure would ultimately be found unconstitutional, granted an injunction prohibiting it from going into effect. The state attorney general of Colorado, who was later appointed to the cabinet of George W. Bush, appealed that injunction and lost in the Colorado Supreme Court. She then took the matter to the Supremes. The case was called *Romer v. Evans*. It is arguably the most important case ever concerning lesbians and gays. The reason for that is that the Supremes listened to the arguments for and against Amendment 2 and rendered a decision in a 6–3 vote, saying that the insidious piece of legislation was indeed unconstitutional and could not be permitted to go into effect. The case was decided by the Supremes four years after the amendment was approved by Colorado voters. In stating that the measure didn't bear constitutional scrutiny, Justice Anthony Kennedy said that the amendment sought to make gays and lesbians "unequal to everyone else. This Colorado cannot do. A state cannot so deem a class of persons a stranger to its laws." The case is important for many reasons, not the least of which it was the first time that the Supremes considered a lesbian or gay matter and actually recognized that rights existed that could not be legislatively taken away.

The Amendment 2 experience is an excellent reminder for all in the lesbian and gay community that rights are not something that are given to you, nor are they something for which you have to fight. Your rights are something you have already. The struggle isn't in getting your rights, but in getting others to recognize that you have them. Straight people do not own the Constitution nor the law.

At some point, they will realize that. Until they do, there are laws that may protect your rights, but unfortunately, they are not uniform, and your ability to use them will once again, as in so many other areas of law, depend on where you live.

Today, thirteen states prohibit discrimination against gays and lesbians, with Maryland and New York being the latest in 2001 and 2003, respectively. However, also in 2001, a coalition was announced to put the initiative on a statewide ballot in an attempt to repeal the Maryland state law, and was passed by the legislature and signed by the governor. The coalition was called "Take Back Maryland," as if Maryland belonged only to straight people and gay people had made a grab for it. However, the effort to get the repeal onto the ballot failed, and the measure went into effect in late 2001.

There is no federal legislation that prohibits discrimination against gays. In the 1970s there was an attempt to introduce such a law by Ed Koch and Bella Abzug, both then congresspersons from New York and later both mayoral candidates. The End Discrimination Act (ENDA) was introduced before Congress in the late 1990s, where it has since sat without action.

Current Events – Four Steps to a Discrimination Case

As mentioned above, protection for you depends on where you live and to what extent the legislation protects you. You will have to look and see if there are loopholes. Only a limited number of states have passed protections, though there are also protections afforded by city and county governments. Sometimes a jurisdiction may not ban discrimination by private employers, but will forbid discrimination in its own hiring practices. Sometimes a jurisdiction will pass legislation that protects gays and lesbians from discrimination, but will exempt religious institutions. All of this means that you have a job ahead of you when and if you ever need to figure out whether you have protection. Below are progressive steps for doing that; if you don't have the first one, you can't go onto the second one . . .

- First, you will need to determine whether you have in fact suffered an act of discrimination;
- Second, if you have indeed suffered an act of discrimination, you next have to determine whether discrimination against gays and lesbians is illegal where you live as well as whether the type of discrimination you suffered is against the law;
- Third, even if you have been discriminated against illegally, can you prove the discrimination, and how should you do it?
- Lastly, if you have suffered discrimination and it is illegal, is bringing suit something that is desirable for you to do?

Determining Whether You Were Discriminated Against

When is someone's action towards you an act of discrimination and when is it simply a reflection of personal choice. There is no pat answer to this question. It is largely a matter of "gut." Listen to your instincts, and if there is something that you think is quite possibly there, your next step may be to confide in someone. As with any instinct, however, you may be wrong. Sometimes people may be inclined to see an act of discrimination where there is none, because they are unwilling to face other problems or issues they may be having at work.

Factors to Help You. With that in mind, your next step may be to test your hypothesis with a friend or even to call a legal hotline. You shouldn't just trust your own judgment in this matter. You should keep an open mind, and if it is possible, you should talk to a lawyer early in the process. At this stage, you aren't trying to build your case; you are trying to determine whether or not there has been an act of discrimination. This means that with whomever you speak to about the matter, you should take care not to rail. State the facts as objectively as you can. Don't embellish. Relay events as they have happened without trying to convince someone of a point of view. One caveat: You would best be advised not to confide in co-workers, as they may be called as witnesses in the event that there is a case.

One obvious consideration is whether the person you believe has discriminated against you knows that you are a gay or lesbian person. If they don't know, or if you cannot prove that they know, then it would be impossible for them to have acted in a discriminatory manner. If a person does not know you are gay, but creates an environment that is unfriendly to gays and lesbians, that may not necessarily be considered discrimination.

While you should not have a knee-jerk reaction, automatically assuming that you have been discriminated against when you have not, don't necessarily assume that because you are well regarded in your employment everything is OK. Sometimes people don't see discrimination when it is there, because they are so stunned. They have been open about their homosexuality and didn't think it that there was any problem, when in fact, there was.

And if you are in the closet, you can't assume that they don't know, and you cannot assume that being in the closet will keep you safe. "It isn't just a matter of what is written on a person's performance evaluation," says Kevin Layton, legal director at the Human Rights Campaign in Washington. "After positive performance evaluations, there could be circumstance that causes a change – a picture or something said that triggers recognition on the part of the employer that you are lesbian or gay. Then you see that their pattern of behavior changes."

There are two essential elements that you need. On the one hand, you need to show that the act was motivated by the knowledge of your sexual orientation. On the other hand, you need to also demonstrate that there is no other possible explanation for what happened. "The more you can do one, the less you need of the other, but you need both," says Matt Coles, legal director of the Lesbian and Gay Rights Project at the American Civil Liberties Union. For example, he says, if you are working in a workplace where you have an excellent work history and the employer finds out about your sexual orientation and then suddenly comes up with something far fetched to hold against you, then you may not need to make a strong showing of homophobia on the employer's part. But, if you have a situation where homophobia is everywhere, your burden in demonstrating that the employer knew you were gay may be less burdensome.

The Perfect Case. Kevin Layton describes a perfect example of blatant discrimination that occurred in Georgia. "It was a written company policy that employees who were gay or lesbian violated the traditional family values of the corporation and should be separated," he says. "The employee had good reviews, but on her termination slip it said that the employee was being terminated because she was gay." That is the best case scenario, because the termination and the reason for it were quite clear. Not everyone, however, is so blunt, and your circumstances are unlikely to be as clear-cut as that.

In the end, what you must find out by talking with your friend or to a lawyer is:

- Did the person you believe discriminated against you know that you were gay or lesbian?
- If you have reason to know that your homosexuality was known, did behavior change as a result of the knowledge?

- If it did change, was the change directed specifically to you, treating you in a manner distinct and apart from others?
- And lastly, are there other circumstances involved that complicate the issue, that you haven't felt comfortable talking about or addressing, such as work performance or attitudinal problems you may have exhibited? (Were you denied a job because you were gay or because your resume shows that you have gone through five jobs in five years?)

You may find that, in considering this, the answers to your questions are not so black and white, but are more in a gray area. That is why, as Matt Coles suggests, you should involve a lawyer as early as possible. Not only can the lawyer be objective, but he or she will be able to bring experience to the discussion that will help you come to the conclusions you need.

Determining Whether Discrimination Is Illegal

Now you have identified the fact that you indeed have suffered discrimination. You talked it over with your significant other, with the friends down the block, and with your family. You even talked about it with your preacher, priest, or rabbi, and they all agree – it sounds like someone is discriminating against you.

Your next step is to determine whether or not the discrimination was illegal. Not all acts of discrimination are. Just because something isn't fair doesn't mean that it's illegal.

Each day, whether you are aware of it or not, someone makes a decision about you based on who you are. Your Aunt Betty doesn't invite you to her dinner party because you are a lesbian and she has invited someone else who she feels will be uncomfortable with that. Or, your Aunt Betty invites you to a dinner party because there is another lesbian there she wants you to meet. In either circumstance, a decision was made to exclude or include you based on your sexual orientation. Of course, you are not going to sue Aunt Betty, though her Christmas present may suffer if you discover her true feelings about your homosexuality. Still, if Aunt Betty left you out of dinner because you are gay, as you may guess, it isn't illegal.

But it may not be dinner. It may be a job promotion. Your boss Betty decides to promote Carol rather than you because Carol is a divorced mother with three kids and you are a lesbian with a cat. You couldn't sue your Aunt Betty, but could you sue your boss Betty?

How You Determine Illegality. There are three things you must ask yourself when trying to decide if discrimination is illegal:

- First – is there a law that protects you against discrimination in the place where you live, work, or where the incident occurred?
- Second – is the action that occurred deemed illegal by statute?
- Third – is there an exception to the law?

What does that mean? Well going back to Aunt Betty for a second, let's say you live in Maryland, where there is a law against gay and lesbian discrimination. Aunt Betty lives there too. She has not invited you to dinner because you are a lesbian. In that case, you live in a place that bans discrimination, but the law does not cover being asked to dinner, it covers employment. Now let's go back to your boss Betty. She overlooks you for the promotion and finds out that you are a lesbian and fires you. In that case, you have a statute that protects you and you have an act that is prohibited in the statute. You have a case. Unless. . .

Unless there is an exception. What was the name of the organization you worked for? Was it St. Betty's Boniface Church Charity? Well guess what? In order to get the anti-discrimination statute passed in the state where you live, the legislature had to tack on an exception for religious employers, meaning that you don't have a case after all. If you had worked for a convenience store instead of St. Betty's you could sue their pants off. But because you worked for religious folk, you can't.

Remember the perfect case Kevin Layton described on page 151? It was perfect except for one thing. Georgia had no statute protecting lesbians and gays from discrimination. That means the company policy was perfectly legal. The plaintiff in that case struggled for a long time to win her job back. The case too place in 1991. In 2002, the company (Cracker Barrel) finally changed its policy, but their discriminatory policy was not against the law.

Huh? What about your constitutional rights? It doesn't cover you either. In fact there is currently no federal law at the current time protecting the rights of lesbians and gays in employment, with the exception of an Executive Order signed by President Clinton that bars discrimination against homosexuals employed by the executive branch of the government.

Where Laws Exist. So where do you find protection? Thirteen states and the District of Columbia have passed discrimination laws respecting employment of gays and lesbians.

States with Anti-Discrimination Laws (and DC)

California	Maryland	New York
Connecticut	Minnesota	Rhode Island
District of Columbia	Nevada	Vermont
Hawaii	New Hampshire	Wisconsin
Massachusetts	New Jersey	

If you don't live in one of these geographies, what do you do? Just because there isn't a state law doesn't mean there isn't a county, city or local law. In addition to the federal and state governments, there are other people who have the task of running the organized society at a more local level – they are county and city governments. They have the right to pass laws and ordinances that affect the goings on in their own communities, as long as they are not against the state or federal constitutions.

The following counties have passed legislation that offer protections.

Counties with Anti-Discrimination Laws

State	County	State	County
California	Los Angeles San Mateo Santa Clara Santa Cruz	Michigan	Wayne
		New York	Albany Onondaga Tomkins
Florida	Broward Miami-Dade	Oregon	Benton
Illinois	Cook	Virginia	Arlington
Kentucky	Jefferson	Washington	King
Maryland	Howard Montgomery Prince George's		

If you have no protections at the state or county level, the following cities have anti-discrimination statutes in place.

Cities with Anti-Discrimination Laws

State	City	State	City
Arizona	Phoenix Tucson	(*continued*)	Mountain View Oakland Sacramento San Diego San Francisco San Jose Santa Cruz Santa Monica West Hollywood
California	Berkeley Cathedral City Davis Laguna Beach Long Beach Los Angeles		

State	City
Colorado	Arva
	Aspen
	Boulder
	Crested Butte
	Denver
	Fort Collins
	Telluride
Connecticut	Hartford
	New Haven
Florida	Gainesville
	Key West
	Miami Beach
	Ocala
	Palm Beach Town
	Tampa
	West Palm Beach
Illinois	Champaign
	Chicago
	DeKalb
	Evanston
	Springfield
	Urbana
	West Lafayette
Indiana	Bloomington
	Lafayette
Iowa	Ames
	Cedar Rapids
	Iowa City
Kansas	Lawrence
Kentucky	Henderson
	Lexington-Fayette
	Louisville
Louisiana	New Orleans
Maine	Bar Harbor
	Falmouth
	Long Island
	Orono
	Portland
	Sorrento
	South Portland
Maryland	Baltimore
	Rockville
Massachusetts	Boston
	Brookline
	Cambridge

State	City
(*continued*)	Malden
	Somerville
Michigan	Ann Arbor
	Detroit
	East Lansing
	Grand Rapids
	Ypsilanti
Minnesota	Minneapolis
	St. Paul
Missouri	Columbia
	Kansas City
	St. Louis
Nevada	Carson City
New York	Albany
	Hampton
	Ithaca
	New York
	Rochester
	Syracuse
North Carolina	Raleigh
Ohio	Athens
	Cleveland
	Cleveland Heights
	Toledo
	Yellow Springs
	Youngstown
Oregon	Ashland
	Corvallis
	Eugene
	Portland
Pennsylvania	Harrisburg
	Lancaster
	Philadelphia
	Pittsburgh
	York
Rhode Island	Providence
Texas	Austin
Vermont	Burlington
Virginia	Alexandria
	Charlottesville
Washington	Seattle
	Spokane
Wisconsin	Madison
	Milwaukee

While a state may not prohibit discrimination in private employment, there still may be prohibitions against discriminating against gays and lesbians in state employment. This includes:

States that Prohibit Discrimination for State Employees

Illinois	New York
Iowa	Pennsylvania
Maryland	Washington
New Mexico	

If You Live in an Area without a Law. In essence, like so many other areas of gay and lesbian law, what you can do in response to your discrimination is largely a factor of your geography. There are some places in the United States where you could live and have several laws protect you from discrimination because you are a lesbian or gay person. For example, if you happen to be living and working in West Hollywood, California, you would find yourself protected by city law, county law and state law. Each jurisdiction will have its own way of enforcing its law and its own remedies for those who suffer discrimination. Deciding which to use will be the job of the professional you choose to help you through your case. On the other hand, you may find if you live in Pierre, South Dakota, and you suffer at the hands of some discriminatory bigot, well, you are out of luck, because there is no law to protect you. You are just out of a job.

But just because the place where you live doesn't have a statute may not mean you don't have a case. If you are really determined, don't give up. Seek out the advice of a lawyer who can investigate other avenues, such as a union contract under which sexual orientation is covered as a protection, or an employment contract that has a provision that will protect you.

Even if you don't work for a government agency, there may still be protection for you within the personnel policy or manuals of your company. There may be language there that creates an obligation on the part of the company that will be enforceable. In some places you can bring various kinds of unfair employment claims even if you don't have a discrimination claim. Don't give up. Contact a lawyer.

Another possibility comes in the form of AIDS/HIV protections. If you are fired from your job because your employer associates your being gay with having HIV or AIDS, then you may have a remedy even if you live somewhere without protection for gays and lesbians. That is because HIV/AIDS is more protected than is the status of gay, lesbian, bisexual, or transgender. There are more laws covering it and there is even federal law – the Americans with Disabilities Act. While those laws do not prohibit discrimination against you for being gay or lesbian, they do prohibit discrimination if you have AIDS or HIV. They also often cover the situation if you are *perceived* to have AIDS/HIV. Because of that, if the facts of your case are such that your employer is discriminating against you because he is concerned about AIDS transmission or the costs associated with your care, you may have a case.

Lastly, Kevin Layton adds that, sometimes, the court of public opinion can be an effective means of waging your case. Whether you can sue and get your job back, there is a public relations opportunity if your case is egregious enough that it will allow you to state your case publicly and, in doing so, educate the public. In his perfect case, the woman who had been fired was able to work with community organizers who in turn helped her make her case in a public forum. She did not get her job back, but the company changed its policy.

Building Your Case

Let's say you have now answered the first two of the four questions we posed at the beginning of the chapter. You do feel you have suffered discrimination and there is a statute that protects you, covering the type of discrimination you suffered, i.e., employment. Next you have to set out to prove it.

Documentation and Proof. You now need to begin building the elements of your case. One of the things that will be essential is proof. Without it, you will get nowhere. "The worst kind of case is where people can't point to anything – they have all these examples of discrimination but can't show how the employer knew that they were gay," says Matt Coles. You have to show homophobia and you have to show that the act was motivated out of that homophobia. You will need more than just your word to convince a court that this is what happened. An essential ingredient in your evidence, therefore, will be documentation of the events and circumstances that led up to the discriminatory action.

Documentation isn't you sitting down with your diary and sounding off about your feelings over your treatment. Your feelings are important, but don't let them get in the way. Your writing should be factual, Coles warns. "If you write about what happens to you, it is not really documentation. You do want to be able to keep an account of things that happen. It shouldn't be a diary with your feelings or your reflections but a straight recitation of the facts as they happened, with dates and times."

This is something essential for your lawyer, says Kevin Layton. "The best cases are those that have a decent chronology – what happened and where it happened and who was involved. A chronology that is detailed is very valuable to an attorney because they can use it in a deposition and in discussing the case with the other side." The straight recitation of facts gives everyone a framework.

When do you begin your documentation? How about when your supervisor tells you that you should act less gay? Is that enough to begin a suit? "The red flag," says Coles, "is when you perceive that your job is on the line. It doesn't make sense to keep a long record. Any time your supervisor says something like that, anything that blatant, you would want to make a record of the event." But again, anything else that tells us how you feel about that event is probably going to be less critical and less helpful to your case and your attorney than the plain simple facts.

Documentation goes beyond your diary's recitation of facts. It includes meeting minutes, transcripts of telephone conversations or messages, or even the saved or recorded messages themselves. It may be a performance review, a bonus memo, or e-mail. In addition, personnel policy manuals or flyers that are posted by management making announcements are all examples of potential proof you may need. Be aware of anything that documents your job and the work that you do, such as job descriptions. You should be careful that you are gathering materials that you are supposed to have access to and not taking things that could cause you to get yourself into trouble, such as patient records.

You have three of the four bases covered. Now you just have to decide whether you really want to sue.

To Sue or Not to Sue?

You are almost done now. You have determined that you have suffered discrimination, you have talked to a legal expert and found that it is illegal and that you are protected, and you have pieced together the proof that can demonstrate your position. You are set to sue. Or are you? You will need to

- Get experienced legal help. Have you got the legal resources to fight the legal battle?
- Examine your motives for the suit. Do you want the remedy you will get as a result of suing?
- Determine whether you feel up to it?

Finding Legal Help. If you haven't done so already, the next step for you is to find a lawyer. He or she will be the best sounding board for whether you truly have a case. How do you find a good discrimination lawyer? While the gay and lesbian community has developed incredible legal resources in national organizations, such as Lambda Legal Defense and Education Fund and the American Civil Liberties Union, getting help is not as easy as calling either one of them up and telling them that Big Bad Betty has booted you out. "Most of the national organizations have to turn away most of the cases," explains Matt Coles, "and only do cases which, in their judgement, are going to affect large numbers of people." These are usually cases that are going to set a precedent and are commonly referred to as "impact litigation." While the organizations would like to take all the cases, those kinds of resources simply aren't there. It makes the most sense for them to litigate the cases that are going to have an impact for everyone. That means if your case is not something that is going to shake things up on that scale, you may be left with having to find an attorney who is going to help you.

"I think the best way to find a good lawyer is to talk to people who know you and know that you are gay and get some names," says Coles. Don't make the judgement call about your case yourself, however. You may think your case is ordinary, says Coles, but one of the national organizations could spot how the case could be useful in creating a precedent that would affect others. You definitely should check it with experienced lawyers. There are legal referral networks (See resources at the back of this book) that can help steer you.

Wait until you find someone who is experienced in this area and with whom you feel comfortable, because litigation is a long and very personal process. Coles says you may have to persevere. "You may not always find that the first referrals you get are people that can handle your case. You want to find someone who is used to dealing with these issues."

Remedies – What You Want, What You Get. You may in fact feel that your case is going to be a case that will shake things up. But if you have taken all the steps outlined already in talking to people, by now you should have developed a realistic and objective viewpoint of what your case is and what it is not. You have to be careful not to let your emotions get in the way. One of the things you need to explore with your lawyer through a good heart-to-heart discussion is your motivation for undertaking a lawsuit. Why you are doing this, and what do you think you can get out of it? Make sure, to the extent that you can, that you know what you are in for and what you want out of the whole thing.

"People have enormous expectations of what they want to get out of a lawsuit," observes Matt Cole, "financially and emotionally. They want the bad guys to make amends. But the bad guys usually feel justified in discriminating against you, even when the case is over." In other words, you can't sue someone with the hope that they are going to repent and ask for your forgiveness. This isn't a made-for-TV movie. Chances are, if the person consciously acted in a way that was discriminatory, they are still the same person they were when they began that action. Your lawsuit may not change them into someone different. You really have to compare what you want with what the cost is going to be to get it – and whether you can really get what is going to make you happy.

No lawsuit is easy – it is a rigorous and difficult process. How difficult? In undertaking a lawsuit, be aware that you are going to have to relive the experience you have had in ways that you might not expect. Part of any litigation is a process called discovery, which involves both sides gathering evidence. Part of that evidence can take the form of pre-trial testimony called a deposition. A lot of questions can be asked in this venue, and you may find that you have to answer extremely personal questions that make you uncomfortable or even embarrass you.

The remedy for suing for discrimination is not a demand from the court that the manager who fired you repents; the remedy is that you get your old job back with back pay. Unless there was an aggravating circumstance in which you were injured or you can demonstrate psychological injury as a result of your experience (a very heavy burden of proof), then you need to be engaged in this lawsuit because you want your job back.

Just because there is a statute that protects you does not necessarily mean that you can sue and win a lot of money. Your remedy is going to be fashioned by the statute that is in place to provide anti-discrimination protection, and it may be very limited. Some of the city and county statutes direct people to file a complaint with a commission that may then have very limited means to create a remedy for you. In other words, if the law that is in place lacks real teeth to fashion a strong remedy for you, you may find that you are trying to sue to gain one thing, when in fact, you will get something completely different.

Once you know the remedy that is available to you, you then have to factor that into the equation when you are putting together your own cost/benefit ratio. Before you go through with it, it may be a good idea to contact one of the national legal organizations or a local lesbian and gay support organization to see if they can put you in touch with someone who has already gone through this. It might be a good way for you to learn first hand just exactly what the benefits and costs will be.

And keep in mind, if you did have a really bad experience, it is something that you are going to have to relive in a number of ways throughout this process, and that alone may make it not worth it for you. You may want to move on. You may want to find a better job, and if you do find one, does it then make sense for you to sue? You may not get the vindication that you think you are going to get or deserve.

This isn't to say that you shouldn't sue if what you are doing is trying to make a point. People are able to accomplish a great deal with a lawsuit in which the final decision impacts the situation of many other similarly situated people. That is one of the factors to include in your cost/benefit analysis. If you are going to engage in a lawsuit, make sure that your eyes are open.

Factors to Consider. Once you have gotten legal help and you have determined that the remedy is one that you want, you next have to decide if suing is something you really want. To do this you may want to write down on a piece of paper just what the benefits and costs of pursuing your lawsuit are. In column A, write down what the case is going to cost you, personally, professionally and financially. In column B, write down all the things that you are going to get if you are successful. Don't embellish it with anything like "watching boss grovel". In column B, you would have to write "Get Job Back." If that isn't one of the things in column B, it may be a problem. If you have no desire to go back to the job, you may have no case.

As part of your assessment, you also have to weigh in on whether you have a good chance of prevailing. You are probably not going to simply file a suit and win within a few weeks.

You also have to factor in costs. Who's going to pay for this?

One other practical and tactical note of caution about suing. Suing may not be the first thing you should do. Before suing, you would be well served to contact your company's personnel department to ensure that it is in fact the company that is responsible – not just some wayward manager – to give them the opportunity to address the situation. If you bypass the company's human resources department, you may find a unsympathetic court that could even send you back to GO and tell you that you first need to start with the company. Once you've documented your evidence, then go through the internal grievance process first and trust the company to do the right thing. Otherwise, the company can raise your neglect to do this as a defense to your charge of discrimination.

This is particularly true if part of the discrimination that you are alleging has to do with harassment. You may find that you are being singled out by co-workers and fellow employees because you are gay – they may make crude sexual jokes, for example. With harassment it is critically important to go to the employer and you have to be smart about how you make the complaint. You want to leave your employer with the impression that this is a good loyal employee with a serious problem – who is being treated unfairly. The one thing you want to avoid is approaching the employer in any accusatory way. You may also find that your employer's policies have stated procedures for making harassment claims. If the harassment seems sexual enough, then it might be actionable under a state's laws on sexual harassment.

As you can see, the issues related to bringing a discrimination suit are complex and are very emotionally charged. What you get for your trouble may not be what you set out for.

Matt Coles raises an interesting point in connection with discrimination situations – and that is how they can make people feel bad about being lesbian, gay, bisexual, or transgendered. "I think the most important thing about suffering discrimination is to make sure that it doesn't screw up your life," he says. "By that I mean that it doesn't damage or destroy your self confidence, that you don't use it as a way to start eating away at yourself because you are lesbian or gay." To remedy that, he suggests that you reach outside of your lawyer for help, because your lawyer, while sensitive to your needs, may not be the best person to help you out with those kinds of issues. "I think you should get whatever kind of help is best for you and spend some time working through this. No matter how sane a person is, most people find a way to blame themselves for what has happened. The goal here is to be happy and to lead a fulfilling life . . . The first person to call is not a lawyer, but someone with whom you can begin to work through the problem to make sure that it doesn't screw up your life. For some people, pursuing the case is very healthy, but for others it can exacerbate the wounds and become an obsession."

Discrimination in Housing

While being booted out of your job can be humiliating, there are, of course, other kinds of discrimination that can make you feel unwanted in a most hurtful and disgraceful way. Being denied the most basic right of a place to live because of who you are can be humiliating. It is also not as uncommon as one might think – and your options may be fewer than with employment discrimination.

If you are living in an area that is covered by a statute prohibiting discrimination and you have suffered housing discrimination, you must look and see what the statute covers. Most likely, your statute or ordinance covers only employment, but some jurisdictions will cover housing as well.

Bear in mind that there are fewer protections where housing is concerned. In some respects, housing is a more difficult problem than employment. The tricky thing about housing discrimination is that it is much more covert than employment discrimination. In other words, it is in the closet.

The problem is less likely to involve eviction, but rather gaining access to the housing in the first place. You apply for a lease for an apartment and you never really know how you are the one to get it. This is particularly true where housing is scarce, such as in New York City, and the number of applicants per apartment is high. "It is quite common and quite easy to cover up," says Matt Coles. "In most places, it remains easy to say 'I had a lot of applicants and I gave it to someone else.' No one has looked at this in any rigorous way, but I'm convinced that it is a very serious problem. It happens more frequently without people understanding that it has happened to them, and so they don't do anything about it."

Where Housing Discrimination is Illegal. There are some enlightened places where you can live and be protected:

States Prohibiting Housing Discrimination

California	New Hampshire
Connecticut	New Jersey
District of Columbia	Rhode Island
Massachusetts	Vermont
Minnesota	Wisconsin

Hawaii, Maryland, and Nevada, while providing employment protections, do not care if you are discriminated against while trying to buy a house or rent an apartment. Like employment however, there are also municipalities that extend local protections.

If you do live in one of the states or localities where there are protections, you should know that there are exceptions to the rules, usually involving small housing facilities where there are few units for rent or where a landlord is renting out part of his own home.

Acting on Housing Discrimination. However, if you do live in a locality with protections, you should try to be aware of any action taken by a landlord, prospective landlord, or real estate agent who asks you about your sexual orientation. If you are renting a one bedroom apartment with a partner and the landlord asks how many beds you have, it is obvious that he is trying to determine your relationship. He may even come out and ask. If that knowledge is accompanied by an action, such as the apartment suddenly becoming unavailable, then you may have the elements necessary to file a complaint. For example, if the landlord or agent may suggest to you that there are a number of children in the building. If his statement comes after a question that was obviously fishing for information on your sexual orientation, he may be trying to discourage you from the apartment, in which case he may be in violation of state law or local ordinance.

As you approach a housing situation, if you suspect there is a possibility of discrimination going into the situation, you need to begin to build your case.

- Like the employment issue, keep a chronology of what happens, your conversations, and who was involved.
- Keep any telephone messages.
- Keep copies of all of the lease materials.
- Keep track of any and all questions or comments made.

Naturally, as in the employment situation, you will have to determine whether you have a case and if you do, whether you have a law to rely on. Since there is no federal protection, if you have no state or local law, your options may be more closed than they are in the employment arena, because you are without a contract or human resources policy to help you out. There is federal law that prohibits discrimination in housing, but guess what? It only applies if you are suing on the basis of race, national origin, religion, gender, disability, marital status, or age. It does not apply if you are gay, lesbian, bisexual, or transgendered.

Future Directions – Making a Federal Case out of It

In polls, a majority of Americans say they do not believe that gays and lesbians should be discriminated against in the workplace. (Sometimes this varies depending on the profession being considered. People don't mind their plumber being a lesbian, but they are not so keen if she shows up as their minister.) This sentiment is evidenced by the growing number of local ordinances that have been passed in some cities, counties, or states that protect the rights of lesbians and gays in the workplace. There has been a great deal of progress, and today, gays and lesbians are more protected than ever from discrimination at the job, in places of public accommodation, and in housing.

The ultimate effect of the patchwork of laws at various government levels that protect or fail to protect the rights of lesbians and gays is that not only are all men (and women) not created equal, but even among gays and lesbians, there is a lack of equity. Some gay and lesbian Americans have their rights protected, while the rights of others are completely ignored.

A federal statute has been proposed that would outlaw discrimination against gays and lesbians in the workplace and in housing. It would provide a federal standard, thereby providing protection for all gay and lesbian Americans, rather than offering protections only to some of them under state and local laws. The proposed legislation is known as the End Discrimination Act (ENDA) and it was first introduced in 1994. However, since its introduction, it has gone virtually nowhere.

There is a strong need for ENDA. "There are people outside of New York City, Dallas, Houston, Austin, Denver, Atlanta," notes Kevin Layton. "There is a great part of the country that may have city ordinances, but there are a lot of places that don't." And, he points out, there are limitations to the local ordinances.

He also adds that when it comes to civil rights, they have usually been granted from the top down – meaning that they are federally directed. Instead, with gay and lesbian rights, the impetus has been at the local level, so that rights are being protected from the bottom up. "In this country we have a federal civil rights machine; the way we protect workers is to have a federal approach," says Layton. "With ENDA, we're talking about a federal law that becomes the policy of the United States. There isn't a much stronger message you can send."

Will we ever see ENDA pass into law? A colleague of Kevin Layton's at the Human Rights Campaign, Winnie Stachelberg, thinks so, because it is legislation that people genuinely would like to see. "There is incredibly strong public support for protections and for the bill itself. Graphing polls from 1977 until now shows increasing support. We are at eighty-five percent support now, and it probably isn't going to get better than that. HRC has done focus groups, and they demonstrate that no matter how people feel about gay people, they do think we should be able to hold jobs – we should not be discriminated against in the workplace."

Should ENDA be passed, what would it mean for you? Well, if you live in a place where you have no protections, you will have a federal statute that will allow you to sue. But bear in mind, the remedy will be no greater than exists now for all intents and purposes. "It is a conventional employment discrimination remedy," says Matt Coles. "You can try to get your job back, you can try to get the money that you lost while you were unemployed, and you can try to get some money for pain and suffering." While there are sometimes punitive damages, "people should never calculate it," says Coles. "They are designed to punish an excessive wrongdoer. Everyone thinks that anyone who's discriminated against them is excessive, but the law doesn't see it that way." While you may hear about people who get millions of dollars in suits that don't sound like they were very bad cases of discrimination, the truth is that doesn't really happen, according to Coles.

Would ENDA really be the enda it? Well, the Constitution and the Bill of Rights have not ended discrimination. The civil rights laws of 1964 have not ended prejudice and bigotry towards African Americans. A bill will not end discrimination. Despite its name, it doesn't really seek to end discrimination entirely.

Like other anti-discrimination statutes, there are limits to what ENDA seeks to achieve, and there are exceptions to the rule. "ENDA has a small business exemption," explains Layton, "as well as a religious exemption. All religious organizations would be exempt. It doesn't apply to the military or to domestic partner benefits, and it does not require employers to keep statistics on how many gay and lesbian employees they have. It is actually a very conservative civil rights law." All of those exemptions are there to increase its chances of passage. But will it be enough – will ENDA pass?

Says HRC's Winnie Stachelberg, "I think there are lenses by which you measure progress and in the civil rights arena, that lens is a very long lens. After all, the 1964 Civil Rights Act took a long time to pass, as did the Americans With Disabilities Act. For ENDA and whatever follows to pass will take a long time, and that is no different at the federal level than it has been at the city and state level." The nature of anti-discrimination law requires that people have time to get used to the idea. But there have been other victories, and there is no reason to believe, absent a lack of impetus from the lesbian and gay community, that ENDA will be any different.

Whether it is ENDA or another federal method to assure the equal rights of lesbians and gays in American society, there does seem to be some assurance that momentum and history are on the side of our community. "I think that the central battle we are having now is over relationships and family," says Matt Coles. "It is over whether we get to protect the people we love and get the same respect for our families. I think we will win it, we are winning it. I don't mean to say that fifty years from now there won't be people who believe in their heart of hearts that we deserve different treatment. Getting the barriers down won't automatically achieve equality. There will still be deep strains of homophobia, but society will be reaching a consensus on the question about whether you should be disadvantaged because of how you lead your life. That will happen."

CHAPTER 6

A Kinder Gender Nation – Transgenders and the law

History and Perspective – Freedom of Expression

AMERICAN SOCIETY IS founded on a cornerstone principle that you have the freedom to express yourself. The range of that expression is pretty far and wide-reaching. You can choose your religion, you can choose who to marry (unless you are wanting to marry someone of your own sex), you can choose where to live and what you want to do for a living. You can decide to have children and how many you want. You can decide not to have children at all. This is called freedom.

You can choose your appearance. You can dye your hair turquoise or orange. If you choose to wear red socks with a blue suit, some may find it a matter of questionable taste, but you wouldn't be barred from entering a club for the evening, or shown the door at your place of employment. People might just think you are expressing yourself or want to draw attention to the fact that you are different.

If you are a straight couple who decides that taking some fertility drugs in order to have a litter of children is your way of expressing yourself, not only are you not discriminated against, you are usually celebrated in the media. You even get to hold your hands out for recognition of your accomplishment and expect many gifts as a result. No one refuses to acknowledge your choice by refusing you birth certificates for the litter, passports, or attempts to annul your marriage.

However, if you choose to express yourself by wearing clothing that is traditionally believed to be of the gender opposite of your own, you may be creating a problem – not just for those around you, but for yourself as well. And if your expression goes so far as to literally cross over the line, and have yourself surgically altered as an expression of your identity, well, you may encounter definite problems, legal and social. And there will be people ready, willing, and able to deny you your right to marry, your right to a birth certificate, your right to a passport, your job, and even the simple act of using a public toilet to relieve yourself.

Ever since there were two genders who dressed differently, it is likely that they cross-dressed.

Nevertheless, despite all that experience, there still exists a tremendous amount of misunderstanding on the part of society at large and the transgendered community. First and foremost is the misconception that a person who is expressing their gender identity in a way that is different from their biological sex is a gay or lesbian person, which is most certainly not the case. In fact, that is the whole point of changing one's gender. Secondly, there is a widespread assumption that to be transgendered automatically means that you are headed to surgery. Lastly, as with gay and lesbian individuals, many consider the issue to be a matter of choice, rather than a self-acknowledgement of who you are.

What all of these sociological challenges mean is that a transgendered person is necessarily going to also face legal challenges. Your birth certificate, for example, identifies you as something you are no longer, as does your driver's license and all of your official documentation. If you subsequently marry someone of the opposite sex, some may challenge the basis of the marriage because, while you have become a person of the opposite sex in appearance, you have not done so genetically. And just the fact that you have done this may cause employers, among others, to treat you in a manner that is discriminatory. This chapter will look at how you handle those situations.

For purposes of clarity, the term sex will be used to describe a person's physical characteristics while gender will be used to refer to a person's identity. Pronouns are assigned to people according to their expressed preference, not their biology. The term transgender means any type of gender modification – meaning transsexual, transvestite, cross dressing, or other activity or affect that is intended to declare some independence from an assigned role dictated by your genitals and/or chromosomes.

Paving the Way

Historically, while surgical alteration of sex organs has occurred for centuries to create a "third gender," also known as eunuchs, it was not until the twentieth century that the surgery was devised for the purpose of altering the exterior gender identity of an individual from female to male, or male to female.

"To me, it was a matter of survival," said Christine Jorgensen of her widely publicized sex change surgery. She was not the first male to female (MTF) transsexual, but she was the first one known to Americans, though most of them only knew her through the media. The year was 1952.

As a man, she had served in the U.S. Army. Born George Jorgensen, she grew up sensing her profound difference. She was attracted to other men, but did not feel that she was herself a man, and therefore not a homosexual. She educated herself on the state of medicine in the 1950s and on pioneering research being performed on gender identity. She relocated to Copenhagen and underwent a series of surgeries and hormonal treatments. When she returned as a woman to the United States and a barrage of publicity, the *New York Daily News* ran the headline "Ex-GI Becomes Blonde Beauty – Operations Transform Bronx Youth" along with side by side before and after pictures.

After her operations, George, now Christine, contacted her parents to inform them of the change. In reply she received a cable that said "[W]e love you more than ever." Christine also had to notify someone else – the American ambassador to Denmark. She needed to let her know that she would need a new passport – one that changed her name and changed her sexual identity. The ambassador said that was fine and issued it without any difficulty. If it had remained that easy for transgendered people, there would be no need for this chapter.

Despite the ease of her passport experience, in fact, when she returned to the United States to the accompaniment of widespread publicity, she found herself a matter of considerable controversy. As she undertook a career in entertainment, she found that some night clubs that booked her would later cancel out of fear of offending the public. And she was unceremoniously banned from entertaining U.S. troops. Apparently, they could face the enemy with honor and bravery, but a transgendered person in a night club act just might make them fold like a house of cards.

There is a fundamental basis for discrimination against transgenders – that is the fact that even with surgery, many regard a woman who has surgery to become a male (FTM) as a woman nonetheless, and a MTF as a man. Surgery doesn't change the chromosomes given to you by God. That is a sentiment that is even expressed in some laws, as you will see.

The International Bill of Gender Rights

In the wake of Christine Jorgensen there have been thousands of others. Some found their way into the media spotlight, either by way of celebrity or tragedy. But as with all the rights reviewed in this book, there has been progress for men and women who are transgendered. While there is growing medical understanding that gender identity is less black and white than one might suppose, and that a spectrum of gender identity is perhaps more appropriate than a classification of two, the law has some serious catching up to do. Still, there is hope and even an ideal put forth in the form of an outline of standards called the International Bill for Gender Rights (IBGR).

Compared to other groups – racial minorities, women, and even gays and lesbians, the evolution of recognized rights for the transgender community is far behind. The legal environment is quite undeveloped. However, in the early 1990s the International Conference on Transgender Law and Employment Policy began to formulate standards to enunciate what the transgender community regards as basic civil rights. Naturally, these do not have the force of law – they aren't part of the Constitution of the United States. But it is a declaration – which any transgender person can hold onto as a life raft outlining basic tenets of respect and decency in what may be a sea of intolerance, ignorance and difficulty.

The principles of the IGBR are as follows. You have

- The right to define gender identity
- The right to free expression of gender identity
- The right to secure and retain employment and to receive just compensation
- The right of access to gendered space and participation in gendered activity
- The right to control and change one's own body
- The right to competent medical and professional care
- The right to freedom from psychiatric diagnosis or treatment
- The right to sexual expression
- The right to form committed, loving relationships and enter into marital contracts
- The right to conceive, bear, or adopt children; the right to nurture and have custody of children and to exercise parental capacity

Unfortunately, there is a very long way to go before these rights are accepted into legal doctrine on a widespread basis. Some states, rather than progress, have actually devolved when it comes to addressing the legal status of transgendered persons. Similarly, at the federal level, there have been efforts to exclude transgendered persons from any laws that offer limited protection.

Current Events – Miles to Go

Discrimination and Transgenders

There is a great deal of discrimination that a transgendered person might face – in public accommodation, housing and employment – that is similar to the discrimination experienced by lesbians, gays, and bisexuals (see chapter 5). However, for transgenders, discrimination can have a further reach into one's life. For example, they may face having to deal with a dress code at their place of employment or even have to deal with issues around the use of a public toilet.

The discrimination faced by the transgender community sometimes comes from surprising sources, for example that which comes from the lesbian, gay, and bisexual community itself. For reasons too complex to go into here, the transgender community has often been left behind when advances were being made for the lesbian, gay, and bisexual community. Thankfully, that changed a great deal during the 1990s.

When faced by discrimination in employment, public accommodation or housing, there are limited avenues open to transgendered individuals. Not only are there few laws, but the extent of the resources available, with the exception of some notable activists and pioneers, has also been somewhat more limited when compared to other minority groups.

Federal Law. The most obvious thing to say about transexuals and federal law is that, for the most part, you have been excluded from it. In 1990 Congress passed the Americans with Disabilities Act to protect people with disabilities from discrimination. However, in passing the Act, conservative senators went out of their way to exclude transgendered persons from benefiting from the law. They specifically stated in the text of the law that a disability shall not be considered to include homosexuality, bisexuality, pedophelia, transvestism, transexualism, pyromania, or beastiality. Other federal laws that offer other approaches to fighting discrimination also fail to include transgenders as a protected group.

There is a possibility that federal law might protect a transgender person if a court is willing to interpret federal laws that prohibit discrimination based on sex to apply to your case. Recently, a federal court heard a case where a man who dressed and presented as a woman, but was physically male, sued because she was refused a loan unless she presented in male clothing. These allegations, the court said, would support a claim of sex discrimination.

One area where transexuals – those who have undertaken medical intervention to change their gender identity – have absolutely no protection at all is in the military. The military absolutely forbids transexuals to serve in the armed forces. Don't look for this to change any time soon.

There is hope for the future and federal law, limited though it may be. There has been, for many years, a proposed law before Congress called the End Discrimination Act (ENDA) that would end discrimination against lesbians, gays, and bisexuals. It is a questionable whether transgenders will be included in this law as, in other federal laws, transgenders have either been left out or specifically excluded. The inclusion of transgenders would have a huge impact on the ability to protect the rights that currently cannot be asserted in many cities and states around the country. See chapter 5 for further discussion of ENDA.

Until such time, however, for the most part, you are without federal law to protect you. Whether you are protected, therefore, as you may have guessed, is dependent on the state in which you live. Some states have decided cases where transgendered people sought protection under disability laws and concluded that the laws do protect them.

Disability Protections. While you may feel fine, it is nevertheless possible for you to use laws that protect people with disabilities. A disability doesn't just mean you have a bad back that keeps you from working; it has a broader definition than that. It is usually defined as a mental or physical condition that has a limiting effect on a major life activity.

So, are you still asking yourself what that has to do with you? After all, you can perform all of the daily functions of your life. Psychologists have a manual called the *Diagnostic and Statistical Manual of Mental Disorders* (DSM). It defines conditions that are usually treated by psychologists, such as generalized anxiety disorder for example. One of the diagnoses is "gender identity disorder." The existence of this diagnosis may be one factor in demonstrating that you have a disability under anti-discrimination laws, so that you can use the protection of these laws in your case. There are other factors as well – if you are undergoing medical treatment, such as hormone therapy or surgery, the existence of such a regimen may in and of itself constitute your disability, qualifying you for protections.

Use of disability laws to seek protection is a two-edged sword. In the first place, it is out of step with the IGBR. On one hand, you are saying that you want to be treated equally, but on the other hand, you are saying that the assertion of your gender is a disability. It doesn't quite add up philosophically, and you may not be comfortable with it. Eventually, there may be changes that will protect you because of your transgender status that do not address your identity as a "condition." However, despite the fact that you may not like the idea of equating your identity with a disability or disorder, if you are discriminated against in a state that has anti-discrimination protections for people with disabilities, use of these laws may be the only way to help you.

Anti-Discrimination Statutes. Obviously, the most expeditious course open to a transgender person facing discrimination is to seek redress under a statute that includes transgenders in its antidiscriminatory statute or ordinance. In spite of the fact that the progress of transgendered rights is not as advanced as it is for many other minority groups, there are still some protections in place in various jurisdictions around the United States. According to the Transgender Law & Policy Institute, they are forty-six in number – two states, six counties and thirty-eight cities. The list is as interesting for those cities that are present as it is for those that are not and it you should note that there are an increasing number of cities that are offering protections.

Jurisdictions Protecting in Discrimination Against Transgenders

STATES	
Minnesota	
Rhode Island	
COUNTIES	
California	Santa Cruz County
Kentucky	Jefferson County
New York	Suffolk County
Oregon	Benton County Multnomah County
Pennsylvania	Erie County
CITIES	
Arizona	Tucson
California	Los Angeles San Francisco Santa Cruz West Hollywood
Colorado	Boulder Denver
Georgia	Atlanta
Illinois	Champaign Chicago DeKalb Evanston Urbana
Iowa	Iowa City, IA
Kentucky	Lexington-Lafayette Louisville
Louisiana	New Orleans
Maryland	Baltimore
Massachusetts	Boston Cambridge
Michigan	Ann Arbor Grand Rapids Huntington Woods Ypsilanti
Minnesota	Minneapolis St. Paul
New York	New York City Rochester
Ohio	Toledo
Oregon	Portland Salem
Pennsylvania	Allentown Harrisburg Philadelphia Pittsburgh York
Texas	Dallas
Washington	Olympia Seattle Tacoma
Wisconsin	Madison

In addition, the Institute reports that the following U.S. jurisdictions prohibit discrimination in public employment.

Jurisdictions Protecting Transgenders in Public Employment

Atlanta, Georgia	Multnomah County, Oregon
Dane County, Wisconsin	Pine Lake, Georgia
Decatur, Georgia	Portland, Oregon
Houston, Texas	

As was stated earlier in this chapter, a transgendered person may not identify themselves as gay or lesbian. Nevertheless, if a state offers antidiscrimination protections to gay and lesbian citizens, then a transgendered person may nevertheless be able to avail themselves of that law to seek relief from a discriminatory circumstance.

In fact, theoretically, a straight person could even gain protection from gay and lesbian legal protections. That is because the laws often extend not only to people who are gay and lesbian, but to people who are perceived to be gay or lesbian.

If you feel you have suffered discrimination and you have some form of statute that offers you protection, there is still one hurdle to cross. You are going to have to prove that the discrimination occurred, and you are going to have to be willing to undertake the rigors of litigation. Lastly, you are going to have to want the remedy offered you by the law, and that may vary greatly depending on the statute. For more about proving a discrimination case, see chapter 5.

Documenting Your Gender

At the beginning of this chapter, the experience of Christine Jorgensen in Denmark – contacting the American ambassador and ordering up a new passport reflective of her change in gender – was quick and easy, and in some respects, nothing short of remarkable. It was the 1950s after all.

You may identify your existence by what you feel on the inside – in your heart, in your soul. However, the law considers you only to exist by what it sees on the outside – and then only to the extent that there are documents that say you exist and also say what you are. Right from the beginning, your first piece of official paper is your birth certificate. School records then begin to accumulate, as do your medical records. You may have insurance bought for you at an early age by your parents. The document that truly marks your passage from a teenager to an adult – your driver's license – is possibly the most important piece of documentation you own. You are made socially secure with a little card issued by the federal government with a ten- digit number on it (if only it were that easy). If you travel or don't have a driver's license, your passport is vital.

There are military records and other various identification cards issued you by professional societies. In short, there is endless paper documenting the fact that you exist, saying where you live, what you look like,, what your gender is. Life is an extensive paper trail. Without it, you are more or less non-existent. Needless to say, if you change in some pertinent fashion – e.g., you gender assignment – the documents need to change with you. That sounds easy. It should be, but it may not always be.

Name Changes. Let's begin with your name. You need to begin here, because you will need documentation of your name change in order to effect changes to other important documents. Maybe you are one of the lucky ones named Lee. In that case your name works for either gender and you can skip to the next section. More likely however, you may be Robert and become Roberta or Roberta and become Robert – in either case you will need to file a petition with the county court where you live. Which court you have to go to may be a matter of the state in which you live.

A name change is quite common, and people are free to do it. Many people do it when they become married. However, anyone should be able to change his or her name. You should be able to choose any name you want, as long as there is not a fraudulent intent (for example, if you are changing your name in order to evade legal authorities who want to arrest you for a bank job you pulled last year – or more likely, to avoid creditors). Some states may have a residency requirement, which means you will have to wait a certain period of months before you can file for a name change. You may have to show that you have not been convicted of a crime. If you have, there may be an extended period of time after serving a sentence that you will have to wait. The intent to change the name may have to be published in a local newspaper. A name change should be easy and, in fact, forms and information are easily available and can be found on the Web.

After you have filed your petition and everything checks out, the court will issue an order effecting the name change. Once that happens, order yourself up several certified copies of the court order. You are going to need them to bring about other changes you need to accomplish.

Social Security Cards. This is the most basic document you need to change. You will need it to change other documents, so you may want to do this one early on. While your driver's license is issued by your state, your social security card is a federal document. You can obtain the form you need either by calling Social Security or by going on the Web. The form is to apply for a corrected card. You will have to correct two things – your name and your gender.

Driver's Licenses. To the extent that it is easy to deal with any Department of Motor Vehicles anywhere, changing your name on your driver's license should be easy as well. You will have to pay a fee, but the amount and the procedure will vary from state to state as to how you effect the change and the documents that will be necessary. Certainly, one of the things you will need is the court order that effected the change of your name. You will also need other documentation, such as a birth certificate. It will be alright if these are in your old name, as long as you have the court order that changes your name. You may find, however, that in changing your gender with your license, you first need to supply a birth certificate. However, if you are a transsexual who has transitioned, your appearance at the DMV may be enough to correct the "mistake" that is on your license.

Passports. It wasn't a problem for Christine, and you should not have a problem either, though you will need a copy of your amended birth certificate. Like your Social Security card, your passport is issued to you by the federal government – specifically the State Department. In addition to your amended birth certificate, you will need a copy of the court decree that changed your name. You can get the forms from your local passport office or on the Web.

Birth Certificates. Your social security card is issued to you by the federal government; your driver's license is issued where you live; and you can change your name in the county where you live. But to change your birth certificate to reflect your new name and gender will require a procedure in the jurisdiction in which you were born. That could be a problem.

Of all the document changes you face, changing your birth certificate may be the most challenging. While some states have specific language in their laws that permit changes in birth certificates after a transition of genders, some states pointedly do not. And you may have to go to extremes to prove that you have made a full transition to another gender. And to the extent you need a corrected birth certificate with any of your documentation changes, you will have a particular problem if you live in one of three states that do not allow sex changes to amend birth certificates. They are Idaho, Ohio and Tennessee. Until recently, Florida was also on this list, but in the autumn of 2002, it changed its policy. Otherwise, if you were born in one of these states, they will not amend your certificate. If you now live in a state where you are applying to change documents and a birth certificate is needed, then you may try submitting an affidavit stating the circumstance, but offering documentation of your transition in other ways.

With the exception of birth certificates, for the most part, effecting these changes should be easy. But that doesn't always mean that it will work out without a snag, and it is conceivable you could meet up with a judge or an official who decides on arbitrary grounds to deny you the name change you seek. It is not a bad idea to maintain a record of your change. Begin a portfolio listing all of the documents you need to change. Make a note of appointments, keep all correspondence and documents, and note anything that happens that is out of the ordinary. This will not only keep you organized; in case you need to pull together evidence of what has transpired, it will help you in establishing proof you may need. If you do find that you are being discriminated against, you need to contact an attorney or a national legal organization for assistance.

States with Statutes Authorizing Gender Change

Alabama	Illinois	North Carolina
Arkansas	Kentucky	Oregon
Arizona	Maryland	Rhode Island
California	Massachusetts	Utah
Colorado	Michigan	Virginia
Connecticut	Missouri	Wisconsin
Delaware	Nebraska	
Georgia	New Jersey	

States Refusing Gender Change on Birth Certificates

Idaho
Ohio
Tennessee

Any other state policies have permitted change, even where there is not specific statute guiding the matter.

Family Matters

It may surprise you to know that not very long ago, in many jurisdictions across the United States, it was illegal for a person to wear clothing that was intended for the opposite sex. While mostly repealed, it is not impossible to imagine that some of these laws are still on the books, having never been eliminated though never enforced – legal relics collecting legal dust.

But there are other legal relics that *are* enforced, having to do with your right to marry and your right to be a parent. If you are making a change in your legal status by name or gender, you may face some of these relics. In fact, some courts have recently issued decisions respecting your right to be married that are relics in the making, so backward are they in their reasoning.

It is perhaps a bit paradoxical, but the rights of transgenders to marry are more established than the rights of lesbians and gays, though there are some judges who consider transgender marriages and gay/lesbian marriages as equivalent.

Marriage before Transition. If you have made a transition as MTF or FTM and you were legally married at the time of the transition, there would seem to be no reason for anyone to consider you not married. The marriage you entered into with your spouse would remain in full force and effect. The fact that you have changed your gender may give your spouse grounds for divorce, but the marriage would not be invalidated automatically by the law of any state in the union. However, that doesn't mean that it couldn't be done, particularly if there were a challenge by a relative after the death of your spouse.

Many states have enacted legislation that defines marriage as an institution between man and woman (see the discussion of DOMA and related laws in chapter 1). If one of the parties to the marriage changes gender, then it is arguable that the marriage ended as of that date. While no jurisdiction may move on its own to invalidate such a marriage, it is possible that a relative of your legal spouse might challenge your right to inherit from your spouse after your transition, citing such laws. It is a complicated set of circumstances, because such invalidation would also have a material affect on the status of children who had been born to that marriage.

If all of this sounds far-fetched, read on – there are other decisions by judges that also sound equally absurd, but have nevertheless become law.

Marriage after Transition. If you can *stay* married after transition, it would make sense that you could *get* married after your transition as well, wouldn't it? If you are MTF who has undergone therapy, by all accounts and appearances and doctor's affidavits, you are the gender you say you are. You may have gone through everything, changed all of your documents, including your birth certificate, and find that everyone in the world is willing to now call you a female. Everyone except a judge, that is.

Many people after transition do get married to a person of the opposite gender, and there is little reason to think there is much that would stop a person who has undergone transition and changed documents from entering into a marriage. However, like the situation described above regarding the right to inherit, when challenged by a third party, some marriages have been declared non-existent.

How could such a thing happen? There are two recent examples, both of which imply that when it comes to marriage after a transition, there are no guarantees that your marriage will be respected by the law. As with so many of the issues you face, it is going to largely depend on where you live.

One case involved a post-surgical MTF who, many years after her surgery, entered into a heterosexual marriage by marrying a man in a ceremony with a marriage license issued by the state of Kentucky. Seven years later, her husband died, and she brought suit against a physician who treated him, claiming medical malpractice. The attorneys for the physician countered that there was no standing to sue.[10] In the case of malpractice, a legal spouse would have such standing, but the lawyers for the physician claimed that, because she was a transsexual, she was a man and a marriage between two men would have no validity. When a judge looked at the situation, he agreed with the physician's attorney. The basis for his decision was rooted in chromosomes. Despite the surgery, treatments, appearances, document changes, and physician attestations to the contrary, the judge ruled her a man and invalidated the marriage, depriving her of her right to sue the physician for the loss of her husband. Despite the validly issued marriage license, the court said she had never been married because they were two men, and people of the same sex cannot be married.

It would be nice to believe that this was a singular case of isolated jurisprudence, but it also happened in Kansas, where a court ruled that a post-operative transsexual could not marry. In that case, a MTF married a man who later died, leaving his MTF transgendered wife to inherit his estate. A case was brought by the son of the deceased husband, who did not like the fact that his transgender step-mother was about to inherit from his father's estate. He asserted that the marriage could not be legal, and therefore she could not inherit, because she was the same sex as the father when she was born. The court agreed.

There may be silver linings. While the trial court ruled for the son, the appeals court stated that a court must look beyond sex at birth to determine a person's legal gender. Unfortunately, when it was appealed to the Kansas Supreme Court, the ruling came down on the side of the son. However, the reasoning of the appeals court was enlightened and may represent the true evolution of legal thought on the matter of transgender marital validity.

Parenting. Speaking of children, there can be complications for transexuals when considering their rights as parents.

10. Standing to sue is a legal expression meaning that a party who is bringing suit (the plaintiff) has a right to sue because he or she is directly involved in the matter at hand. For example, if you see a car crash, you can't sue the driver who caused it, because you are not involved in the matter – only the person he hit would have standing to sue.

In either of the examples noted above, in which the marriage of post-operative transexuals was rendered invalid by a court of law, there would have been a question of what that would mean to the children involved in such a marriage. The couple could have adopted or the children of one birth parent by a former marriage could have been adopted by the transsexual parent. (For more on adoption, see chapter 2.) A marriage that is declared invalid by a court would not be like divorce; it would be like annulment – it would be deemed to have never existed in the first place. That would leave any children without a legal relationship to the transsexual, unless they were biological children born or conceived before a transition.

But perhaps more importantly, there are considerations for a transsexual when facing a custody or visitation battle. The standard for deciding custody among courts is supposed to be the best interests of the child (see chapter 3 for more information on custody standards). That means that a judge must examine all of the circumstances and evidence to look at each case for itself and decide what the bests interests of the child dictate. However, it would not be at all far-fetched to consider that an uneducated judge could enter a decision on custody not by looking at the evidence. Rather he or she could infer, based on his or her belief that the existence of a transsexual parent could never, by definition, be in the best interests of any child. There has even been a case where parental rights of a transsexual were terminated entirely. If you are faced with such a circumstance, it is extremely important that you contact one of the national organizations for assistance and gain a referral to an attorney who is experienced not only with the legal aspects of such cases, but with the ability to educate judges and courts on matters related to transgenders.

Dressing and Undressing – Dress Codes and Public Facilities

Even where there is a somewhat less hostile legal environment for transexuals, the issue of bathroom use is vexing. In fact, it may be easier for you to change your documentation than it is to use a restroom.

At places of employment, while dress codes can often be negotiated, the issue of bathroom use is often a point on which even the most progressive can falter. In places such as a gym or club, it can even result in physical harm. And in the end, there is actually very little law to support you, though there are things that might be done. Still, it is hard to believe that we are talking about something as simple as going to the bathroom.

If you are about to begin the process of transition, it is a subject you may need to address with your employer. Some employers are eager to find ways to retain good employees and will go to lengths to accommodate you. There are a number of compromises that can be struck in the workplace, depending on the circumstances. Your employer may support your transition but seek to effect a workplace transition as well, so as not to bring about a great deal of disruption to the workplace. That may mean that he is willing to undertake education efforts with staff and to set up bathroom rules, schedules, or facilities. It may also mean that they look to you to be consistent in your new role.

Other employers may not be as evolved in their thinking. They may see this as a way to get rid of a troublesome and uncomfortable situation and may focus on the bathroom issue as a way to do it. If your employer demands that you use a bathroom that causes you serious discomfort, your options may be limited. If you are not living in an area that offers legal protections that prohibit discrimination against transgendered persons, then you may have to explore whether disability laws or gay and lesbian protections are open to you and your situation. If they are not, or if you do not wish to consider using disability law because it conflicts with your outlook on transgender rights, then you may be without a remedy. Still, without law, as with any discrimination case, it is worth working with an attorney to explore all possibilities.

Whatever your employer's outlook, you will also have to face the opinions of co-workers. Even if your employer wants to be supportive, there may be some at work who feel that your use of the "their" restroom infringes upon their rights. In some of those cases, they have brought suits and won. In fact, in Minnesota, there was a case where a co-worker won in such a situation, while during the same here in the same state, another lawsuit was won by a transexual. Whose right is it to say who gets to use the restroom? Unfortunately, legally, there is no clear way to tell at this point. It would seem logical that you would be supported by the law and that this is discriminatory pure and simple. Sadly, it is not pure and it is not simple.

If you are faced with an untenable situation, it is extremely important that, before you quit your job or submit to demands that make you feel uncomfortable, you seek help. There are attorneys who specialize in transgender issues and who themselves are transgendered. Don't give up until you seek advice. There is no reason for you to be uncomfortable – until there is a reason. That isn't meant to be a riddle, but you should not feel defeated until you have sought help from an experienced attorney or from one of the national organizations. One of the advantages of being involved in such an underdeveloped area of law is that there is a better chance that the situation you face may in fact turn into impact litigation. That would mean that a national legal organization serving the lesbian, gay, bisexual, and transgendered community might be able to take the case and make a difference in winning it that will affect many more people in the future. The disadvantage in being in such an underdeveloped area of law is that you may consult with experienced attorneys and find that there is nothing you can do. That is what is meant by not being uncomfortable until there is a reason.

Future Directions – Refuse to Be Left Behind

There is growing support and understanding for people who are transgender. However, it is reasonable to expect that, like advances made in gay, lesbian, and bisexual rights and protections, that advancements will necessarily mean some defeats.

Nevertheless, as a broader understanding of the spectrum of human sexuality emerges, there will also be a greater understanding of the spectrum of gender.

There are only three states that forbid you to change your birth certificate. In time, there will be none.

But perhaps the greatest thing that could happen for the transgendered community is inclusion in the End Discrimination Act (ENDA) and the passage of that bill into law. In the first place, it would offer transgender people all over the United States protection, rather than the lackluster piecemeal protections they have now. Secondly, it would begin to make up for some of the phobia expressed by lesbians, gays, and bisexuals toward transgenders. Lastly, it would make a powerful statement that inclusion, rather than exclusion, is the way that it must be from now on.

CHAPTER 7

Serving Your Nation

History and Perspective – Denied, but Present

THERE HAVE BEEN GAYS AND LESBIANS who have served in the military since the dawn of time. King Solomon sang his songs and was a great warrior. Alexander the Great conquered the world. Queen Christina of Sweden disguised herself as a man to lead an army and nation. Richard the Lionhearted led the Crusades. Edward II led England. Frederick the Great of Prussia was a great military figure and a great composer. There are countless others who are either well known to the pages of history or lost in the obscurity of the ages. But clearly, we have fought in many great battles – leading armies, in some cases, even leading nations. We not only look snappy in a uniform, but we know how to play the game with the best of them.

Yet despite a track record throughout history that bears scrutiny and even demonstrates prowess and cunning in the military field, gays and lesbians and the military have an uneasy relationship. That has been particularly true with the American military, even before there was an America. Nevertheless, in spite of the ban, throughout our relatively brief American history, books have been filled with stories of the bravery and courage of gay men and lesbian women. They were called upon to exhibit the greatest courage and not only had to battle the enemy at the front, but battle the enemy at home as well. There are, of course, the ones we know – the ones who came out of the closet after their experience and talked about their service to their country. Then there were those who never got the chance to come out of the closet because they took a bullet, stepped on a land mine, or were blown to bits by a bomb. They made the ultimate sacrifice for a country that wanted no part of them and that would even go out of its way to persecute, humiliate, and desecrate their fine service.

Early American – Colonial Gays

Even though officially banned in the military, stories of gays and lesbians in the ranks are often tales of two cities. One is a place where gays and lesbians serve with distinction and honor and the other is a place where they are, at great expense, hunted down and dragged out of the closet and the military simultaneously. In his seminal work on gays and lesbians in the military, Randy Shilts describes these two cities through the experience of two men living in colonial America.

Then, there were thirteen small, sparsely populated settlements decided to stage a rebellion even though they were entirely lacking the necessary ingredients of a standing army. In spite of that, the leaders of the colonies were determined that they could toss off the most powerful nation on earth. The men who came to fight were farmers for the most part, existing as a mere collection of undisciplined militias, without training. The army they faced was one of the most trained and disciplined in the world. Given those circumstances, it is no surprise to learn that in the beginning, things weren't going so well for young America. The colonial armies met with defeat after defeat and, in fact, General George Washington had more defeats than victories to his credit. At one point, when the British outnumbered and outflanked him in Brooklyn, New York, the general and his troops had to sneak out during the night and take boats to Manhattan to escape certain capture and defeat. It became apparent that the success of the revolution and even the lives of the very people who led it – Washington, Adams, Jefferson, Franklin – all depended on a better trained Continental Army, without which there would be no United States.

That need coincided with the emerging needs of a young military genius from the court of Frederick the Great – king, conqueror, military genius, and composer – in Prussia. Unspecified difficulties emerged in the all male court of Frederick II for one Baron Frederick von Steuben, who decided that it would be wisest to beat a hasty retreat from that continent to the new world of colonial America at the same time that General Washington was looking for a way to make the militia into an army. Baron von Steuben applied for the job. Washington watched him drill a few troops for a few days and, upon discovering that the baron was unparalleled in his talents, hired him. His success was dramatic and his work is credited with developing the militias into a fighting force that would eventually defeat the British. He may have been the first well-known gay man to serve in the American military with distinction. For him, the term "serving" in the military is almost the wrong word. There was no military until he came along. He transformed it, he instructed it, he mobilized it, he gave it discipline, he gave it order.

You can meet his likeness today if you should pass by the small square in front of the White House in Washington, D.C. There his statue sits, appropriately enough, surrounded by a few other statutes depicting well-built naked male warriors. Ironically, one of them illustrates military instruction by depicting an older soldier showing a sword to a younger soldier, both nude.

But there is also the story of another soldier who served in the Colonial army and who would acquire distinction as well. For him, however, there is no statue in front of the White House or anyplace else, for that matter. Still, presumably he fought for his budding country, though his service apparently did not win him the honors and distinction of the baron. He was not royal, but he did share one trait with the baron – he was apparently gay, and it is for that which he is remembered. His name was Lieutenant Fredrick Gotthold Enslin. He would become the first person to suffer court martial and banishment in the United States Army. Needless to say, he would not be the last. But the disparate stories of Baron von Steuben and Lieutenant Frederick Gotthold Enslin, you could say, are at the very root of the armed forces current policy respecting homosexuals – "don't ask, don't tell." Apparently, von Stueben was asked no questions and told nothing, while Enslin had a little slip of the tongue, either literally or figuratively. Perhaps the baron's prestige shielded him from inquiry. The lieutenant however, had no such shield. He did not have an important position. In any case, it would appear that don't ask, don't tell was the policy of the Colonial military, and today, 225 years later, nothing much seems to have changed.

Minority Report – The Roles of Non-Whites and Women

The men who primarily served during the Revolutionary War were, like the Congress and the people who would eventually be granted the right to vote, white and they were men. Women, African-Americans, or anyone else who did not fall into the category of heterosexual white man, the power structure had little time for. And so it is no surprise that the U.S. military, the very heart of that power structure, has always had an uneasy time with the integration of people into it who were not straight, white males. The fact that the society it protects is not made up only of straight white males does not seem to figure into the logic of the situation very strongly. Still, as military needs grew and as society progressed, the old paradigm would break down, so that non-whites and women could be included in the military ranks.

During the Civil War, troops of blacks were raised to fight on the side of the north. However, they were not allowed to fight side by side with whites, but rather fought separately from their fellow soldiers who were white. It was a segregated war for the freedom of a race, if that isn't an oxymoron.

That was in the 1860s. It would take almost eighty-five years for the military to change that policy. President Harry S. Truman issued an executive order in July 1948 to desegregate the troops. That was only after African-Americans had fought separately from whites in the Civil War, the Spanish American War, World War I, and of course, World War II. White soldiers strenuously objected. They did not want to shower with African Americans, they did not want to share barracks with them, and they did not want to be integrated. In fact, some branches did not permit the participation of African Americans at all. It was argued that morale would suffer. It was argued that the integrity of the military was at stake. In fact, all of the arguments used today to maintain the ban against gays serving in the military were used then to prohibit people of different races and different genders from serving.

There was also a time when women, serving in segregated units, were secretaries and drivers for the servicemen of the United States. Women were not allowed in combat roles in the armed services. That was a tradition that lasted a long time – well into the second half of the twentieth century. The wall came tumbling down, however, in July 1978, when Judge John J. Sirica issued a federal ruling that stated that it was unlawful for the Navy to prohibit women from serving at sea. This change in policy was eventually adopted by the Marine Corps and then finally the U.S. Army, dismantling the separated areas of service. Today, women are helicopter pilots and serve aboard ship. Objections to integrating women into the military included the argument that they would cause fighting among the men, sexual relationships would compromise morale, and that the integrity of the military was at stake – again arguments heard to keep gays from serving with heterosexuals in the military. The transition was not so easy as a court order followed by immediate integration; there was resistance. And while there are still tensions today, in fact, the military has not fallen apart because these lines of discrimination were erased.

Somehow, despite the integration of all of these security risks and morale busters, we continue to have the greatest military in the world.

Ruined Lives

The military was able to segregate racial minorities and women because they were able to identify them merely by looking at them. That made segregation easy. But sexual orientation is not visually apparent, so gays and lesbians are admitted to the ranks of the straight fighting force when they would otherwise be turned away. As a result, homosexuals are subject to witch hunts to root out their existence, while blacks and women were simply denied entry at the outset or given menial jobs once they were in the armed services. Another distinction of gays and lesbians is that while other minorities were minorities because that is simply the way they were, gays and lesbians were (at least in the early days) considered mentally ill and therefore unfit to serve. Today gays and lesbians are considered morally unfit.

During World War I, homosexual conduct while in the armed forces was codified as a criminal offense. Being gay meant jail time if caught, though there was a school of thought that it should only lead to exclusion from the military, not imprisonment. By the time World War II came around, while the entire world was going a little bit insane with killing one another, homosexuality transitioned in military eyes from a crime to a mental illness. During World War II, regulations were put into place that authorized the exclusion of gays and lesbians from serving in the armed forces as they were deemed unsuitable for military service. Homosexuality was determined to be a personality defect and, as such, would handicap any person so inclined who tried to serve in the military. In spite of this characterization, during times of armed conflict when bodies were short, it would seem that discharges for this reason declined.

There are people who can bear excellent witness to how the military has treated gays and lesbians since World War II. One of them is Frank Kameny, who lives in Washington, D.C. He is not only a pioneer in the lesbian and gay rights movement; he has helped countless soldiers who were accused of homosexuality before the advent of don't ask don't tell. He speaks from years of experience providing this help before there were organized efforts, such as the Service Members Legal Defense Network. And, he can speak from his experience as a veteran of World War II who fought under enemy fire. He remembers Pearl Harbor, he remembers enlisting, and he remembers being fired from his job when he came home because he was a homosexual. He had a job under the federal civil service, which had a policy that mirrored that of the military and excluded homosexuals. In 1957 Frank was one of those excluded. He fought his dismissal at a time when there were no protection statutes or much gay case law on which to build. He is one of those people who, in fact, did take his case all the way to the Supreme Court. While not a lawyer, he wrote his own petition. However, when he got there, they didn't open the door. The Supremes can do that – they get to decide what cases they are going to hear, and they decided not to hear Frank's case. The year was 1961.

Frank Kameny was there when no one else was around and for the following four decades worked on behalf countless men and women in uniform who were accused of being gay or lesbian and who decided to fight back.

Gays and lesbians have always been excluded, but prior to the 1970s, when the gay and lesbian movement began in earnest, gays and lesbians when discovered were summarily discharged from military duty. The discharges that people got when they were expelled from the military for homosexuality were the kind that ruined your life. "In earlier years, you never got to have an honorable discharge," says Frank Kameny. "They were almost always under 'unsuitability' or other than honorable. In real life, if you don't have an honorable discharge, you might as well have a dishonorable one." The damage that could be done to an individual who was discharged under these circumstances was immense. "It permanently threw people onto the human trash heap. It was a very, very nasty thing."

At the time, it was perfectly permissible for gays and lesbians to be asked about their homosexuality. In fact, during investigations, they would also ask about the homosexuality of others as well, perhaps even offering some leniency in return for the exchange of names. Once they got a name or names from a person being interrogated, they would then go and find them and try to get more names. "In those days they would get their claws into one person and haul them in and then question them and haul in some more, and the thing would just grow and grow and grow," recalls Kameny.

A variety of tactics would be used to extract information that would allow military authorities to try to root out large numbers of lesbians and gays. There were any number of tactics, including overt threats – the informing of parents, for example. In short, interrogation tactics were used to the fullest, and there was case after case in which people were pulled out of the closet by military tactics and subjected to discharges that would, in effect, brand and ruin them for life.

Gays and Lesbians Fight Back

All of this happened in an era when there was no organized establishment to help people who were faced with these types of situations or even to inform them that they had a right to such help. There were only a few attorneys in Washington who would take such cases. The Mattachine Society of Washington tried to change that. The advice they gave was to say nothing, sign, nothing, get counsel, and fight back. As harsh as the era of Frank Kameny was, there was eventually a softening of the military stance. Gradually, through the 1970s and 1980s, the military pulled back from its intransigent position on discharges. While they never backed off from their policy, discharges were no longer always so harsh, and people began getting honorable discharges in spite of their homosexuality. However, this big step only took place after gays and lesbians began to fight back.

One case that came to Kameny for help was that of Sergeant Leonard Matlovich. A decorated Vietnam Air Force hero, Sergeant Matlovich challenged the military policy in a court of law and the court of public opinion in 1975. Though he was discharged, he did win a monetary settlement. The following year, a lesbian in the military challenged the Army Reserve and became the first person to be reinstated. With the benefit of organizations such as the National Service Member Defense Network and the Lambda Legal Defense and Education Fund, others would follow. They traveled their way through the morass of trials, appeals, reversals, and more appeals, many having their stories told in books, television, and on film, including Margarethe Cammemeyer and Keith Meinhold.

Once service members began to challenge their discharges in court, and the military had to defend its actions, the nation became kindler and gentler. But still the basic policy did not change – gays and lesbians continued to be excluded from the military.

The time from World War II, when homosexuality was declared a personality disorder, was one that was insane for the people who were victims of that policy. To the sane and level heads of men such as Frank Kameny, and the clients who had the courage to fight their eviction from the military, those to come will owe a debt of thanks. These people and others like them were not only brave enough to execute military discipline, to the point where they were heralded and decorated by their commanders, but they were brave enough to fight the policy and to try to effect change. One thing became clear with this kind of push back from members of the lesbian and gay community: the policy would have to change. And change it eventually did.

Current Events – They Repeat Themselves

Gay men and lesbian women are not tolerated in the military because they are considered to be bad for morale. The men don't want to shower with "them" or share barracks. There is fear of sexual relationships causing fighting. The integrity of the military is supposedly at stake.

Despite the bravery of our armed forces, there is one thing of which our military chiefs are deathly afraid. One thing will apparently bring this, the most powerful force in the world, it to its knees: Gays and lesbians. If you remember from chapter 1, the one thing that would seem to end straight marriage is the idea that gays and lesbians could marry each other – so they have gone out and passed laws like the "Defense of Marriage Act."

Actually, if you think about it, it is kind of empowering. Apparently, gays, lesbians, bisexuals, and most certainly transexuals are so powerful that not only are we able to disrupt heterosexual marriages by having our own, but by serving in the military, we take it from being the strongest force in the world to one that is compromised. This is in spite of the fact that the armed forces of Europe nearly all accept gays and lesbians into their ranks, and they are also our staunches allies.

Forging a New Policy

Given the successful history of integration of other groups into the military, coupled with more aggressive resistance by lesbian and gay service members to their expulsion, it was logical to assume that gays and lesbians would likewise be eventually accepted. It made sense therefore, that in 1992, candidate Bill Clinton stood in a theater in Los Angeles during his first presidential campaign and made the promise that the ban on gays in the military would come to an end in his administration. The crowd went wild. Here was a candidate coming to meet with the gay, lesbian, bisexual, and transgender community, in and of itself it was historic. He was issuing an historic promise and signaling acceptance at unprecedented levels.

No longer a candidate, President Clinton was true to his promise and made ending the ban on gays and lesbians in the military one of his first acts of business by issuing an executive order, not unlike the one issued by Harry Truman in 1948. The tumult that followed was extreme. The crowd went wild again, but not quite in the same way as they did in the Los Angeles theater. The lifting of the ban became *the* story in the press for weeks. *The New York Times* ran a picture on its front page of Senator John Warner (R-Virginia) inspecting the cots on board ship with an intense scrutiny, as if he were expecting these cots to tell a story. The picture was meant to point out how unacceptable it would be to be sleeping so close to homosexuals. It was an eerie echo of the military's reaction a generation before when white soldiers said they didn't want to shower with black men. It leaves many questions, not the least of which is, why are white straight men so afraid of everyone else – and if they are so afraid, why do we want them fighting the enemy?

In the battle that ensued, the Clinton executive order was emasculated into a vastly different policy, popularly known as the "Don't Ask, Don't Tell, Don't Pursue" policy. However, rather than succeeding at integrating gays and lesbians into the military, Don't Ask Don't Tell has been responsible for ejecting more

American service men and women than under any previous Administration. Candidate Clinton's vow turned out to be the *Titanic* of campaign promises.

The intention of the new policy of Don't Ask Don't Tell was to weave a compromise between President Clinton, who moved to lift the ban, and the military which did not want the ban lifted. The art of compromise is just that, an art. Some who craft a compromise are daVinci's, others only finger painters. The compromise that resulted in the crafting of Don't Ask Don't Tell was an exercise in bad finger painting. Somehow, what began as the idea of easing the restrictions on gays and lesbians serving their country turned into a policy that continues and even exacerbates oppressive practices and discharges. The executive order issued by President Clinton eventually morphed into legislation passed by Congress that set new military policy in 1993.

While employment discrimination against gays and lesbians is illegal in many parts of the United States, the truth is that it is still perfectly legal for the largest employer of people in the country, the U.S. military. In between the time of Baron von Steuben and the policy formation of Don't Ask Don't Tell, a lot of stuff happened. But the one thing that never happened was a lifting of the ban on gays and lesbians in the armed forces. The one constant over the years was the rationale for keeping gays and lesbians from serving – they are a security risk and a morale buster and, as such, endanger the lives and success of the war effort. With the advent of the new policy, there seemed to a perceptible shift in the argument.

You may find yourself asking whether the new policy of Don't Ask Don't Tell isn't an infringement on your right to free speech? Good try. You'd think so wouldn't you? It is a little ironic that the military, which is formed to protect our most basic rights, including free speech, is saying to you that you have no right to be able to utter the very words that may identify who you are. But in fact, the courts have not seen it that way. Lower courts have stated that Don't Ask Don't Tell does not abridge your free speech and the Supremes have so far refused to hear a case involving that issue. That means that, at least for now, by someone's twisted logic, it does not abridge your free speech when the military forbids you from honestly answering the question, are you gay (or lesbian)?

How "Don't Ask Don't Tell" Works (or Doesn't)

The unofficial name of the new policy is "Don't Ask, Don't Tell, Don't Pursue." Perhaps the only good thing about this new military policy is that the name sort of captures it all. The military are not supposed to ask, and you are not supposed to tell, and they are not supposed to pursue – meaning that the witch hunts described by Frank Kameny should be a distant memory. In effect, the new policy was meant to allow homosexuals to serve in the military as long as they did not engage in homosexual acts while serving and as long as their sexual orientation is kept secret.

Perhaps that sounds like a welcome change and even a fair compromise. But it isn't. Let's break it down to its most simple components. First, the no-asking thing. You have to keep in mind that just because they aren't supposed to ask *you* doesn't mean that they're not supposed to ask *anybody*. They can ask anybody they want to. Second, the no-telling thing. They mean it. As far as you are concerned – with respect to the telling part – you aren't supposed to tell anybody. They mean anybody. Anywhere. Anytime. For any reason. Lastly, the no pursuing part sounds good, but in effect, the number of discharges from the military on the basis of sexual orientation has increased, not decreased, meaning that while the tactics have changed, the overall aim of the military has not.

The only significant difference between pre-Don't Ask Don't Tell and post-Don't Ask, Don't Tell is that the idea that the military can ask a person entering the military whether they are gay is no longer allowed. Prior to the policy, when you entered military service, you were screened by a question posed to you: are you a homosexual? After the policy, that question was no longer used to screen personnel – meaning that, theoretically, anyone who wanted to serve their country who also happened to be a lesbian or gay individual could do so if they entered the service without ever mentioning their sexual orientation.

Sharra Greer, legal director for the Servicemembers Legal Defense Network (SLDN) says that while the witch hunts described by Frank Kameny have declined dramatically, the nuance of Don't Ask Don't Tell policy doesn't translate so well down to actual practice in the various armed services. Witch-hunts still do occur and inappropriate questions are still asked. In fact, even though the policy went into effect in 1993, in 2002 the Air Force Reserve was still asking recruits on the application whether they were homosexual. What this means is that there is a very uneven understanding of Don't Ask Don't Tell regulations and very individual interpretations of the provisions of the policy. After all of the rigorous hoopla on the issue, the fact is that the only thing that has changed is that the military can no longer ask you whether you are a gay or lesbian. They can, however, ask you a whole lot of other questions, and upon getting the answer, they can discharge you.

Sharra Greer puts it this way: "The policy is a failure – for everyone. It is bad for the military, in that they are losing record numbers of people and at a time when the military is having a hard time keeping people in. They are losing record numbers of gay, lesbian, and bisexual soldiers, which isn't good for the taxpayer or for the commands who are losing soldiers. Don't Ask Don't Tell is not real progress; in fact, it didn't make anybody happy."

How is it that more people are being discharged when, in fact, no one is supposed to be talking about the homosexuality that is resulting in the discharge? You can kind of sum it up this way: There are two ways that you are going to be expelled from the military.

The first way is that something you say or do causes someone to rat you out.

The second way is that you decide to take off your camouflage and come out of the military closet.

Tripping the Wire

The wire is tripped and you are potentially on your way to an investigation when someone brings it to the attention of a commanding officer that you may be a homosexual. What causes them to do that? It could be something you said or did that provided a hint, or it could merely be spite.

Perhaps one of the very worst parts of a policy such as Don't Ask Don't Tell is that it can subject a service member to the charge of being gay or lesbian merely because someone doesn't like them. The charge may not even be true. Sharra Greer recalls a case in which a service member was accused of being a lesbian by another service member. She said that the accused made a pass at her. But the service member defended herself, asserting that she was not a lesbian, and when her matter came before a discharge board, she had the testimony of ex-boyfriends to prove her case. But how do you prove what your sexuality is? In reality, you can't prove anything. The discharge board voted for her removal. No one offered proof that she was a lesbian. She did offer proof that she was not. In fact, women are more vulnerable than men in this regard. A spurned pass by a male officer could earn a straight woman the title of lesbian. There are other circumstances that can bring about suspicion. Says Greer, "If you are a woman in a non-traditional field – Military Police, helicopter pilot – and if you are not dating a man, then you are probably going to be called a lesbian. We see that quite a bit." While none of those things is enough to result in an investigation absent a trigger of Don't Ask Don't Tell, nevertheless there is a red flag that may cause an individual to be more closely scrutinized for any particular way in which she might "tell" on herself. The vulnerability of women is evidenced by the fact, Greer says, that "women are discharged at twice the rate of their representation in the services."

In the final analysis, the effect of the policy is to render any gay, lesbian, or bisexual person who enters the military (transgendered people are absolutely forbidden) to forget who and what they are entirely and to essentially put aside their identity and think of themselves only as military personnel. “I think that is a fair assessment,” says Greer, “The kind of closet that you have to live in for most service members is pretty complete, and that is a pretty unpleasant place to be for anyone.” And for anyone who is not willing or is not able to do that, then the degree of risk they are running begins to increase.

If there has been a suggestion that you have made a statement that you are a gay, lesbian, or bisexual person, either by statement or by deed, then you may be subject to an investigation. You are not subject to an investigation because your wrist is limp or, as a woman, you aren’t dating a man. It will only be triggered because of some action that you undertook or someone alleges that you undertook. To use an example provided by SLDN, suppose you are seen marching at a gay pride event. Affiliation with a known gay person or persons is not supposed to be enough to trigger an investigation. However, if you are carrying a sign that says the Pentagon should drop the ban, then you may have tripped the wire. You may have just “told” on yourself.

If someone rats you out, that means that you either said or did something that tipped someone off that you were the person you are. What does that mean? With respect to the thing that you said or did that tipped someone off, it can be almost anything. The “Don’t Tell” part of the policy is interpreted very broadly. In other words, the act by which you tell someone of your homosexuality could be verbal or non-verbal. That is not the way it was originally intended to be, points out Sharra Greer. “There was supposed to be a zone of privacy for service members. There was some thought that certain kinds of telling wouldn’t get you kicked out. Telling your mom, telling your doctor, allowing people to have a little private life. As long as people weren’t out there, you would be permitted to serve, but the legislation and regulations didn’t reflect the intention of the rhetoric around the issue.” That is to say, the “zone” that Greer was referring to got pretty small, in fact so small that it practically doesn’t exist outside the mind of the service member.

And the result is that any telling in almost any manner imaginable has the potential to get you into serious trouble. It could mean you told a friend who serves with you, or it could mean that you told your chaplain, or you told your best friend who is off base, or you told the base doctor when you had a physical, or you told a high school chum. It means telling anyone – anyone at all. But telling can also be non-verbal. It can be holding hands with another person of your gender or displaying some other type of affection. It can be wearing a T-shirt that gives it away. It can be your online Internet screen profile.

An Example of the New Policy in Action

What's in a name? This is a story about names. For starters, a man who was named Timothy McVeigh – not the Timothy McVeigh who was executed for his crime in connection with the Oklahoma City bombing, but a different one who was serving in the Navy on board – the *U.S.S. Chicago*. This Timothy McVeigh served for seventeen years in the Navy and was a decorated senior chief – he was the most senior enlisted man on board his nuclear submarine.

He had another name besides Timothy McVeigh, a screen name on his America Online account: "boysrch." In his online profile, he identified his marital status as gay, and he listed his interests as including collecting pictures of young studs and "boy watching." He did not give his identity in the profile. How did the Navy connect the dots, discover this profile, and find out who it belonged to?

A woman who was a civilian Navy volunteer was organizing a toy drive for the children of the crew members of his ship. He sent her an e-mail about the toy drive using his boysrch tag name and also signed the e-mail with the name "Tim." She saw the name and called up his profile. His profile stated his preferences, though not his name. She only knew that he was "Tim." She tipped off the Navy about the e-mail and the fact that one of their ranks, presumably aboard the nuclear submarine, was saying online that he was a "boysearcher." An inspection began. The military went to America Online without identifying themselves as the Navy to confirm the identity of the individual. Amazingly, America Online told them. This was in spite of the fact that there was this little law called the Electronic Communications Privacy Act of 1996 that forbade the government from obtaining information from an Internet service provider without a warrant or without notice to the Internet subscriber. But when the Navy contacted America Online, according to the company, they did not state that they were with the government. The military then moved to kick Timothy McVeigh out of the Navy, saying that he had violated Don't Ask Don't Tell by having this profile and name on the Internet. He had a discharge hearing, during which he actually admitted writing the e-mail about the toy drive. Bear in mind that he did not have the profile connected with his identity. The Navy told McVeigh that they had information that he had "told" – that he made a statement that he was gay.

An administrative discharge proceeding then ensued in short order. At the hearing, McVeigh presented evidence that he had been engaged and had several other heterosexual relationships. But the outcome was that it had been shown by a preponderence of the evidence that McVeigh had admitted that he engaged in homosexual conduct. Just before his discharge, McVeigh took the matter to federal court and requested an injunction against the Navy, saying that if they discharged him, it would do him irreparable harm. To get such an injunction, McVeigh would have to show that he would be likely to prevail on the merits of his case.

When they got to court, the court looked at what the Navy had done. They had a tip without a certain identity. They then went and looked up that identity and connected it with one of their own, a decorated naval officer. They then moved to dismiss. As such, the Navy lost, because the court perceived that McVeigh had not really "told" but that the Navy had pursued, and pursuing is something they aren't supposed to do under Don't Ask Don't Tell. The court stated that "all the Navy had was an e-mail message and user profile that it suspected was authored by the Plaintiff. . . . When the Navy affirmatively took steps to confirm the identity of the e-mail responders, it violated the very essence of Don't Ask, Don't Pursue by launching a search and destroy mission."

According to Sharra Greer, it was one of the rare cases in which the court actually says, "Military you are out of line and I am going to enforce your regulations." McVeigh won his injunction, and the Navy was enjoined from releasing him, because he had convinced the court that he was likely going to prevail on the merits of his case against the Navy. With the injunction in place, the parties negotiated a settlement whereby all of McVeigh's legal costs were paid for by the Navy. McVeigh, two years short of his ability to retire with pension, was allowed to do just that.

Still, it may have been a matter of winning the battle, but losing the war. On the one hand, you could say that the Navy was not successful in their efforts, but on the other the guy was finished. "His career was ruined, and he settled and retired, though they weren't able to kick him out," says Greer. So it was a victory, but a small one. The effect was still the same; he no longer had a military career.

Don't let the outcome of the case make you think that you can be fast and loose about being out. The McVeigh case does demonstrate that there are limits to what it means for you to "tell." But the reason McVeigh won his injunction against the military is because the court was able to find from the facts that the Navy pursued him. His online profile did not have his name on it – so the Navy had to go and find out that it was him. That was pursuing, in violation of the regulations that support the Don't Ask Don't Tell policy. By no means should you consider it license to be glib online and do anything that would connect your sexual orientation with your identity.

Will There be an Investigation?

Once there is an assertion that you are lesbian or gay, it will be up to the discretion of your command whether an investigation occurs. If the command, as he or she is known, intensely dislikes the idea of homosexuals in the ranks, then he or she will appoint an inquiry officer to begin an investigation. If he or she does not care much about it, then there will be no investigation. Other factors exist that may mitigate the chances of having an investigation launched. According to Sharra Greer, "A lot of people serve without a problem, particularly officers who, because of their position, have more privacy. Lots of service members live out their twenty years – it can be done. Some commands are more liberal, some professions – such as medical – are more liberal." She notes that profession can also go a long way toward mitigating your chances of being investigated. Just as the military did not want to lose soldiers during the Persian Gulf War, there are some professions that are just too valuable to toss out lightly. "There is no good statistical evidence to prove this, but skilled professionals may have less of a hard time than unskilled, particularly linquists, doctors and dentists. They may have more leeway. You get into the infantry, it may be a lot more likely that you will face an investigation."

The bottom line is that it may heavily depend on your command, because their discretion to investigate or not, to push on the evidence or not, is very strong. Sherra Greer also states that it may very much depend as well on how interested the command is in getting rid of a particular person. She cites an example in which the command was not interested in getting rid of one individual. In that case a diary was found during a search. In it, Greer states, the service member talked about his deep affection for another man. There was nothing stated that was sexual and nothing talked about other than deep friendship. He was investigated but he continues to serve. "If the command really wanted to get rid of him," says Greer, "he'd be gone."

As well, there may be some differences in the way that the various branches of the military handle the situation. "There is definitely some difference among the branches and it changes from year to year as to what is going on in each of the services," says Greer. According to her, Navy ship commanders are loathe to have discharges from their ships and may be more tolerant and less inclined to launch an investigation unless the circumstances cannot be ignored. Still she stresses, individual commanders make a much greater difference than the branch of service. This is not to suggest you should come out to your commander, but some of them simply see a gay claim as a way to get out of the Navy. "If you are in the Navy and assigned to a ship and you came out, the chances of you being believed would be low," says Greer.

Still, it does of course, happen and there is no reason for gays or lesbians in the Navy to be careless. But it is one of the examples of the way that the regulations guiding gays in the military are enforced with such unevenness. According to Greer, each service has its own regulations, there are various Department of Defense memoranda. In her words, "you end up having to look in twelve different places to understand what the rules are. That is why there is such a difference among the various commands about what the policy means and the way it is enforced."

The fact that the military may have a great need for your services does not necessarily mean that you won't be booted out. In late 2002, the U.S. Army gave honorable discharges to nine soldiers who were linguists specializing in languages desperately needed in the war on terrorism. That need did not create a safe harbor for them.

In the end, there is no way to predict with certainty whether you will have an investigation. It will depend on a number of circumstances, mostly beyond your knowledge and control. These include your branch, your profession, your level, your commanding officer's outlook on homosexuality, and the nature and circumstances regarding how the information that you are gay or lesbian came to the attention of the military.

If You Are Being Investigated

If there is going to be an investigation, than the inquiry begins by either asking those around you or coming directly to you to inquire of the circumstances. *You will need to get immediate legal assistance that is available to you, but under no circumstances should you speak to any representative of the military about your investigation or circumstance.*

You may start looking for assistance by using the Internet. But you even have to use caution in that regard. The use of any computer anywhere has some risk associated with it, because during an investigation, it might be searched. It is even possible that a search could as a result in something other than a gay or lesbian investigation – a criminal investigation – and that matter would then come up. The use of government property for your personal use can get you into additional trouble. This is complicated for those who need help but who are on base or on board ship. If you have a personal account and you need to make contact with an organization that is going to assist you, you still need to be cautious, and you need to use a computer that does not belong to the government.

If there is going to be an inquiry and the investigation reaches you, you really have only one option advises Sharra Greer:

Don't say a word.

They may not be able to ask you directly if you are a gay man or lesbian woman, but they may ask you other forms of the same question. Do you have romantic feelings for someone in particular of the same sex? Are you aroused by same-sex pornography? Have you ever had sexual relations with another individual of the same sex?

Say nothing. This is the most important legal advice you will get in this chapter. In the face of any investigation that comes your way, you should state that you are not willing to answer any question until you have legal representation from an experienced non-military attorney.

If you have ever watched television, then you should remember the civilian Miranda warnings you have heard a thousand times – words uttered by a police officer when placing someone under arrest: "Anything you say or do can be used against you in a court of law."

That applies in spades here – anything you say or do at this point can be and will be used against you, only it won't be in a court of law, it will be in a discharge hearing. If you are confronted with an inquiry, say nothing except that you are going to seek legal representation. Do not ask questions, do not chat with any of the investigating personnel, do not respond with anything other than your desire to get an attorney. Do not admit to anything, do not deny anything.

You may be sorely tempted to deny the charges and when asked whether you are gay or lesbian, to just say no and walk away. You may look at the situation and decide that they don't have evidence, and therefore you may want to deny it. After all, how are they going to prove it? That would be mistake of the first magnitude. Lying can only compound your problems. You do not want to be in a position where you are lying or destroying evidence. Lying during the course of an investigation can take what would have been an honorable discharge and turn it into something else. You have the right to remain silent – it is a right worth using.

You have to be aware that you do not necessarily have all of the rights you had when you were a private citizen if you are a member of the armed services and you are living on a military base. In that case, you must know that a search warrant is not necessary to go through your belongings. If you live off base, a search is supposed to be accompanied by a warrant, but that doesn't mean that it will necessarily happen. If you are faced with the prospect of a physical search, SLDN advises that you never try to physically stop a search. You may state your disagreement with the action, but getting in the way may only result in worsening the charges brought against you or even in getting physically hurt.

Once underway, the scope of the investigation can be very broad.

Who can they ask? They can ask you mom, your dad, your doctor, your therapist, your roommate, your chaplain, your friends, your enemies. This list may surprise you. Don't let it. While in a civilian proceeding, you enjoy confidentiality from your doctor, your minister, and your shrink; in the military, protected confidentiality is non-existent.

Who can you tell? None of those people. None of them.

Telling means more than just saying in this regard. As you could discern from the SLDN example of going to the gay pride parade with a sign to drop the ban, your act of "telling" is not just verbal. If you can answer yes to any of the following questions, you may be telling.

Are you keeping a diary that talks about your feelings or details your life?

Do you have any gay or lesbian magazines laying around?

Do you have a T-shirt that has a gay or lesbian rights slogan on it?

Have you kissed a person of the same sex in public?

Have you held hands with a person of the same sex in public?

Do you use your computer to write letters that discuss your feelings?

Do you have a computer that contains downloaded pictures that might give you away?

Do you exchange love letters with anyone?

If by some chance you are living off base with a same-sex partner, you probably should take steps to "sanitize" your home. Greer asks that people remember "that anything you do that tells the outside world about your sexual orientation puts you at risk. Off-base homes cannot be searched without a warrant or without your permission," she says, "so you can have things that reflect you life in your home, but if they do get a search warrant, then you are at risk. While they cannot get a search warrant to find out if you are gay, they can get one for other reasons. It is not inconceivable that they could get a warrant for something else with the real reason wanting to find out something gay or lesbian."

Does all this mean that you should get rid of all your identifying personal effects before going into the military? Not necessarily, but what it does mean is that, while you are in the military, the more "out" you are, even as expressed through your personal effects, the more risk you run. This is especially true if you live on base or on board ship. Any effects, such as a diary, magazines, or love letters, can be evidence in a discharge hearing. The more sterilized your life is with respect to your personal effects and behavior as related to your sexual identity, the less risk you run.

It is even possible that you are unsafe in areas where you should be safe. For example, according to SLDN, on your insurance forms, you should be able to list someone who is the same gender as you and not related to you as the beneficiary of your life insurance. However, even though the Department of Defense has stated that doing so should not trigger an investigation, it is nevertheless information that could be used against you during an investigation. If you want to provide for a friend or partner with your insurance, but don't want to run this risk, you can leave your estate as your beneficiary. Then if you should die, the money would be paid into your testamentary estate. In order for this to be successful, you must have written a valid last will and testament (see chapter 4), and in the body of that document, you can provide for your friend. You can keep your will private, but don't store it on base. You may consider leaving it with your attorney and making sure that your executor knows where it is. There is a serious drawback to this, however, in that with an insurance policy, the benefits automatically transfer directly to a beneficiary on your death. By putting it through your estate, it will not be a quick process, and any money in your estate must first be used to pay all of your debts and expenses. Therefore, while an option, it is an option that has risks.

As you can see, the investigation is pervasive and complicated, and any weakness you have may be exploited. It is also unevenly applied, meaning that the regulations are not clearly understood by all who would use them. That is why it is imperative that you do not provide any grist for the mill by saying anything, and why it is vital that you seek legal assistance as soon as you understand that you are the subject of an investigation. The hallmarks of success, or mitigating damage, involve getting help and getting it early. It is essential to assert one's right to an attorney and to not respond to any question about your sexual orientation.

Taking Off the Camouflage – Coming Out in the Military

If an investigation begins, you may be tempted to just throw in the towel and admit that you are a homosexual and get on with your life. Even without an investigation, you may decide that you want out. The military closet is small and uncomfortable and nearly impossible to stay in. To the degree you can't stay in, you increase the danger of being found out. The rigors of staying within the confines of the policy are taking their toll, and that is one reason why the number of gays and lesbians leaving the military is on the rise. Ironically, as more open mainstream society becomes more open to gay culture and the open and visible presence of gays, lesbians, and bisexuals, life for recruits just gets that much more difficult.

"It is getting harder to lead a straight life in the military when in the larger community there is such a visible gay community. It makes it harder to try to blend in, which is causing a lot of recruits to give up," says Greer. She adds that there is another factor at work. The reason many gay, lesbian, and bisexual people enter the military in the first place is not only because they want to serve their country, but because the values of the institution appeal to them. Those values involve truth and honor. It becomes a little difficult to live up to those values when, because of the policy, you have to lie to everyone you meet or at least to conceal the truth about who you are. It adds pressure to what is already a very difficult situation, and people do get fed up and leave.

So how do you leave? You raise your hand and you tell. But it is not that simple, and you need to be very careful how you do it or else you run the risk of doing yourself a great deal of damage. In fact, more and more people are leaving the military by virtue of this than for any other reason. They just don't want to do it anymore. But before you raise your hand to signal your intent, there is something you should do first. Get legal help. This is not something, no matter what the circumstances, that you should handle on your own.

You may feel that you have a pretty good relationship with your command and think that he is OK with gay people, and that it would be OK if you went into him to discuss leaving the military. You would be ill-advised to do so. As nice of a guy or gal as your command may be, they still have an obligation to execute military policy, and military policy does not allow anyone gay in the military. To go to your command without legal help can result in jeopardizing your retirement benefits or cause you to be the subject of efforts to recoup the losses the military will be suffering as a result of your admission of homosexuality (see the section below entitled "Payback").

If you are wanting out, it is vital that the first thing you do is get in touch with a non-military lawyer. A lot of people are inclined to go to the legal officers who serve with them, but that can also be a mistake. These people are not always lawyers. And, more importantly, even though you may feel that they are open minded, they are never on your side. You need the benefit of an experienced non–military attorney, because it is essential that you do not say or do something that will lower your discharge characterization, subject you to criminal prosecution, or complicate your retirement.

Coming out to your command means constructing a letter advising the command of the circumstances. The biggest advantage of legal assistance is that they have experience in helping people to craft their statements in a way that foregoes the kind of damage you don't want. Experienced help on drafting your coming out statement will tell you what you can and cannot say. For example, you don't want to talk about your boyfriend or girlfriend who is also in the military – it will get you both in trouble. The letter you write will be in your own words, but legal assistance will help you understand the rules. A further reason to have help is that your command may not know what the rules are either. The implementation of policy around Don't Ask Don't Tell has been somewhat uneven, and the level of understanding of the policy by commands can vary widely. Your legal help will submit your letter with a cover letter of their own and will also outline for the command what the rules are.

You would think that coming out while you are serving in the military is an automatic speedy exit ticket. It might be, but there might also be complications. In the first place, it could be that your command simply doesn't want you to go. Not every command is anxious to get rid of a valuable employee. They may ask you to take your statement back and pretend it never happened. It is the exception, not the rule, but it does happen.

Being Harassed

One of the most vulnerable situations faced by a service member is when he or she is being harassed. Harassment comes in a lot of forms, verbal or non-verbal and it can end in serious bodily harm and even death. To not report it means that you have to put up with uncivil or even dangerous behavior. To report it may make you feel that you are signaling your command that you are in fact a gay man or lesbian woman.

"It is one of the trickiest situations out there," says Sharra Greer, "particularly because most members don't understand the difference between saying that I'm being harassed because I'm gay versus people who believe that I'm gay."

That kind of slip can result in getting yourself discharged. As with the other situations, if you are in a situation involving harassment, get legal advice as soon as you can. Gay or lesbian harassment is different from that based on sex or race. In those cases, the Equal Employment Opportunity Commission steps in and begins their work. But for gays and lesbians, the matter is less formalized, and anyone filing a complaint will be sent through the chain of command, the chaplain or the inspector general's office. Even if you go to one of the latter, you may be sent through the chain of command. And to none of these people can you say that you are being harassed because you are gay or lesbian, but only because someone thinks that you are.

In any case, it raises a red flag. Having recently suffered the embarrassment of a widely publicized death in the barracks from harassment turned deadly, the Army is making a concerted effort to engage in education in an effort to stem harassment. "The Department of Defense had always maintained that there was not a big problem with harassment," says Greer, "but the Inspector General's office did a survey of 75,000 members, and the bottom line of the report was that harassment was a huge problem." As a result, a working group was commissioned to come up with a way to address harassment in the ranks. They developed a thirteen-point action plan. Greer says that there hasn't been a lot of follow up, and though it was sent to the various services for implementation, the Army is the only one to take it seriously by developing a manual.

Discharge

If that flag is raised and there is an investigation, what then? If the investigation finds that you have "told" and your command is determined to see this to its conclusion, then the outcome is only one thing: discharge. That is a funny word – discharge. It is not usually associated with anything attractive. Think about it.

In military terms, there is something called an honorable discharge and now, unlike long before Don't Ask Don't Tell, you should be able to obtain an honorable discharge if your record is a good one. If your record does not merit an honorable discharge, then you will get a general discharge. However, if there are circumstances, such as criminal conduct, that accompany the issue of your homosexuality, you may receive something called an other-than-honorable discharge.

Benefits that are yours as a result of your military service are determined by the type of discharge you have. An honorable discharge means that you will have all veteran's retirement and education benefits. A general discharge will not get you the education benefits. But an other than honorable discharge means that benefits may be determined on a case by case basis. The other effect of your discharge respects your future employment. When you leave the military, if you lack an honorable discharge, there may be questions or reservations on the part of your prospective employer.

For the most part, being gay or lesbian is not a criminal offense, however acts of sodomy under military law are. There is guidance in the Department of

Defense document that gay or lesbian matters are not to be treated as criminal unless people get caught in parks soliciting, on ship or barracks while having sex, or doing other illegal activities. While it is believed that most cases are not treated as criminal, there are no centralized records that would confirm that. The records are maintained by individual commands. However, if the circumstances of your outing involve a sexual act, then discharge not only leans toward dishonorable, but there may be criminal charges as well. Needless to say, any forcible or unwanted touching or involvement with a minor can lead to criminal charges. If it is illegal in civilian life, it is illegal in military life.

If there is no criminal activity, but you are leaving by virtue of being found out or raising your hand and informing your command so that you can leave, then the type of discharge you receive will largely depend on your record of service, and of course on your command. According to Greer, a vast majority of people who get discharges have honorable ones, a policy that began prior to Don't Ask Don't Tell. The rule is that when you are discharged you are to be given a discharge consistent with the character of your service. Therefore, if your service record is a good one, you should have an honorable discharge. If you have a couple of citations, then you can get a general discharge, but it has to be more serious than violating dress code. Says Greer, "You will perhaps get a general discharge if you have one serious infraction, or lots of small ones. If you have had lots of disciplines unrelated to your being gay, you can get a dishonorable. If you've been caught having sex on a ship, the way the military views it – it has nothing to do with being homosexual; you have violated a criminal law in the military. On ship, in public in the barracks, for money or with a minor – those can be aggravating factors in considering your discharge."

When you receive notice of an inquiry, there will be forms given you to fill out. Consult with non-military counsel before filling out and returning the forms. They are important, because they will affect your rights in the hearing. There will be a deadline by which you must return the forms. Don't let the deadline pressure you into filling them out, but rather let it motivate you toward finding non-military legal help as soon as possible.

Payback

If you were educated by virtue of being in the military service, then you may have another issue to deal with. It is entirely possible that they will want their investment back. This is called "recoupment." This also may apply to any other perks that you have received during your time in military service. They want it back, and they want it back badly. In fact, says Greer, the Air Force in particular will go after every penny they see owing to them.

Supposedly, the policy in place does not demand recoupment from any service member who is discharged involuntarily for making a statement regarding one's homosexuality or bisexuality, though it would be most certainly required if there were an aggravating circumstance accompanying the discharge. But this policy is unevenly enforced, and there are no guarantees that a long and involved recoupment claim will not be made. When they do demand their money back, they go to great lengths to get it.

Frank Kameny attests to that. He is still handling cases, and he has two in which he is representing physicians in New York City. Each of the physicians received their education through the Air Force, with the understanding that they would serve in the Air Force afterwards for a period of three years. "But," explains Kameny, "they were discovered to be gay and kicked out. Now the Air Force is seeking recoupment for their education. Both of these cases are being accused of putting homosexuality on the record in order to avoid their military service. Both of them are willing to put their careers on hold and provide service for the Air Force." However, in spite of the fact that they are willing to serve, the military simply wants its money back. The case is now ten years old. Everyone involved seems very, very determined.

Future Directions – Liberating the Troops

Are things getting any better? Yes and no. There has been a gradual change in the way that the military deals with gays and lesbians in the ranks. The bottom line policy has never changed; you are still not allowed in. But over the course of the twentieth century, there was progress: from criminal charges to dishonorable discharges to general discharges to the current system of honorable discharges. The practice of "witch-hunting" is far less frequent now than it used to be. However, with the advent of Don't Ask Don't Tell, the uneasy alliance that was supposed to exist in which gays and lesbians could serve as long as they didn't talk about being gay, has resulted in extremely high levels of discharges and, in that respect, things are definitely not better.

Not every nation bans gays in the military. Australia, Canada, Great Britain, and even Israel all allow gays to serve openly in the military. In fact, every one of our NATO allies allows gays and lesbians to serve in the military, except for

Turkey. They do not seem to be any less able as allies than if they did not allow gays to serve in the military.

Israel in particular needs every soldier that it can get, but it also needs armed forces that have excellent morale and strength of spirit. Great Britain, Canada, and Australia have all served honorably as allies of the United States in the war against terrorism. Interestingly, since allowing gays and lesbians to serve in the military, none of these nations have fallen. Their militaries are strong and intact. Their policy of inclusion does not appear to negatively impact their national security. They are not less reliable allies than they were before they lifted their bans. In fact, you could argue that the policy makes the country less secure. The policy that seeks to exclude an entire class of people and also belittles them and even endangers their lives and well-being. It results in a waste of taxpayer dollars, time, and resources, and encourages insubordination and, at the very least, confusion about how to carry out orders. Perhaps it makes a less secure military force for our country than our allies. It is warped logic at best that can conclude that such a policy is in fact good for national security.

This is perhaps evidenced by some of the high profile cases that have evolved over the past few decades since Frank Kameny began his work. The records of such people as Sargeant Leonard Matlovich and Margarethe Cammermeyer were all exemplary. They were all decorated soldiers, and they were all held up as ideals to other soldiers by the military until the military found out that they were gay or lesbian. Then the military spent an inordinate amount of time, effort, resources, and, importantly, hundreds of thousands of tax dollars to get rid of them. Remember the case of Timothy McVeigh? In order to settle the case, the Navy had to not only pay its own legal expenses, but the legal expenses of McVeigh as well. In the end, the McVeigh case cost the Navy tens of thousands of dollars. Still, each year, the armed forces expend efforts to discharge hundreds upon hundreds of gay and lesbian service members, whatever the evidence on record.

While evidence of exemplary service records exist on the one hand, on the other, there is no evidence that supports the military position. The only evidence is a policy statement that says that homosexuality is not compatible with military service. That is not evidence, it is merely a statement. Sooner or later, someone in a position of authority and responsibility within the military will have the wisdom and ability to realize that. There is no evidence at all that gays and lesbians are unable to serve in a capacity that is strong and able within the military. No evidence rebuts the records of these fine soldiers. And what better proof of that than the record of Baron von Steuben – without whom, there would have not been a United States military. His record is recorded on the base of his statue in front of the White House:

> After serving as aide-de-camp to
> Frederick the Great of Prussia
> He offered his sword to the American
> Colonies and was appointed major
> General and inspector general in
> The Continental Army. He gave
> Training and discipline to the citizen
> Soldiers who achieved the independence
> Of the United States.

CHAPTER 8

Crimes of Passion – Sex and the Law

History and Perspective – A Legal Tradition Against Gays and Lesbians

THERE ARE A LOT of laws about sex. This chapter is going to look at a few of them. There are, first of all, laws against gay people having sex of any kind. These are called sodomy laws and they exist in several states. Sometimes sodomy laws are directed to gay people, and sometimes they are generalized in order to outlaw certain sexual practices that are not deemed wholesome.

There are also laws that prohibit sex in public areas, and these exist in every state and apply to everyone, gay or straight. There are also law-enforcement methods used that try to entice gay people to break sodomy laws or at least to break the laws that prohibit sex in public areas. And with the advent of HIV, lawmakers passed laws seeking to prohibit the intentional transmission of HIV to an infected sexual partner.

Laws that attempt to regulate sexual behavior are passed by states, though the federal government has had a role to play as well, in that challenges to the laws can be based in constitutional arguments. This chapter will tell you where these laws sprang from, overview the types of laws that touch your body, and tell you where these laws have been struck down and where they still exist. Most importantly, this chapter will also explain why these laws are, for the most part, an insult to you and, as far as sodomy laws are concerned, need to be struck down by court action or repealed by responsible legislatures.

In the Beginning – The Bible and Homosexuality

From the very dawn of written law, legal codes often picked sodomy as a heinous crime. For those caught engaging in that crime, the result would often be death or torture or maiming, or simply death by virtue of torture, mutilation, and maiming. Homosexuals, mind you, were not outlawed, since the term has a relatively recent introduction into society and people were not truly classified as homosexuals – there were merely people who engaged in homosexual behavior. And for those behaviors, you could pay a heavy price. These laws were not based on any interest in protecting the public good or seeking to shelter an innocent person from victimization. Rather, the law was based merely in the belief that such acts were immoral. In modern America, they are deemed immoral because, it is said, the Bible says that they are immoral.

Sodomy, of course, is named after the famous biblical city referenced in the Book of Genesis. It was a place where, supposedly, people of the same-sex were running sexually amuck with one another. Having a reputation for this, the city gave birth to the name of same-sex copulation. Religious scholars can often be heard in debate over just what was occurring in that famous city of Sodom and whether sodomy actually in fact was referring to same sex relations or to other practices. For our purposes, the outcome of that debate is immaterial. Sodom gave name to sodomy, which in biblical terms is popularly defined as the act of a man lying with another man as if he were lying with a woman, language taken from the King James version of the Bible, and it is the Bible that is the basis for American law on the matter.

American Sodomy Law Development

The American history of sodomy begins with a harshness that was nothing less than Biblical in proportions, as it was punishable as a capital crime by colonial American law in the 1600s. The American historical roots of sodomy law begin in none other than the Commonwealth of Virginia. Virginia, as we have seen, was not a seat of very enlightened thought on matters of marriage and sex (see chapter 1). It was the first colony to pass a law making sodomy punishable by death. In fact, four centuries later, it is still not legal in Virginia. Making sodomy a capital crime was a trend that caught on, and other states soon followed. An interesting exception to this was Pennsylvania – home of Philadelphia, the city of brotherly love. Though Pennsylvania did make a crime out of sodomy, they did not immediately make it punishable by death. However, early in the following century, they changed their minds and went with the crowd, opting to kill the faggots. Most early statutes forbidding sodomy did not mention women, though a few did. Death occurred in many imaginable ways, including drowning and even choking, both of which seem a difficult way to go about it.

In the latter part of the seventeenth century, the sodomy laws were modified and liberalized somewhat. If one of the partners engaged in the act of sodomy was under the age of fourteen, or if it were a matter of rape, then these parties were not put to death. That, one must suppose, represented progress.

Other Biblical prohibitions have not seemed to carry the same moral weight in American law. For example, there is a Old Testament prohibition against charging interest for the loaning of money. Can you imagine where our banking system and entire economy would be if lenders were as persecuted as gays and lesbians? And where would companies like Gillette be if the Biblical prohibition against shaving were as rigidly enforced here as it was in Afghanistan? It is hard to imagine the American farmer really enjoying a moral prohibition on eating pork. The farm lobby would not like that. And then, lawyers would find a moral ban on divorce truly oppressive. Fortunately for them all, the only Biblical prohibition which really stuck in American law as a victimless crime is the one against sodomy.

It is hard to believe, but it is true. Across America, in various places, there are men and women who have the capacity, intelligence and where-with-all to enter into a campaign for public office, win a hard-won election and carry the responsibility of governing on their shoulders. These are people who are therefore, by process of elimination, arguably intelligent. Yet remarkably, many of these same people are under the impression that if you make certain sexual acts against the law – well, then, people just won't do it. Because, after all, everyone would rather obey the law than have sex wouldn't they?

Eventually sodomy laws were modified from penalities that embraced the more lethal extremes to those that were merely life-ruining, meaning imprisonment. The acts of sodomy now universally include acts between people of the same sex, and women are included. Progress with respect to these laws, how ever, was glacial, and it would take 300 years from the time of colonial America before states would begin dropping sodomy statutes altogether.

Today, while no longer a capital crime, the fact remains that sodomy laws at one time existed in every single state in the United States. Sodomy as a sexual act was defined under many names under the statutes – sexual misconduct, crimes against nature, unnatural acts, unnatural intercourse, or sometimes just plain old sodomy. The statutes forbidding sodomy sometimes went, and still often go, into great detail as to what constitutes a violation, and were fairly explicit – all about mouths on genitalia and such.

The Beginning of the End – When Sodomy Laws Began to Fall

The law is funny about sex. Legislators like to pass laws against it. Yet to read the headlines, they are spending a great deal of time doing it themselves, mostly outside of the confines of the precious institution of marriage and often with partners who are the age of their adult children, which is just plain creepy. Yet they deem the marriage institution so sacred that they are also passing laws to try to protect it, perhaps out of guilt for their own behavior – against gays and lesbians (see chapter 1). Yet try to get those legislators to repeal a sodomy statute, and you have a real task on your hands. There are two ways that the statutes can go away – one is to repeal them, the other is to overturn them in court.

The state statutes themselves tend to be years old and they are not the product of recently introduced legislation nor enlightened thought. Still, when there is a challenge to one of them in states where they still exist, states tenaciously enter the battle and attempt to defend these statutes with all their might. This is in spite of the fact that the acts prohibited by them occur on a daily basis with great frequency amongst most of the populace and probably amongst most of the legislature.

In 1962, one state began a wave of enlightenment that has not yet run its full course. You might think that this sexual revolution would have begun on the shores of California or in the sophisticated and swinging Empire State, with New York City leading the charge. Perhaps it would be seductive Miami, convinced that no one could walk around in bathing suits all the time without committing at least a little bit of sodomy. But it wasn't any of these cosmopolitan meccas, it was the humble Land of Lincoln – Illinois.

Illinois did not exactly set the prairie on fire with its progressive sexual stance. Nearly a decade ensued before other states followed, but they too might not be who you would think would be the ones to pick up the baton. Connecticut followed suit in 1971, followed by Colorado and Oregon in 1972. In 1973, Hawaii got bold, which is maybe understandable, but then they were followed by that sexual trail blazer, North Dakota. Go figure.

Where were those havens of iniquity throughout all of this? California did not repeal its sodomy law until 1976, New York had to have its law struck down in court in 1980, and Florida – well if you are committing sodomy in Florida, let's put it this way: you are wanted not only by your partner, but by the law. Sodomy is still illegal in the state of Florida. It kind of makes you wonder if all of those people in South Beach are voting. Still, the Illinois action was succeeded by several states that also repealed their sodomy laws. Today, many states have done so, but several still outlaw sexual activities defined as sodomy. Remarkably, some, as you will see, exempt married couples, some only refer to gay couples, and some just outlaw it no matter who is doing it.

What the Supreme Court Says About Sodomy

In the 1980s, an opportunity presented itself to do away with sodomy statutes in the entire United States when the Supreme Court took under consideration a case brought by way of Georgia that challenged the constitutionality of that state's ban on sodomy. The case was called *Bowers v. Hardwick.*

Now you can't make this stuff up – the guy who was charged with sodomy was named Hardwick. Really. Georgia's sodomy law made it a criminal offense if you either performed or submitted to an act that involved the sex organs of one person and the mouth or anus of another. It was not limited to homosexuals who did this, but in fact, applied to heterosexuals as well. The punishment for this act in Georgia was imprisonment for a term that would be not less than one year, but not more than twenty! Yet despite the fact that the law was on the books, there had been no prosecution of the sodomy statute for several decades.

It seems that, one day, Michael Hardwick was at his home, enjoying consensual sexual relations with another individual, who also happened to be a man. This sounds like something that perhaps happens every day in every state of the United States. It also sounds like a perfectly logical place for it to be happening. He was not at a rest stop or a park; he was in his bedroom. Unfortunately, his driving skills seemed to lack the same finesse as his sex life, and an officer of the law happened to arrive at his door to serve him with a traffic violation warrant during the time of the sexual liaison. As a result, the officer serving the traffic violation happened to notice that Mr. Hardwick was in the middle of another kind of violation – that of the Georgia sodomy statute. This resulted in his placing Mr. Hardwick under arrest, not only for poor driving, but for committing acts in violation of the sodomy statute of the state. Instead of finding himself on his way to traffic court, Mr. Hardwick found himself on his way to the Supreme Court.

Believe it or not, that is what happened. It took years, of course. The alleged incident occurred in 1982, but Mr. Hardwick did not see the Supremes until

1986. Mr. Hardwick challenged the law in Georgia and the court he went to found it constitutional and enforceable. He then appealed, and that court determined that Mr. Hardwick was right and that the sodomy statute violated his fundamental rights. That moved the discussion to the nation's highest court – the Supremes.

This was important, because Mr. Hardwick was claiming that the United States Constitution offered him a right of privacy that was necessarily violated when people passed laws saying what he could and could not do in his bedroom. Americans, it was argued, have a right to expect privacy from government intrusion into the most intimate aspects of their lives, and one of those aspects is sex. Sodomy, whether the gay kind or the straight kind, fell into this zone of privacy. His argument was, in essence, that it was unlawful under the United States Constitution for states to pass such laws.

But when the Supremes got this case, they stated that they were only going to address the issue of homosexual sodomy under the Georgia statute, and not any other kind of sodomy (presumably heterosexual). They limited their decision because it was homosexual sodomy in which Mr. Hardwick was engaged at the time of his arrest. Therefore, they would decide the case as to whether the Constitution of the United States conferred a right on an individual to have this sort of sex in his own bedroom. This was just silly. In the dissenting opinion, Justice Blackmun wrote that the claim that the statute is a violation of the right to privacy is not dependent on Mr. Hardwick's sexual orientation. The case, they said, was about whether he had a right to intimate association, regardless of who it is with and who he is. But the majority of the Supremes decided that the case would only apply to whether homosexuals had this right. And to find that there was such a right "invalidates the laws of the many States that still make such conduct illegal and have done so for a very long time." They would decide, in a 5–4 decision, that in fact the Constitution does not give you the right to make love to anyone you desire in the confines of your own bedroom. To get to this point, the Supremes had to torture logic.

The Constitution, through the Fifth and Fourteenth Amendments, has been interpreted to give people a right to privacy in leading their lives. This right to privacy, for example, protects you if you want to have children, get married, not have children, not get married, whether you take contraception, etc. In other words, these articles of the constitution are deemed to give you the ability to pursue life, liberty, and happiness in your own way and to allow you to make private decisions about the way you run your life.

However, when it came to considering whether you have the right to commit sodomy in the confines of your own bedroom, the court said that you do not, at least not homosexual sodomy. To justify this, they looked to the long tradition there has been in law to condemn acts of sodomy. One justice, used some of the more colorful references: "a heinous act," "a disgrace to human nature." The majority opinion went to lengths to mention that sodomy was illegal in all of the thirteen colonies when they ratified the Constitution, thereby implying that the right to privacy sought could not have existed as far as sodomy went.

Of course, it bears noting that at the time of ratifying the Constitution, people in the colonies also *owned* other people, in an institution known as slavery – an institution that also had ancient roots and basis in law. It is difficult to see the logic of the Supremes.

With respect to your privacy, the Court said they had to draw a line. After all, they said, if you take the position that the law can never follow a person into the bedroom, then how could the law justifiably outlaw the use of drugs, firearms, or possession of stolen goods? What drugs, firearms or stolen goods have to do with making love to someone in your own bedroom is not explained by the Supremes. They sort of realized that, so they went on to say that even if you only considered sexual consensual acts, the state still had a right to enter your bedroom to prohibit certain acts – incest and adultery to name a few. Therefore, the court concluded the state does have a right to proscribe acts in the bedroom, and there is no fundamental right to privacy in this regard in the Constitution.

Despite this decision by the Supremes, it is a safe bet that there is no less oral sex occurring now than when the gavel came down on this decision. However, as was evidenced by the fact that the Supremes were not of one mind themselves by reason of their 5–4 vote, this is an issue that continues to resonate, and sodomy statutes continue to be challenged. In fact, the Georgia sodomy statute, the same one under which Mr. Hardwick was arrested, was declared not in keeping with the constitution of the state of Georgia by the Georgia Supremes.

The *Hardwick* case might have been the last word on the subject, until one day when the police came across a same-sex couple in Texas were engaged in sexual acts deemed no appropriate by the Texas sodomy statute. Texas is one of the states that outlaws only same-sex sodomy, not heterosexual sodomy. The police entered the home of one of the men on a false tip regarding matters unrelated to sodomy. When they came into the bedroom, they arrested the couple, who were charged and fined. Their conviction was challenged by the Lambda Legal Defense and Education Fund. In December, 2002, the Supremes said they would hear the case, presenting a second opportunity to overturn the case. There are two means to do so. One is whether the court accepts the argument that this is an invasion of privacy. If they do that, it may be possible that every sodomy statute in the nation would be deemed unconstitutional. However, they may overturn the conviction by accepting the argument that the application of the Texas law to homosexuals only deprives a class of people from equal access to the law. Or, as surprising and illogical as it would seem, they may uphold the Texas law, just as they upheld the Georgia law in *Hardwick*.

Current Events – Sodomy Laws and Their Impact

Why Do Sodomy Laws Still Exist?

With the end of federal hope, lawyers began to focus their sights on the states themselves. While the federal Constitution was said not to ensure privacy, that might not be true in some of the state constitutions. In Tennessee and Arkansas, lawyers argued that the state constitution itself did not permit the passage of such laws. In this way, they did not need to talk about whether it was legal or not under the U.S. Constitution. Many of these state challenges were successful and began to make a big difference. While the Hardwick case would have done away with sodomy statutes everywhere, now it is a series of state by state battles. Success is not always guaranteed. A recent court challenge to overturn the Virginia statute did not succeed. And so, in many places, sodomy statutes still exist, and your acts of sex may be against the law.

The fact that making love in your own home may, in fact, be illegal in your state may come as something of a surprise to you. You may stop and ask yourself the question, "If oral sex is legal in the White House, why not in my house?"

Most people aren't aware of sodomy statutes, because they don't perceive that they directly affect their lives. In fact, most people probably don't even know they exist. After all, any reasonable, bright, and intelligent person would tell you that in America, the law has no business in your bedroom, wouldn't they? And even if you are aware of the fact that they exist, has the existence of a sodomy law in your state ever acted as a deterrent? When was the last time you were on a romantic vacation and, gripped in the arms of passion, stopped to ask yourself, "Is it legal to do this in this state?" Your answer is probably "never." And it probably never will be. So why then are there sodomy statutes, and why do we even care?

The real use of sodomy laws has very little to do with what two consenting adults do in their bedroom – at least when it comes to using those laws to prosecute people. So if sodomy laws aren't used to prosecute gays and lesbians in their bedrooms, what are they used for?

First, remember that the term sodomy is not limited to sex between two people who are of the same gender. Legal sodomy definitions often include any sexual contact that includes oral or anal sex – between gay people or straight people; it doesn't matter. However, there are some states that have limited the definition of sodomy to refer only to sex between people of the same gender. Second, another aspect to sodomy is that not all acts of sodomy are consensual. Therefore, the existence of sodomy statutes allows a prosecutor to press additional charges against an individual who has committed forcible sexual acts. In other words, a defendant might be charged not only with rape, but with forcible sodomy as well, even though these laws, according to experts, are enforced on a spotty basis. And even if the evidence does not support a conviction for forcible sodomy, there may be a conviction for consensual sodomy.

Whether or not sodomy statutes are enforced in the bedrooms of lesbians and gays, there is another point to be made with respect to their existence. For gays and lesbians, the only way to express their love for another person is by breaking these laws. Heterosexual people, if so minded, can choose never to commit sodomy. Gays and lesbians only have that choice if their choice is celibacy. In reality, sodomy statutes are more than an inconvenience.

How Sodomy Laws Affect the Lives of Lesbians and Gays

In practice, these statutes are rarely enforced. They are a little like the prohibition you see on your pillows when you purchase them – that removal of the tags from your pillows is against the law. It's not like there are pillow police going around to make sure that those tags were on your pillows when you bought them. They also aren't checking to see that what you are doing while you are using that pillow is against the sex laws of the state. It does make one wonder under what circumstances people find themselves being charged with sodomy crimes.

Unfortunately, as we have seen, for a number of reasons, sodomy statutes are a lot more serious than the pillow-tag laws. Every so often, someone does get arrested for sodomy or solicitation to commit sodomy, and when they do, there is an opportunity to challenge the statute's validity in court.

Though they are not generally enforced against gays or lesbians in their homes for consensual sexual acts between adults, they can be and have been. For some, sodomy statutes can even be a tragedy. A closeted person who is arrested on a sodomy or solicitation charge may be effectively outed in a way that will damage him or her for life. Perhaps those who favor forced outing are not saddened by the notion, but it is unfortunate when an arm of the state is involved in the adventure of outing gay citizens who would rather remain in the closet, for whatever reasons.

Sodomy statutes tell an entire class of people that they are "dirty" in the eyes of the law. They institutionalize the notion that there is something wrong and inherently unseemly about homosexuals.

There is another very damaging aspect to sodomy statutes. Though it may not be immediately apparent, sodomy statutes can inhibit people from taking advantage of important laws that are designed to protect their well being. For example, a lesbian who is beaten in an episode of domestic violence or a gay man who is being stalked by another man may feel disinclined by sodomy statutes to call the police and avail themselves of the laws against domestic abuse and stalking. The laws that are there to protect all in effect may only protect heterosexuals, because homosexuals are too afraid to use the laws and out themselves in front of the police.

It is not merely the fact that the laws intimidate people; they can be used by courts against people when other legal issues, such as child custody, are under consideration. A lesbian or gay parent may find that the court does not want to award custody, or severely limits it, because the gay or lesbian parent is actually considered to be a felon under a particular state's law. Every gay man and lesbian woman is considered a criminal in the eyes of the law of any state with a sodomy statute. That status – that of a criminal – can then be used as a wedge to deprive a gay person of other rights. The statutes have been used as an excuse to deprive people of their desire to serve as a foster parent or as a reason to offer employment.

Lastly, sodomy laws affect the lives of lesbians and gays in another way – one that has nothing to do with the law. Acts of sodomy are the only ways that gays and lesbians have to make love with the most important people in their lives. By declaring that love illegal, whether or not it is enforced in the bedroom, the law says that you are, by your very nature, a second class citizen. It is an institutionalized way to say the lives of gay and lesbian Americans some how count for less than do heterosexual lives, and that you are, in fact, not equal. Sodomy statutes, joke that they are, are no laughing matter.

State Laws Against Sodomy

It is important to note that some of the states have statutes that are gay/lesbian specific. On its face that strikes one as necessarily discriminating – picking out one group of people and making their sexual activities illegal. Today, only a handful of states have gay-specific statutes. However, even in those with statutes that are generically written to cover heterosexuals as well (Georgia had one), it is clear that prosecutions would be primarily aimed at homosexuals. In the *Hardwick* case, the state of Georgia readily admitted that. This would necessarily mean that the state would be guilty of selective prosecution of the law, which could make it inherently unethical.

Of the fewer and fewer states that still have sodomy statutes on the books, the penalties for a conviction are as varied as the states themselves. Needless to say, no state still lists it as a capital offense, though in some foreign countries, it could be. The Georgia statute allowed for imprisonment that was not less than one nor more than twenty years. Other states allow a year as the maximum, and still others punish it merely with a fine (in Texas, $200).

Except for the rare circumstances noted in the recent Texas sodomy case that is going before the Supreme Court in 2003, there is no cadre of bedroom police crashing into the homes of individuals to determine whether the inhabitants are engaging in unlawful forms of oral and anal sex. However, if an individual is arrested in connection with another crime, such as solicitation, public lewdness, indecent exposure, or public sexual indecency, or any act in which a person is discovered to be having sex in a public place, then a prosecutor may want to prosecute not only for the violation of that law, but for the violation of a sodomy statute as well.

State Laws Repealed through Legislative Action

Alaska (1980)	Iowa (1978)	Oregon (1972)
California (1976)	Maine (1976)	Rhode Island (1998)
Colorado (1972)	Missouri (1999)	South Dakota (1977)
Connecticut (1971)	Nebraska (1993)	Vermont (1977)
Delaware (1973)	Nevada (1993)	Washington (1976)
District of Columbia (1993)	New Hampshire (1975)	West Virginia (1976)
Hawaii (1973)	New Jersey (1979)	Wisconsin (1983)
Illinois (1962)	New Mexico (1975)	Wyoming (1977)
Indiana (1977)	North Dakota (1973)	
	Ohio (1974)	

Source: American Civil Liberties Union
www.aclu.org/issues/gay/sodomy.html

State Sodomy Laws Invalidated by Court Action

Arkansas	Maryland	New York
Georgia	Minnesota	Pennsylvania*
Kentucky	Montana	Tennessee

*The state legislature later repealed the law in 1995

Existing Same-Sex Laws – States with Sodomy Laws Targeting Only Same-Sex Acts

Kansas
Oklahoma
Texas

SOURCE: American Civil Liberties Union
www.aclu.org/issues/gay/sodomy.html

Existing Same-Sex and Opposite-Sex Laws

Alabama	Louisiana	North Carolina	Virginia
Florida	Minnesota	South Carolina	
Idaho	Mississippi	Utah	

States with HIV Criminalization Statutes

Alabama	Kansas	North Dakota
Arkansas	Kentucky	Ohio
California	Louisiana	Oklahoma
Colorado	Maryland	Pennsylvania
Florida	Michigan	South Carolina
Georgia	Missouri	Tennessee
Idaho	Montana	Utah
Illinois	Nevada	Virginia
Indiana	New Jersey	Wisconsin

SOURCE: Lambda Legal Defense and Education Fund

Entrapment

It is impossible to consider the effects of sodomy statutes without talking about entrapment. This is a delicate situation, and one that is sometimes difficult to understand for a person who is not steeped in the sometimes meandering logic of the law.

There are other laws, in addition to sodomy statutes, that you may be breaking if you are someone who is inclined to having sex in public places. For example, you can be arrested on solicitation charges. In other words, it is alleged that you ask another person, who just so happens to be an undercover police officer, to engage in an act that is a felony. If you are in a state with a sodomy law, you might be charged with asking that person to commit sodomy, but if you are instead suggesting sex in a public place, then that is the law that you are seeking to break. There are laws against sex in public places. Sex in public is not legal anywhere.

The public policy against sex in public is used as a basis for police undercover activities to try to prevent it. Parks, public restrooms, and any popular outdoor cruising spot are the venues for those activities. If there are complaints from the public about a particular venue, police may set up an undercover operation to try to discourage it. That is one side of it. On the other side, however, are efforts that may go beyond that type of law enforcement.

In 1999 the Michigan Triangle Foundation released a report reflecting police activity in that state that was aimed at the arrest of gay men under circumstances that are difficult to comprehend today. They describe police officers going to "cruising" spots and flirting with gay men who, when the notion of sex is broached, arrest their suitors for breaking laws against solicitation or for disorderly conduct. According the Triangle Foundation, these practices are known as "Bag a Fag" activities. The report describes frequent efforts by the police in this regard, even extending to venues such as gay bars, with police justifying these actions by stating that they are responding to citizen complaints regarding public sexual activity. The foundation reports that many individuals who did nothing more than talk about having sex with another adult are fined, suffer the impoundment of their automobiles, and must pay probationary supervision fees or other costs. In 2002, the Detroit City Council was reported to have approved a settlement brought on behalf of men arrested for violating an ordinance that, while designed to deter lewd public behavior, was allegedly used by police to entrap gay men who were reportedly flirting or even sitting and talking in a car.

Perhaps the most well-known entrapment case occurred in 1998 in Beverly Hills, California, and involved singer George Michael. He was arrested in a restroom in a park where, apparently, things got a little frisky. The incidents in the Triangle report describe just that sort of thing, except no one makes music videos about them afterward.

But is this what entrapment really means?

Entrapment is not about a cop flirting with you and you grabbing him, if you were so inclined, first. Instead, entrapment is when a police officer actually originates the crime – persuading you to do something that you were not otherwise inclined to do.

What would George Michael say to that? If a man enters a public restroom and encounters another man who flirts with him and there is a response by the soon-to-be defendant, who began the crime? Well, that would not be entrapment in the eyes of the law. That's not the way it works, explains Sam Garrison.

Samuel A. Garrison III is an attorney in Roanoke, Virginia, where he has a practice that deals in criminal, traffic, and family law, as well as an assortment of other cases. In his earlier career, he served counsel to Vice President Spiro

Agnew, as well as a liaison to members of the House of Representatives. Later, he was chief minority counsel for the Presidential Impeachment Inquiry for the Judiciary Committee of the House of Representatives. What could he possibly have to say about sodomy laws? Plenty – he brought the most recent challenge to the sodomy laws of the Commonwealth of Virginia.

"It may be true that the defendant was not intending to have sex, but if he were there with that in mind, then he has not been entrapped," Garrison says. "If he was there looking for sex and hoping that something might develop, the officer only provides the opportunity, but did not cause the defendant to commit the crime." In other words, it would be perceived by the law that you went into the notorious restroom pre-disposed to the notion that if you found a sexual opportunity, you would take advantage of it. It would be a difficult matter to dispute, and in fact, if you claim in a court of law that you have been entrapped, according to Sam Garrison, you are not likely to prevail.

Sex and the Internet – E-trapment. The Internet has brought many changes in the way we do things – developments that were previously unimagined. You can type in the address of where you want to go and instantly receive directions, whether you are driving three miles or 3,000. You can shop with the entire world as your catalog and have the merchandise delivered to your home the next day.

You can attend classes, join support groups, or find people to "chat" with whom you will never see. Some will join a chat room that is somewhat general, based on one's geography or some other interest. Some of those interests can be sexual. Some of those sexual interests can be very specific. "Men 4 Men Big Feet." "Women 4 Women in Chains." You get the idea. The Internet has provided a way for people to reach out and find many others of similar interests. People sometimes end up meeting in person; they date and some even end up in life-long relationships. Others end up in jail.

The relative anonymity of Internet chat rooms allows some people who are shy by nature to talk with others in a way that they might not otherwise be able to. But that anonymity is a two-sided coin. The other side allows people who have sexually predatory instincts to pursue sexual contact with minors. It is not only an amazingly selfish activity on the part of any adult, it is also very much against the law. Soliciting a minor to have sex, to meet for sexual relations, or to pose for pornography is illegal. This is of course true if one is doing this in person, but if one is doing this over the Internet, you are not only breaking the law, you are providing the evidence of it. It is sort of like the Watergate school of thought regarding the commission of a crime – let's talk about doing a whole bunch of illegal things *and* let's make a recording of it! No one will ever know!

Well, not exactly. The Internet is only somewhat private. The fact that you are sitting in your own home, or office when you are chatting doesn't really translate to an act that would occur in your own home because you are communicating in a public forum.

There is an even greater risk. In your efforts, you may find that the person you think you have been talking to is not, in fact, the person you have been talking to. Anyone who's ever gone on a blind date has learned this hard lesson. But here, instead of soliciting a minor, which is creepy in and of itself, you may be soliciting a major legal problem when you find out that the person on the other end of the ether is a police officer posing as a teenager. If you ask this police officer to meet you, chances are he will not stand you up. You may not, however, enjoy the date. You will find that you have broken several laws that can, and quite possibly may, result in jail time. This is true in all states, though the number of laws you have broken and the penalties will vary. For example, in states where there are sodomy laws, there may also be laws prohibiting the solicitation of sodomy.

Remember, the fact that you did not have sex does not mean that there wasn't a crime, and the fact that there was no teenager does not mean that you have been entrapped. If you went into a chat room looking to pick up a teen and thought you did, then you are likely without a defense of entrapment, or rather "e-trapment."

If You Are Arrested

What would you do if it happened to you? A man in a bathroom flirts with you, and you respond without thinking. We'll forget for the moment about calling you a slut; what would happen if some handcuffs then came out? Depending on your proclivities, it might excite you more. But if it is followed by a badge and a reading of rights, you are bound to feel a little less enthusiastic. Have you committed a crime? Would you have committed the crime if the police officer hadn't been there? The answer is, of course, no. But if you invited him to have public sex and he did not invite you, then you may have a problem.

It is not always that simple. What if the undercover agent is the first to approach the topic of sex? That may not be enough to protect you from the charges. You would probably have to demonstrate that the police officer was positively domineering in the situation – a circumstance that would be difficult to demonstrate. Police who work in this area may cross the line and be more than suggestive about a possible short-term relationship that will begin and end in a public place. Here the line gets very fine. The Triangle Foundation in their report certainly describes circumstances in which the suggestion does, in fact, seem to come from those working undercover.

If you find yourself in this situation – what do you do next?

Sam Garrison's advice starts out with that which you should *not* do. You should not run. Running away never solves any problem, but if you are in the process of being arrested, that can make matters worse, because you can be charged not only with the solicitation or sex charges, but with an attempted escape if you are caught.

Secondly, you should not talk. You should shut up until you have had access to your attorney. Getting chatty or argumentative or even trying to talk your way out of this can dig the hole you are in a little deeper. You are under an obligation to identify yourself, but whatever you do, don't discuss any of the facts. "Clam up," says Garrison. "You are obliged to identify yourself, but don't discuss any of the facts. You may find that there is a good defense, given how aggressive the police officer may have been in trying to get your guard down."

Third, get a lawyer, preferably one who is experienced.

Punishment and fines depend on the circumstances. It is not uncommon for persons to be charged with a misdemeanor and a fine, but more serious charges can be filed. However, if police are acting in an effort to "clean up" a public sex situation that they have deemed serious, or if there is a desire to truly persecute gay men, entrapment can provide a means for doing so and charges can escalate. It is not unheard of for people to have their cars impounded and for the nature of the charge to be made public, which in a small community can be devastating. It is a situation that evokes the need for the utmost caution.

Criminalization of HIV

The HIV epidemic has spawned more law than any other disease in history. As the epidemic spread across demographics and geographies, the law sought to keep up with it by anticipating situations and addressing them. As well, because the epidemic was so intimately connected to both sex and drugs, there were also expressions of indignation in the law. Perhaps nothing fans public indignation as much as the willful and knowing transmission of HIV from one person to another.

It is difficult to imagine circumstances by which one individual would knowingly and wantonly infect another human being with HIV. Sadly, not everyone lacks that imagination, resulting in a number of high profile cases in the media of people who, out of anger or carelessness, knowingly passed on their HIV infection to others.

Emotions on this issue run high. One man in New York was alleged to have engaged in unsafe sexual practices with as many as forty-eight women, several of whom subsequently tested HIV positive in a highly publicized case. As a result, many states passed statutes that made such transmission a crime – often a felony, punishable by imprisonment and/or a fine, though in some states it is a misdemeanor that incurs less punishment. Imprisonment can last from months to years.

It is not just about transmitting HIV through sex, but having HIV while you have sex. Some statutes are written in a way that state that it is not the transmission that is being punished, but the exposure to HIV. For example, the Arkansas statute punishes exposure and defines it as "an act of anal or vaginal intercourse, cunnilingus or fellatio, by a person with AIDS or who tests positive for HIV, without informing the other person of the presence of HIV."

Prosecutions do happen and they can have serious consequences. In South Dakota in 2002, two men were indicted with several counts of knowingly transmitting HIV. The charge is a felony, carrying up to a fifteen-year imprisonment and/or a $15,000 fine. Actual transmission of HIV is not required.

The statutes are sometimes aimed at other transmittable diseases besides HIV. The Virginia statute makes it a crime to transmit HIV as well as syphilis or hepatitis B. Older laws allowed civil actions where a person with a sexually transmitted disease knowingly acted in a manner that transmitted the disease. But with HIV, rather than civil penalties, or relying on existing criminal law to punish those who endangered others, HIV-specific statutes were enacted to exact criminal penalties that can be imposing. In other words, don't ask, don't tell is not a policy that you can incorporate into your sex life if you are a person with HIV.

There is also a possibility that one's HIV status may increase the penalty one may face if being tried for a sexually related crime. In California in November 2001, a man was convicted of attempting to arrange a sexual liaison with a minor, in addition to several other charges that were sexually motivated. When he was sentenced, his HIV status was taken into account and his sentence was considerably longer than that normally given a violator of the laws with which he was charged. While he did not have sexual relations with the minor, the prosecutor stated that the defendant had been intending to have unprotected sexual intercourse with the minor, thereby exposing the child to HIV.

HIV by itself is a "crime" – an insidious virus that has destroyed many lives. Society and the law have seen fit to punish the intentional transmission of the virus, but as this particular defendant found out, even the intent to have unsafe sex can be punished.

Whether such measures are necessary is up to debate. Existing laws that protect people against reckless endangerment should theoretically suffice to punish individuals who deliberately infect sexual or needle-sharing partners with HIV. Some of the statutes differentiate between acts that expose another individual to HIV and those that actually result in the transmission of the disease.

Future Directions – Will Sodomy Laws Stand?

The ability of the law to regulate sexual behavior is practically non-existent. However, the ability of the law to punish certain activities is very strong and will continue to be so as long as there is a public will to do so. For example, there is a strong public condemnation of people who knowingly transmit HIV to others, and statutes criminalizing sex for people with HIV will likely continue to be passed and enforced when egregious circumstances present themselves.

Public sex is illegal, and that isn't going to change. Police will enforce that law. However, in their zeal to enforce the law, gays can be unfairly targeted and subject to questionable police tactics. If that is the case, it is ideal if there exists an organization of concerned citizens who can address the situation in an effort to bring balance and to move both sides to the center of the discussion. The benefits of such interventions are enormous. If this can be accomplished it not only protects gay men, but can result in police departments becoming more sensitized to other issues that affect gays and lesbians, such as proper intervention in domestic disturbances and protection against hate crimes.

However, other sex laws may find their way into the history books.

For example, sodomy statutes are not here to stay. But they may not all go at once, and it will vary from state to state whether the love you make is against the law or not. While it is doubtful that this will be a factor for you should you fall in love, bear in mind that should you fall in lust, and should you do it in the wrong place, sodomy laws could still complicate matters for you considerably.

Public opinion has been ebbing away from the notion of gay sex being illegal. A historical overview of the relevant Gallup polls shows that, in 1977, there was an even divide among the general public. Then 43 percent feeling that homosexual relations should be illegal, 43 percent stating that it should be legal, and 14 percent expressing no opinion – presumably either not caring or not wanting to really think about it. By 1982, the number of people who thought it should be legalized grew by 2percent to 45 percent, with 39 percent saying it should be illegal. The explosion of the AIDS epidemic, however, and the looming public health threat seemingly posed by anyone who even looked like he (or she) might be gay brought about a reversal. A large number of people shifted from the undecided column toward embracing the belief that homosexual relations should be outlawed, with 44 percent saying they should be legal, 47 percent saying they should be illegal, and only 8 percent undecided. The following year, when the epidemic dominated newscasts and public hysteria reached a zenith, for the first time, a majority (54 percent) stated that gay sex should be illegal, and only 33 percent thought it should be legal, down 12 percent from just four years before. Those sentiments intensified in 1987, with 55 percent believing in outlawing sex between members of the same gender. However, in 1989, there was another flip-flop, and the number of people favoring in illegal status plunged almost 20 percent to 36 percent. However, it was not until February 1999 when the number of people who believed that there should not be legal constrictions on gay sex finally reached 50 percent – though still not a majority.

There may be a sense of complacency about the existence of laws that seem to make such a negligible difference in our day-to-day lives. But their very existence is testament to the continued stigmatization of the gay and lesbian community, and they provide the means for some of us, if not all of us, to be oppressed and to continue to be regarded as an amoral subculture.

From a broader perspective, surely no thoughtful American should view laws that deal with consensual adult activities of the bedroom as something that should be the subject of government regulation. There is no room for government in the bed of any American.

CHAPTER 9

No Kidding — Hate Crimes

History and Perspective – Can Feelings Be Legislated

IT COMES AS NO SHOCK to know that gays and lesbians are not a well-liked subculture. From the time a gay or lesbian boy or girl first begins to sense his or her difference, others sense it as well, and they begin to act on it. Anyone who grew up gay or lesbian remembers all to well what it meant – all of it was hurtful.

There was the name calling. Sissy or tom-boy when you were really little. Later, they took on a more serious nature – queer, dyke, faggot – and sometimes even a sexual overtone: cocksucker, muffdiver. Whatever the term, they all stood for the same thing. They were all meant to call out your difference, and they were all meant to belittle you. They were never, at least not until you grew up and were with friends, meant as an endearment. They were never words uttered sweetly, but they were usually shouted or yelled at you. They were used as a threat – to call you out on your difference and to show anger because of it. They were words meant to shame you.

Later, when you grew up, they lost some of their sting – maybe even all of it. And many of the people who used those words when they were young, would remember the moment with embarrassment. However, others would carry that behavior with them always – and would no longer use names, but act out on them, through vandalizing property, intimidating behaviors, assault and battery, and even murder.

When aimed at you, some states call these actions hate crimes and seek special punishment for them when they are committed. Other states don't call them anything at all. This chapter will discuss how hate crimes are used, what states have enacted them, and where you can get help if you are the victim of a hate crime.

What Is a Hate Crime?

Hate crimes have long been a factor in the history of humanity (irony intended) and in particular, in American society. There has been a long tradition in this country of people who are different not only being discriminated against, but also being singled out and hurt because of that difference. One could argue that the entire institution of slavery was one big organized hate crime. Lynchings brought to you by mob "justice" killed countless innocent African Americans after the Civil War. Race riots and gang rapes have been frequent and ugly elements of the nature of our society. At one point in American history, the United States government interned people based on their Japanese ethnic heritage as a security measure during World War II, which upon challenge was found to be constitutional by the Supremes. Many hate groups vent their disdain for various religions in our society. The existence of hate groups has proliferated in recent years, though the perpetrators of the vast majority of hate crimes do not belong to such groups.

Today, hate crimes against all types of people are common and are still the stuff of headlines. Hate crimes can be directed against property, such as the burning of a cross on a lawn or the destruction of a church by arson. Most hate crimes occur against a person. They are acts in which a victim is chosen for particular violent treatment, based on race, gender, religion, nationality, or sexual orientation. It is pretty clear what constitutes violent behavior. Every gay man or lesbian woman has at least once in his or her life feared being beaten up because of being gay. We are talking assault, battery, and even murder. If someone picked you out for being gay and then created a situation by which harm comes to you or your property, then it is a hate crime. It might be a cross burning on your lawn, it might be a noose dangling from broken furniture in your home, or it might be a beating after you've been tied to a fence post. That is what a hate crime is.

One thing that hate crimes are not – speech. When you are walking down the street with your girlfriend having a chat about your grocery list and some Neanderthal who walks with his knuckles scraping the ground yells out, "Hey Dykes!" it is not a hate crime. It is perhaps hateful behavior, but it is not against the law. If he gets another thought into his head and yells out, "I hate all queers," he again is letting people know that he is not an enlightened thinker, but he is not doing anything which could be considered by the law to be a hate crime. Let's say he goes further and yells out that he "wishes all dykes and fags would die of AIDS." He is merely letting us know that he does not wish to be on our Christmas card list – he is not breaking the law. Even if he is in the process of addressing a small group of similarly minded "people" like himself with a megaphone, and he says that he believes that people "should kill queers when they have the chance," he is merely exercising his right of free speech. If, on the other hand, he accompanies this series of verbal assaults with the hurling of a brick that hits you or even your car, he may have, depending on the state where you live, committed a hate crime. Speech alone can be hateful, but cannot be a hate crime. Speech coupled with action = hate crime. Across the United States, it is a scene that is played out for anyone who is "different" – African-Americans, Hispanics, Latinos, Asians and women.

If you have been involved in an incident that you believe is a hate crime, it may help you to look at it from the point of view of the police. You may feel that the incident had all the elements of a hate crime – but then, maybe not. Sometimes, not even the legal authorities are able to sort it out easily. In the autumn of 2002, authorities in Los Angeles had a difficult time coming to a decision in the case of an actor who was hugging a friend good night, when out of the dark, two men appeared with baseball bats who beat one of the men into a coma.

To help you out, the following chart is a checklist followed by the Washington, D.C., Metropolitan Police Department Gay and Lesbian Liaison Unit.

Checklist for Hate Crime Determination

- What are the perceptions of the victim(s) and witnesses about the motivation behind the crime?
- Were there any comments, gestures, or written statements by the perpetrator that reflect bias?
- Was the victim engaged in activities promoting his/her group or community at the time of the crime?
- Did the incident coincide with a holiday or date of significance to a particular group?
- Were there any differences between the perpetrator and victim, whether actual or simply perceived by the perpetrator?
- Have there been similar incidents in the same area that indicate a possible pattern?
- Did the incident occur in an area that has seen activity by organized hate groups?
- Is there an absence of any other motive, such as economic gain, that would explain why the crime was committed?

Recent Examples of Hate Crimes

Gays and lesbians have recently suffered a spate of hate crimes that have been shocking in their brutality and have raised the level of debate about the need for hate crime legislation.

A female-to-male transgender in Nebraska begins to live his life as a man. He dresses in men's clothing, cuts his hair short, and dates women. At a Christmas party he is "outed" and is discovered to have female organs by two men who then beat and rape him. Bleeding and injured, he reports the crime to the police. The rape is confirmed by medical examination. The questioning that is conducted by the sheriff immediately after the rape is accusatory and abusive. His two male attackers are not arrested but are made aware of the complaint. In fear of them, the victim does not return to his home, but stays with two friends. The attackers hunt him down and kill both him and his friends. His family then sues the county police for their failure to offer protection. As damages for her loss, the mother of the victim now must suffer the indignity of a damage award of zero. Fortunately, that is overturned on appeal. The county police officials are held by a unanimous Nebraska Supreme Court to be held liable. The victim's name was Teena Brandon, but he went by the name of Brandon Teena.

A diminutive young male student attending the University of Wyoming leaves a bar with two men one October night. They take him out to a lonely stretch of cold prairie and tie his hands to a fence post. As tears wash his bloody face, the two attackers pistol whip him with a .357-caliber revolver. They crack his skull. The next day he is found. Still alive, he is taken to a hospital where he is placed on life support. Five days after the beating, while still on life support, he dies. His attackers are arrested, and their families explain that they had been enraged when the young man made a homosexual pass at them. At the young man's funeral, a minister pickets carrying signs to remind the public that "God Hates Fags." The young man's name was Matthew Shepard.

Six months later, a shy man, too devoted to his parents to leave their small town in Alabama, is invited from a pool tournament to his death by two men. They had decided ahead of time that they would murder him. After beating him, they stuff him into the trunk of his own car and drive him out to a boat ramp, once the scene of river baptisms in a bygone era. There they beat him further with an axe handle and then slit his throat. They pour kerosene on some tires, set them on fire, and then throw his body on top, creating a pyre. For good measure, they burn his car as well. After their trial and conviction, one of the attackers states that he has repented for his sin since the murder. But their victim? Well, since he never got to repent, said the killer, he would be spending eternity burning in hell because he was a homosexual. The shy man's name was Billy Jack Gaither.

In Virginia, an ex marine by the name of Ronald Gay walks into a bar frequented by gay men and lesbian women in Roanoke and orders a beer. Then he takes out a revolver and beings shooting the patrons of he bar, killing a telephone operator named Danny Overstreet and injuring several other people in the bar. He says that he killed them because he didn't like the association of homosexuals with his last name – a circumstance that brought even more shame to him when three of his children legally changed their surname. When he is caught and brought before a judge, he has little to say and seems to have little remorse about his crime. "Yeah, I killed them," he said.

There are, of course, many, many others.

The crimes described here were not crimes of passion – they were not motivated by robbery or revenge. In each and every instance, the murderers were motivated by one simple drive: hatred. The hatred was not premised on something the victims did to their attackers; it was solely based on what the victims did with their own lives. They wanted to kill their victims, not because of what they did or what they knew, but simply because of who they were. They were gays, lesbians, bisexuals, and transgenders.

Current Events – It Ought to Be a Law

Each day, roughly four or five lesbian women or gay men are the victims of a hate crime in the United States. Over the past decade the rate of hate crimes against lesbians and gays has almost doubled. The Human Rights Campaign reports that FBI hate crimes statistics demonstrate that, in 1981, gay and lesbian hate crimes made up 8.9 percent of the hate crimes reported, but by 1999, that number nearly doubled, to 16.7 percent. Not only have gay and lesbian hate crimes doubled proportionally, but the number of crimes reported has also doubled, from 767 reported in 1992 to 1,317 reported in 1999.

One note about the statistics regarding hate crimes – for a number of reasons they are called into doubt as to whether they reflect reality. On the one hand, it is thought that there is a great deal of under-reporting, though others argue that gays and lesbians are more likely to report hate crimes than other groups. Tracking of hate crimes statistics only began in 1990 and the system is not perfect. A number of police departments that did not report them in the early 1990s are today reporting, thereby inflating the count. However, for anyone who has been the victim of a hate crime, or has watched with horror the most extreme cases we have seen in the news, one hate crime is one too many.

The Great Hate Debate – The Point of Hate Crime Legislation

In the minds of many, it is time for the victims of these crimes to receive something more than pity – they deserve legislation that would punish those who commit such crimes. They deserve to expect, some say, that the perpetrators of these crimes receive the sternest rebuke that society can hand them. Accordingly, many states have reacted by passing hate crimes legislation, which is sometimes inclusive of gays and lesbians and sometimes not. Some of the statutes offer enhanced criminal penalties, while others enhance civil lawsuits that support the victims in bringing suit against the person or persons who committed a hate crime. This type of legislation exists today in many states and the District of Columbia, and some include lesbians and gays specifically in their statutes.

But can hate crime legislation really make a difference? If Nebraska or Wyoming or Alabama or Virginia had hate crime legislation that punished the perpetrators of these crimes for what they have done, would any of their victims be alive today?[11] In fact, the criminals who committed these crimes are all serving time in jail. The men who killed Brandon Teena are in jail, one of them on death row until his execution was stayed in March 2000. Matthew Shepard's murderers, Aaron McKinney and Russell Henderson, both have life sentences without parole. The men who killed Billy Jack with rubber tires are both in prison, one of them making the statement that he'd have to get accustomed to "prison sex." The man named Gay who walked into the Roanoke bar and opened fire plead guilty to his crime and is in prison; he was given four life sentences for his crime. Once you have four life sentences, can you be punished any further and still be alive?

Would any of these criminals have thought differently if there had been a law saying that, should he act on his hatred, he would be severely punished? Can the passions of people be legislated? Can you enact laws to dispel hate? It would indeed be a comfort if you could simply legislate hate away and ensure that no one else joined Matthew Shepard, Billy Jack Gaither or Brandon Teena.

---

11. Nebraska does, in fact, have hate crime legislation that includes lesbians and gays. Wyoming has no hate crime legislation at all. Alabama and Virginia, while having enacted hate crime legislation, do not include lesbians and gays under its protection.

On the one hand, gays and lesbians would argue that it is important for society to condemn crimes based solely on hate as a matter of principle – that society must express its moral outrage at hate crimes through legislation. Unfortunately, this same argument can be applied by those who support anti-sodomy legislation – it may not be a deterrent, but it does express society's outrage for the homosexual "choice" of lifestyle. Is there a principle at stake? Can one legitimately propose hate crime legislation as a moral mandate while at the same time opposing sodomy statutes considered by others on the political spectrum to be a moral mandate as well? There are arguments on both sides of the fence.

The Case Against Legislation. Why would anyone be against making hate a crime? For some, the idea that a malicious crime – such as assault, battery, mayhem, or murder, becomes more of a crime simply because a person is motivated by hate, is a difficult concept. After all, no one goes up and murders a person motivated by love. Presumably, murder is most likely connected with a negative feeling. Therefore, how can you punish a wrongdoer any more sternly based on the motivation for the crime?

First, there are people who oppose any hate crime legislation based on broad principle. Then there are people who may in fact support hate crime legislation, but oppose the inclusion of gays and lesbians in the law. Those in the first camp would argue that there is no difference between a regular run of the mill crime and a hate crime – crime is crime whatever the motivation. The beliefs and even hatred of individuals will not be mitigated by legislation. Nor does hate crime legislation act as a deterrent. Further, there is a concern expressed that hate crime legislation does not punish the action, but rather punishes an individual for his beliefs, not his actions.

Proof of a crime is in the evidence. The evidence of a hate crime is not usually the physical part; the evidence is usually speech that accompanies the crime. Proof of the "hate" in the crime necessarily involves statements and actions of the person who committed the crime. Therefore, if you punish the criminal for those statements, you are infringing on their free speech and right to association. If I hit you because I disagree with you, I can be punished for hitting you, but how can you punish me for disagreeing with you?

Then there are the opponents who cling to more narrow principles: first, that gays and lesbians who are victims of crime do not deserve the law's special protection – all victims of crime are created equal. Why should a criminal receive greater punishment for shooting someone because they are gay than for shooting someone to steal a wallet? Opponents of hate crime legislation would argue that such laws elevate gays and lesbians as victims giving them more protection than other victims, which is unwarranted, and that all people under the eyes of the law are equal and under the Constitution are afforded equal protection under the laws.

Secondly, there are some who feel that to offer the sanction of a law to protect gays and lesbians in fact also offers sanction to the lifestyle of gays and lesbians. It is an argument heard in connection with any legislation that mentions lesbians and gays – that the state cannot offer an endorsement of the lesbian or gay lifestyle. It is difficult to get this group to see past this tortured logic to the perhaps unintended effect of their position. In the case of hate crimes, this would mean that it is a better influence on youth to see that people can commit a crime based on bigotry and that the law will treat them the same as any other criminal than it is to consider that gays and lesbians be accepted as a part of our society.

The case for legislation. Many people feel that the laws of society should be reflect the values of that society and that where a government fails to enact laws, it sends a message. For proponents of hate crime legislation, enactment of such laws is an important expression of society's moral outrage. Society, it is felt, must respond when someone becomes a target for violent crime merely on the basis of their identity. Hate crimes stand apart from other crimes because of the motivation. None of the killers described in this chapter – the ones who killed Brandon Teena, the patrons of the gay bar in Roanoke, and Mathew Shepard – were motivated by greed or avarice. They were motivated by hate. They picked their victims solely because of their identities. And while there are laws to punish them for the acts they committed, there should also be laws that punish them, not for their hateful thoughts, but for expressing those hateful thoughts through harmful actions. Hate crime legislation is not an attempt at creating thought police, but rather is aimed at assuring the targets of hate crimes that the state does not sanction their victimization, even though, in cases involving murder, laws don't really help a dead victim at all, they will help survivors as well as families.

National Gay and Lesbian Task Force former Executive Director Lorri Jean admits that dead is dead: "Whether it is a random drive-by shooting, or the murder of a man because he is gay, the end result is that both of them are dead." Why then do we need hate crime legislation? Because "an antigay hate crime has the impact, if not the intent, of terrorizing a whole group of people. We have all experienced that fear at one time or another – the fear of being beaten up or hurt because of who we love." That, in the final analysis, may be one of the most important arguments for hate crime legislation. No civilized society should sanction, through its lack of legislation, that sort of terrorism.

According to recent Gallup polls, a large majority of Americans favor hate crime legislation at the state level, and three-fourths of those who do, favor the explicit mention of lesbians and gays as well as other minorities.

Does hate crime legislation inhibit free speech? The Supreme Court was polled on this issue when a case came before it in 1993. A man who committed assault and battery was given an enhanced sentence because he chose his victim, who was otherwise unknown to him, simply on the basis of race. He appealed this sentence, stating that the statute infringed upon his free speech and punished not the deed, but his thought. While the state court agreed with him, when the matter got to the Supremes they were unambiguous. In a unanimous decision, they cited the fact that many criminal statutes already provide enhanced punishment based on the intent of the criminal and that this has been long-established in American law. Intent is always a factor in determining the degree to which a person might be guilty of crime. While you cannot punish a person for their beliefs, they said, you can punish a person whose illegal act is motivated by those beliefs. "[T]he Constitution does not erect a per se barrier to the admission of evidence concerning one's beliefs and associations at sentencing simply because they are protected by the First Amendment," said the Supremes. Further, they could not see that one's free speech or ability to hold such beliefs would be chilled by allowing for enhanced punishment for action based on those beliefs.

In Defense of Hate – The Gay Panic Defense

Speaking of intent, what was the intent of the victim? Often when it comes to defending oneself against charges in a hate crime against gays, lesbians, bisexuals, or transgenders, the guilty party seeks to absolve himself of guilt by claiming that the victim had intended to seduce him. Assume, for the sake of argument, that even if this were true, it would be sufficient reason to beat or even kill someone. How many straight men each day make unwanted and unwelcome advances at straight women? Imagine if those women had the right and the ability to beat the crap out of every man who did that?

The relatives of Mathew Shepard's murderers said that Matthew made a pass at them. Billy Jack Gaither's murderers said that he used to talk to them in a suggestive manner. Is there a mitigating circumstance involved if a homosexual makes a pass at a heterosexual – in other words, if a pass is made, is murder somehow a little justified?

Of the people known to commit hate crimes, nearly four-fifths of them are male, according to the National Center for Crime Victims. When the hate crime involves a gay man, a common defense asserted by the murderers is called the "gay panic" defense. According to this doctrine, the perpetrator of the crime is instead himself the victim. The other victim (the one lying dead or hurt) was himself the perpetrator. In other words, the gay guy made a pass at the straight guy, and so the straight guy, being very sensitive to that as a result of some past experience, overreacted and just sort of lost it and killed the gay guy. If that is hard to imagine, think back to 1995, when the *Jenny Jones* talk show taped a show about crushes. A young gay man named Scott revealed to the audience that he had a crush on his neighbor, Jonathan. The show had not aired when a few days later, Jonathan thanked Scott by taking a gun to his apartment and shooting him to death. He said that he was so mortified by the implication that he could be attractive to a gay man, and that it was blurted out on national television, that even after a few days to assess the situation, he felt compelled to commit the crime.

He tried to assert the gay panic defense, plus mental instability, and his defense even tried to paint the victim as a stalker, but it didn't work out. In 1996 the killer was found guilty and received the maximum sentence for second degree murder, which was twenty-five to fifty years in prison. The case was overturned on appeal in 1998, but in August 1999 there was a retrial, during which it was again emphasized how humiliated the murderer had been. The jury returned the same verdict in just three hours and the killer got the same sentence.

In fact, while that type of result is increasingly the case, it wasn't always true. Gay panic has been successfully used as a mitigating factor in cases involving the beating or murder of gay men. Happily, the success of those who seek to assert such a defense is less and less likely. Fewer courts are buying it, and it is technically a difficult defense to assert.

When Aaron McKinney, one of the murderers of Matthew Shepard tried to assert a "rage" defense, it was rebuffed, because the court did not see "homosexual rage syndrome" as fitting within the construct of an insanity defense.

The State of Hate – Where Is It Illegal?

Less than six months after the death of Matthew Shepard, the Wyoming legislature also killed – but their victim was a proposed hate crimes bill for their state. It was perhaps a very tragic punctuation to the death of Billy Jack Gaither in Alabama, when, in the wake of his violent death, a proposal was introduced in that state to add gays to the hate crime statute but was defeated by a vote of that state's legislature. In other words, the state is saying that, while there should be legislation that condemns biased crimes committed against people for their race or religion, it is OK to commit a hate based crime against a gay person.

Where hate crime legislation does exist, it can vary greatly in the way that it is enforced. In the first place, as stated, some states have hate crime legislation but do not include lesbians and gays nor gender identity. As well, there can be differences regarding whether the statute addresses civil or criminal matters. Some of the states with hate crime legislation enacted it for the purpose of enhancing criminal statutes. This means that the sentence of the criminal is lengthened, parole considerations are different, or the degree of the crime inflates. However, other states only provide for civil relief, meaning that there is no enhanced criminal penalty for the crime, only the penalty already in place for committing the crime. The civil provision, however, allows the victim support should he or she decide to sue the perp. Lastly, there can be differences among the states, as to what defines a hate crime – for some states it is merely picking out a person because of their differences and doing violence to their person or property. However, there are a few states where the act of violence against the person must have occurred in such a way that it interferes with the exercise of a federally guaranteed right – the right to vote, for example.

Over half of the states have enacted laws that include lesbians and gays in their definition of hate crimes, including four (and the District of Columbia) that have included gender identity in their list of hate crimes.

Current federal hate crimes law does not cover lesbians and gays, except to the extent that the Hate Crimes Statistic Act requires that the Department of Justice track crimes against lesbians and gays. While there is a federal hate crimes statute, like many of its state counterparts, it does not cover lesbians and gays. Nor, for that matter, does it cover gender or disability – it only covers race, religion, and ethnicity. During July 2000, however, there were signs that the federal outlook on hate crimes might change. When the Senate leadership switched from the Republican side of the aisle, legislation entitled the Local Law Enforcement Enhancement Act of 2001 received a positive vote from the Senate Judiciary Committee, enhancing its chances of seeing a floor vote. If passed, the legislation would allow the federal government to assist local governments in prosecuting hate crimes, or if local government refuse to enforce laws, the feds can come in and do the job.

States with No Hate Crime Legislation

Arkansas	New Mexico
Hawaii	South Carolina
Indiana	Wyoming

States with Legislation Not Including Sexual Orientation

Alabama	Mississippi	Pennsylvania
Alaska	Montana	South Dakota
Colorado	North Carolina	Virginia
Idaho	North Dakota	West Virginia
Maryland	Ohio	
Michigan	Oklahoma	

States with Legislation Including Sexual Orientation

Arizona	Kentucky	New York
Connecticut	Louisiana	Nevada
Delaware	Maine	Oklahoma
Florida	Massachusetts	Oregon
Iowa	Nebraska	Tennessee
Illinois	New Hampshire	Washington
Kansas	New Jersey	Wisconsin

States with Legislation Including Both Sexual Orientation and Gender Identity

California
District of Columbia
Minnesota
Missouri
Vermont

States with Legislation Motivated by Prejudice, but Without Categories of Bias

Georgia
Texas
Utah

States Offering Support for Civil Action

Arkansas	Louisiana	Oklahoma
California	Massachusetts	Oregon
Colorado	Michigan	Pennsylvania
Connecticut	Minnesota	Rhode Island
District of Columbia	Missouri	South Dakota
Florida	Nebraska	Tennessee
Idaho	Nevada	Vermont
Illinois	New Jersey	Virginia
Iowa	Ohio	Washington

SOURCE: Human Rights Campaign

What To Do If You Are a Victim

In each of the cases described at the beginning of this chapter, men were motivated by their hate to harm and destroy other individuals. However, the victimization did not necessarily stop with the beatings and murders. First there is the crime itself, the murder, the rape, the torture. Then there are the crimes that come after that: the insensitive police, the bigoted clergy, the misguided notions of repentance, insensitive juries, deaf legislatures. The system lets many hate crime victims down after the crime in ways that are, at the very least, insulting, and at the very worst (as in the case of Brandon Teena) fatal. In other words, the hate does not stop with the crime. Hate is an every-day part of the lesbian and gay life.

The point is made because if you have been the victim of a crime, you may have several options to consider. One of them is to do nothing. That sounds like a bad joke, but it isn't – doing nothing is a serious option. Reporting a crime necessarily means that you are going to have to deal with the police and you are going to have to be open with them about who you are, what happened to you, and why it happened. For some people, that may be a very rigorous proposition, while for others, it isn't even a consideration. Only you can decide where you are on the scale, and it is probably not something you can decide ahead of time, but only when you actually have to make a decision. The system may serve to extend your victimization rather than to extinguish it.

In addition, there are also psychological considerations. The crime is probably something you would like to forget rather than live out over and over again. You may fear retaliation. The nature of the crime, being one that is aimed at who you are, is naturally one that is taken more personally than other types of crime. You will recover from a car theft much easier than you would from being beaten while being called "dyke" or "faggot."

Lastly, you may not be out. While there are gay activists who feel that everyone should be out whether they want to be or not, that may be a consideration for you.

Ideally, reporting the crime need not be anyone else's business, but in reality, that is not likely. If Billy Jack Gaither had lived and reported his crime as a hate crime, he would have had to come out to his parents, which he had not done. Whatever positions activists take, it is your decision, not someone else's.

For these reasons, if you are the victim of a crime, then you may elect to do nothing. Don't fault yourself or let others fault you for your choice – it is, after all, your choice and your life, and you should not feel compelled to report the crime simply because others may want you to. If you are not comfortable reporting it, there is no point in forcing yourself and victimizing yourself even further.

That being said, while it is an option, it is not a recommendation. The people who victimized you will not be punished if you do not report the crime. In addition, in each of the hate crimes described in the opening pages of this chapter, all of the criminals are behind bars. It is highly unlikely that any of them will ever again perpetrate a hate crime, at least not one that is outside of prison walls. One obvious reason to report therefore, is to punish.

Psychologically, it could benefit you. Reporting the crime may make you feel better – less like a victim and more like you are asserting some control over the situation. Reporting the crime may be saving someone else's life. Reporting the crime says that you simply are not going to take it.

If the crime is reported, it is also then counted as a statistic. While no one wants their experience reduced to a statistic, together, the statistics paint a picture of hate crimes against lesbian and gays that will serve to help in the development of sounder public policy and stronger protections.

On the very practical side, reporting the crime may be necessary if you are going to avail yourself of the considerable amount of help that may be out there for you, because when you are the victim of a crime, there are resources to which you can turn. Several states have funds that have been set up for the victims of crime to assist them in their efforts to recover. In the 1980s, Congress enacted the Victims of Crimes Act of 1984 (VOCA). This act directed that federal funding should be set aside for states to access in order to assist persons who have been victimized by violent crime. This assistance takes the form of various services, and states may supplement those services with additional ones. For example, California law provides for compensation for losses connected with medical need, mental health counseling, wage and income support, funeral and burial assistance, and even job retraining. The persons who may get assistance can include the victim and anyone who is close to the victim who was with him or her at the time of the crime. There are a few prerequisites to gaining assistance, however. First and foremost, the crime must be reported, and the victim must assist in the prosecution of the perpetrator of the crime. Secondly, the victim must not have contributed to the crime in any way.

Perhaps the most important reason to report the crime, however, is to get it to stop. If you know the identity of the person who attacked you, it is likely they know you as well. It is possible, perhaps even probable, that they may not be willing to leave you alone. Whether or not your jurisdiction has hate crime legislation, you may wish to report the crime as an assault and battery and to seek the protection of the court by issuing a restraining order against the person who committed the crime against you. (See chapter 3). A restraining order may not sound like a lot of protection, but if someone violates it, then that is a basis for their detention by the police. However, it is a possibility that in reporting the crime and seeking a restraining order, you may run the risk that the person against whom you – obtain it may state that you have also been harassing *him* – and will seek a restraining order against you as well.

To help you through the process, there are a number of anti-violence organizations that can help you manage the process, and many are in the lesbian and gay commmunity. They can provide counseling that will not only be of assistance in working through the bureaucracy, but will also provide you with emotional support as you try to deal with what has happened to you. Several of these organizations are lesbian and gay specific, but there may also be others that have capable counselors for lesbian and gay situations.

Future Directions

Hate crimes span an enormous range of emotion. Sometimes they are motivated by passion. In the wake of the September 11 terrorist actions against the United States, persons who appeared to be of Middle Eastern descent were beaten and killed, and damage was done to religious property. Those crimes were born from passionate feelings about what had occurred. But still, the underlying premise is the same for all hate crimes: acts against other people based solely on who they appear to be, not based on something the victim did to deserve punishment.

There is no way that hate crime legislation can make hate crimes go away. It cannot legislate people's feelings. It will not make nice people out of bigots, and people will not like homosexuals any better because there is legislation that says that they should not hate. Hate crimes legislation is not the answer to hate. Some people may even believe that by creating hate crimes legislation, we are furthering differences between people by creating a special protected status for some.

On the other hand, perhaps such legislation is part of the answer. Because the laws that are passed and put forth by our legislatures reflect out beliefs and ideals as a society, hate crimes legislation is an important expression by our society that crimes motivated by bigotry are morally unacceptable. It is not to say that the victims of hate crimes are more deserving or are more special than other crime victims. If a person is killed – well, dead is dead, no matter their color, religion, ethnicity, or sexual orientation. But in a society where differences between people have been so callously dealt with and where, in particular, the hate that exists for homosexuals has been enshrined into federal and state laws with the passage of anti-gay marriage laws, perhaps hate crime laws have an important role. They may balance and counter some of the institutionalized discrimination inherent in law. In this sense, perhaps, the statement made by the passage of such laws is more important than the actual effect of the statutes themselves.

CHAPTER 10

Conclusion

What's Your Problem?

As you have seen in the pages preceding, the lesbian and gay community has witnessed changes in the past fifty years that have not only been without precedent, but, when taken together, catalog remarkable legal, cultural, social, and political progress. Merely idea of being "out" in the first half of the twentieth century meant that you would almost inevitably be subjected to persecution that could involve loss of job, family, and even of life. There were few safe havens – you would nearly everywhere have been regarded as mentally ill and perverted. Stereotypes that would have defined you in the minds of others abounded and included notions of child molestation and efforts at "recruitment."

While all of these things are entirely still possible in the twenty-first century, today such persecutions are much closer to being the exception rather than the rule. The gay, lesbian, transgendered, and bisexual community is quite visible. And, whereas fifty years ago you could be persecuted without much help available in the way of legal options, today there are laws that are not only protecting you against discrimination, but there are actually laws stating that you have a right to your partnership. That partnership, at least in one state (Vermont) offers you the protection of the law to the same extent that heterosexual married couples would have. The degree to which the societal outlook and hence, the legal support for lesbians and gays has changed is incredible. We now have domestic partnerships; sitcoms that feature gay characters; legal marriage-like status in Vermont; anti-discrimination statutes; a policy that allows you to serve in the military; and increasing numbers of gay and lesbian parents. Whereas fifty years ago, there were more laws persecuting you than supporting you, today there are more laws supporting you than persecuting you. It has truly been a remarkable change of events.

That being said, the progress of the past doesn't mean that the world has changed so dramatically that gay, lesbian, transgendered or bisexual persons are citizens equal to any of their heterosexual brothers, sisters, moms and dads. It is impossible to read this entire book and not realize that gays, lesbians, bisexuals, and transgenders have been living in a legal ghetto in America. In a family of four with a straight father, straight mother, straight son and lesbian daughter, three of the people in that family have equal rights, while the fourth member does not. While gays and lesbians have seen a cultural revolution around their acceptance that has had important legal effects, that alone has not raised our status to that of equality. Things have changed in the last fifty years, but as you've seen in these pages, there is more change to be done than change that has occurred. Consider the following:

- You can be fired from your job because of who you are in most circumstances and in most places in the United States.
- Even if there are anti-discrimination statutes in effect where you live, religious organizations may seek exemptions, because they are able to assert a legal right to object to your very existence based on the fact that they regard you as immoral.
- You may be denied housing for the same reason, again in most places.
- If you fall in love, you cannot be legally married in any state. The only other class of people discriminated against in this way were American slaves.
- In fact, if you fall in love, the mere act of making love for you is illegal in almost half the states.
- If you want to have a family, you may be forbidden to adopt a child or even to serve as a foster parent to one, even if the child is HIV positive and may find the most supportive home with you.
- The fact that you are gay is considered "anti-family" by many heterosexuals in this country.
- If you leave a heterosexual marriage and you have children by that marriage, the fact that you are gay or lesbian may limit your custody of your child or children. If you have a new partner, your visitation can be sharply curtailed and supervised.
- If you and your same sex partner break up, the law has no structure for supporting you and ensuring fairness for both parties.
- You can vote, but you cannot openly serve your country in a military uniform, and in fact, despite the presence of a policy known as "Don't Ask,

Don't Tell," record numbers of gays and lesbians are being hunted and hounded out of the military.

- If your partner, who you are not allowed to marry, dies without a will naming you as a beneficiary, you could wind up not only emotionally devastated, but financially as well, because you cannot inherit.
- If someone kills your partner, then you probably will not be seen as someone important enough in the eyes of the law to be able to sue for your loss. To be allowed to take care of your lover's remains, you will need the permission and cooperation of his or her family.
- If your partner falls ill, without the proper documents filled out, you will not be permitted to make medical decisions for him or her.
- If someone beats the crap out of you because they hate "fags" or "dykes," laws that punish that action for other minorities may not work for you. In fact, in some places, there have been active efforts to ensure that gays and lesbians are not included in the definition of hate crimes.
- If you get battered by your same sex partner, the laws that cover domestic violence may not pertain to you. If you live in a state with sodomy laws, seeking help from the police in effect is turning yourself in as a lawbreaker.
- Despite the fact that you and your love have lived together in a monogamous relationship for twenty-five years, the law does not regard you as anything but single.
- As single people, you pay *more* taxes than married people and you receive *less* in the way of legal rights than any other class of people in the United States.

What becomes apparent after reviewing this very partial list of some of the many rights that you don't have is that you don't really have a legal problem. A legal problem involves a dispute around a way to interpret a law between parties. But if there is no law to protect you in the first place, then it would be hard to say that you have a legal problem. As a lesbian, gay, bisexual or transgendered individual, there is often little that law itself can do for you. That may sound funny after an entire book about the legal issues faced by lesbian women and gay men trying to carve out a normal life in society. Of course you do have the other kinds of legal problems brought on by circumstances – a fender-bender for example, but those are the legal problems everyone faces. When it comes to the core of you, the laws that protect your most basic identity are sadly lacking, in spite of the successes that have made the invisible gay and lesbian life that existed prior to the 1960s as much a relic as a dinosaur bone. But in essence you don't have a legal problem. Rather, the problems portrayed in this book – those that are particular to lesbians and gays – aren't legal problems at all. They are political problems.

Law is nothing more than the reflection of political will and nothing else. It has been the political will of the heterosexual majority to suppress the rights of the homosexual minority. That sounds a little scalding. Most people you know don't choose to oppress you. Most people you know may be quite accepting of who you are. But it is one thing to accept who you are; it is another to support it in a way that will make a meaningful difference in the way you are treated by the law. Acceptance of your identity as a homosexual does not equate with supporting your right to be married. The fact that your neighbor says you should have equal rights does not equate with your neighbor wanting a gay kindergarten teacher to instruct his kid's class. While most people are accepting and even support anti-discrimination, the majority do not believe in gay marriage. While the passage of sodomy laws is the legacy of a long-dead era of sexual mores, the fight to keep them is a modern decision – one that is filled with malice. The exclusion of gays and lesbians from hate crime laws is one that is meant to hurt us and is successful, because those laws reflect the political will of the population represented by the state legislature that crafts them. Efforts to deny homosexuals protection from job discrimination by not enacting laws, or by trying to repeal those passed, are based on nothing less than politics.

And while there has been incredible progress over during the last half of the twentieth century, it is equally important to acknowledge that there have also been tremendous setbacks. Gays and lesbians have achieved newfound rights and freedoms to be sure, but they have also been named in legislation that is passed for the purpose of discriminating against them: the anti-gay marriage laws. Bigotry aimed at gays and lesbians is being written into the law and even into state constitutions. Nothing could pose a more serious challenge to our ability to live as equal citizens in this country as the codification of hate. Our legal problems have been a manifestation of our political stuggles.

The reason that gays and lesbians do not inherit from each other without a will is political – not legal. The reason we have to work so very hard at having children is political. And as most of us are single, the reason that each of us pays more in taxes that are spent sending other people's children to school is political – it is not a legal issue. Have you ever heard a candidate for public office stand up and propose that we lower the tax rate on gays and lesbians? No, you haven't, and you won't – it would be political suicide. Yet the truth is that a single gay man or lesbian earning $100,000 pays much more in taxes than does their married counterpart with children. Heterosexuals are given a tax break for getting married; we are not allowed to be married. That would mean that the desire to know your rights is directly linked with the desire to be engage in activities that guarantee those rights you have, and assert those rights that are not yet recognized in law. Politics and law different sides of the same coin. What is your problem? Politics.

The Best of Times, The Worst of Times

Charles Dickens used those immortal words to begin his novel *A Tale of Two Cities*. As they were fitting for the novel, they are also a fitting description of the past fifty years for gays and lesbians in America. We have been living in two cities. In one city we there are openly gay members of Congress, gay and lesbian relationships have a legal foothold, there are job protections, and we even have our own law firms. In one city we got together and took care of ourselves during an epidemic and set an example of caring and compassion that was unprecedented in the history of American public health.

The other city however, is a place where hatred of gays and lesbians has been woven into the fabric of constitutions that are supposed to protect rights, not take them away. In the other city, the very act of making love was declared subject to government whim by the Supreme Court. In the other city, people have tried and succeeded for a time to make it illegal to protect us with anti-discrimination statutes. Incredibly, in the other city, people have blamed gays and lesbians in America for the September 11 terrorist attack on the United States. We have seen progress and we have seen folly. After fifty years that brought both the best and worst of times for lesbians and gays, we are still second class citizens.

In the last five decades, beginning with the formation of the first lesbian and gay societies, there has been a tremendous flexing of gay and lesbian political muscle. It is evidenced through the progress we have made and in the large crowds of people who participate in the increasing number of gay pride celebrations throughout the country. Gay and lesbian families are abounding. There are openly gay and lesbian members of the United States Congress.

Political progress didn't just happen. Perhaps the most important achievement of the past fifty years has been the development of an infrastructure of effective organizations that have systematically and bravely fought for the progress we have witnessed. They are legal organizations, such as the Lambda Legal Defense and Education Fund and the National Center for Lesbian Rights – and they are also political, such as the Human Rights Campaign and the Victory Fund.

If we are going to continue to see progress, it is vital that the gay and lesbian community does not become complacent. If anti-discrimination protections exist in the larger more important states, we cannot afford to say that the rest of the states don't matter. If hate crimes legislation is supported in over half, there cannot be anything less than an all out effort to pass it in all states. If our relationships earn the legal respect that they are entitled to in a handful of states, that cannot be good enough. If there is one state where gay and lesbian couples cannot adopt, then parenthood everywhere suffers. If there is one man fired for a limp wrist . . . if there is one place where hate is written into the law . . .if there is one place where we cannot adopt a child . . . then each of us, no matter where we live, are less than full citizens of this country.

And it is not as if the advances we have seen are safe. That is another measure of how the gay and lesbian struggle is different from that of other groups that have had to assert their rights in the past. There are well funded, well organized groups – often rooted in religious fundamentalism – who are dedicated to tearing down the progress that has been made. They would happily turn the clock back to a time when homosexuality was regarded as a mental illness, as the "love that dare not speak its name," to a time when the closet or the grave was the place for someone who is gay. It is they who have opposed anti-discrimination legislation when proposed – it is they who sought its repeal when it has been passed. They have even proposed their own counter-legislation, making it illegal to pass legislation conferring rights upon lesbians and gays. Ironically, they are able to market hateful actions by couching their positions in the bosom of morality. Meanwhile, gay and lesbian people who are merely trying to lead their own lives are cast as immoral. The obstacles they pose are not legal, they are political. Keeping your legal rights is not a legal problem for you, it is political.

Despite the fact that you belong to the most legally disadvantaged class in America, your political future may not be all that bad. Each of the experts who generously gave their time and insights for this book was asked what they thought had been the best and the worst of times for gays and lesbians in the past fifty years. Then they were asked what they thought would come to pass during the next fifty years.

With respect to the best and worst of times, each of the attorneys interviewed for this book offered viewpoints that varied widely, given their areas of concentration and perspective. Sherra Greer felt the thing that bothered her the most from the past is how little attention was paid to the issues of gays and lesbians in the military. Sam Garrison and Kate Kendell both felt that the greatest setback seen was the decision in *Bowers v. Hardwick*, when the Supremes said that it was perfectly within the realm of constitutionality for a state to outlaw sodomy. "Not only was this the most significant setback of the last fifty years if you are a lawyer," says Kendell. "But also, if you are a lesbian or gay person, because it signaled from a sacrosanct place that discrimination and antipathy against lesbians and gay men were perfectly appropriate and acceptable. Once *Bowers v. Hardwick* was decided by the Supreme Court, it began infiltrating lower court decisions on issues addressing any lesbian and gay question, from child custody to employment to the military to gay clubs. There was not any portion of the spectrum of lesbian and gay equality or inclusion that *Bowers v. Hardwick* did not have a decimating effect on – and continues to." Sam Garrison agrees: "It could have been the death knell of all sodomy laws and the repercussions of them, and had it been decided the other way, it would have been as momentous in a positive way as it has been in a negative way."

Yet Lori Jean, from her perspective as a community organizer, saw *Bowers v. Hardwick* as an opportunity. The decision was so outrageous – so biased and so politically motivated – that the gay and lesbian community responded by becoming more organized than ever before. "Hardwick was an issue that we couldn't believe, in that day and age, that we could lose on – it was about our privacy in the most penultimate way. We were able to build upon Hardwick as a movement in this country because it was appalling not only to our community but to many of our allies. That loss turned into an ultimate victory for us."

Kate Kendell of the National Center for Lesbian Rights says that "There is no doubt in my mind that the last fifty years have brought about an enormous sea change in the legal treatment of our families and relationships. The overall tone – it is an almost atmospheric change." When it comes to the single most important event of the past fifty years, she states that "as a lawyer, the greatest legal achievement is having the U.S. Supreme Court acknowledge a modicum of our existence in *Romer v. Evans*. But more important and significant than that, but very much related, are the gains we've made in visibility and understanding and acceptance, which has largely grown out of the mantra that was a drumbeat in the mid 1980s, for lesbians and gays to come out of the closet." In other words, decisions like *Romer v. Evans*, in which the Supremes stated that Colorado violated the U.S. Constitution to pass a law (Amendment 2) that made it illegal to pass anti-discrimination legislation, ended up providing a way for closeted gays and lesbians to feel safer in coming out.

Sam Garrison also feels that the change has been atmospheric, and he sees the evidence of it not so much in the law as in our culture. "There is no one isolated event that made a difference, but a process by which our culture has become comfortable with gay characters in television and movies and accepting of a positive presentation of gays and lesbians. I think that cultural trends drive the progress we make in terms of social acceptance more than does anything that has happened politically."

At the end of fifty years of progress, it would not be accurate to say that gays and lesbians are accepted in American society. Accepted people are not as legally disadvantaged as we are. However, it would be accurate to say that, as a result of our own political will, while not accepted, we have become tolerated.

But being tolerated just isn't good enough.

The Future Doesn't Suck

Given our past, what can we reasonably expect in the future? Will our rights continue to flow in dribs and drabs until we are equal partners in American democracy? Or has the balloon expanded as far as it can? If heterosexual society still regards our existence as immoral and our relationships somehow undermining the very foundation of their own marriages, how will we ever find our way to being regarded as anything more than a tolerated subculture at best, or as pariahs of the supposedly religious right wing?

Respecting the future, there was no disagreement among the experts. To a person, they each thought that the gay and lesbian future was one that offered the most positive of outlooks. The thing that almost everyone agreed upon was that the example of the Vermont Civil Union would be widely followed in a number of states. Says Kate Kendell, "I actually do believe that over the course of the next fifty years, there will be a greater acceptance and understanding of the ways lesbian and gay couples and our families have been marginalized. That will result in far greater legal protections and recognition than we have currently, including marriage, or something very much like it." She states that she believes a lot of that progress will be based on the transformative power that the gay and lesbian movement has had on the way people view gender. "I think that there will be a more nuanced understanding of gender and gender discrimination and its role in sexual orientation discrimination which will result in greater protections for lesbians and gay men generally and for transgendered folks specifically." Does that mean that she thinks that gays and lesbians will become more like straight people and be assimilated into straight society because we've gotten marriage? Not quite. She envisions an outcome in which the entire system is going to change for the better: "I think that the achievements of gay and lesbians will have an enormous impact on marriage law, notions of gender, understandings of relationships, parenting constellations. In fifty years, the country will be much more diverse and dynamic for lesbian, gay, transgendered, and bisexual people, rather than us becoming like Ozzie and Harriet and everyone else, with two kids and a dog. The way we live and the way we articulate our issues has a tranformative power. It is much more powerful to say what we want the legal system to adapt to than it is to say 'I'm just like you so why can't I have rights.'"

Judy Moats has pretty much the same outlook. "I really do think that there will be a redefining of the family and a redefining of marriage and partnering – you will fashion your own commitment that suits you," she says. "I just think that if we are going to survive, we really have to extend our circle of encompassing family. We've hurt ourselves by going to nuclear families as a civilization. I think we need to come back around and recognize extended families."

Winnie Stachelberg of the Human Rights Campaign also sees a bright future, but she and Lorri Jean both caution against complacency. The extraordinary progress of the past half-century should not make us feel that the future will come without a price and an effort. "I think that our opponents will continue to become fewer and more shrill. As we see the march toward acceptance and against intolerance, the intolerant group, while shrinking in number, is becoming louder in volume," says Lorri Jean. "By virtue of our successes, the opposition is angrier and angrier, even as they themselves become increasingly marginalized. I do think that our relationships will become recognized in time. I don't know if we'll be there in the next fifty years. Our opponents will be fewer and our relationships recognized, but I think there will still be expressions of bigotry that will have to be fought just as they have for racial discrimination today."

Sharra Greer of the Servicemember Legal Defense Network doesn't want to wait fifty years – she says that gays, lesbians, and bisexuals will be serving openly in the U.S. military within the next ten to fifteen years.

There was a poignant tale reported in the November 25, 2001, edition of *The Washington Post* that perfectly illustrates what we have accomplished and what we have yet to gain. The terrorists who attacked the United States on September 11, 2001, did not discriminate – they killed black, white, latino, and straight and gay people. In the aftermath, Governor George Pataki of New York announced that his state would also not discriminate and that state agencies would offer support to the domestic partners of the victims, regardless of sexual orientation.

However, it was a different story for one Virginia woman who lost her partner of eighteen years, a civilian employee of the Army, in the attack on the Pentagon. She found tremendous support from her partner's family, who regarded the couple as married. She even found that the military was supportive of her – she received an official letter of condolence that acknowledged the nature of their relationship from the office of the Secretary of Defense, and she was accorded respect in her dealings with military counselors and chaplains, according to the article. However, when she turned to the Virginia Criminal Inquiries Compensation Fund, state law did not allow her to receive assistance, because she was not deemed a relative. When she went for the body, she had to have a signed power of attorney from her partner's family. And in seeking assistance, she may be regarded as ineligible by some agencies because she is not "next of kin."

While we have come so far as to have our own families recognize our relationships, and even some governors and secretaries in the Cabinet, there is nevertheless a stigma that is associated with gay and lesbian relationships that is far from dead. It is a stigma that means that these relationships will not be recognized as fully legal for a long time to come, and that is a political, not legal problem. As the story of the September 11 survivor attests, we cannot allow our progress to cause us to be short sighted about the challenges we have left.

Perhaps Frederick Hertz put it best when it comes to the need for our vigilence on issues related to our civil rights: "The greatest disappointment is that, having entered the mainstream, we are still second-class citizens. Most openly gay people have no idea to the extent to which they are second class citizens. They don't realize the taxes they pay, the rights they are denied. What is so disappointing is that, with so much progress, this next level of rights seems so hard to achieve. It is like we should be grateful we are not being murdered and therefore accept being second class."

Even though the bulk of issues faced by lesbians, gays, transgenders, and bisexuals are political, that is not really to say that gay and lesbian people don't have legal problems – they do in abundance, and when they arise, there are things to do about them. But something stated in the beginning of this guide bears repeating. If you do have a legal problem, you are greatly advantaged by finding a good attorney. In fact, there are times when trying to do things yourself can increase your problems rather than decrease them. It is a little like *The Cat in the Hat Comes Back* – cleaning up one little stain can result in a whole mess to clean up. No book that you buy, no form that you get, and no information you get off the Internet can substitute for the knowledge and skills of a good attorney. Fortunately for us, our community has them in abundance, you only have to find them. With their help with your legal problems and the focus of the community's resources on our political problems, there will be nothing but success in our future.

To the extent that we can understand our second-class nature and do something about it, then there is every reason to be optimistic about the future. But for now, the greatest legal problems you face can't be solved by a lawyer, they can only be solved through the exercise of your own political will. Unless and until we as a community find a way to address our political problems with the same zeal, dedication, and direction that we as individuals employ to pursue our individual legal solutions, we will remain nothing better than the second-class citizens we are today. It is a role we can shed. As Frederick Hertz so wisely put it, we are not seeking to be assimilated into straight society; straight society has to move to embrace us, and our families, for who we are. That is our future.

To get there requires commitment. The churches that fight advances in gay and lesbian rights benefit from the practice of tithing. Many who attend weekly church services donate a portion of their incomes by dropping checks into collection baskets. That money, in turn, often feeds the poor and provides social services, but it is also used to fight advancements in gay, lesbian, and legal rights, especially those laws that affect our families, in an effort to "protect" theirs. The point is, the GLBT community needs to be aware of its tithing needs. The national organizations listed as references throughout this book could move mountains if they had a weekly check from each and every GLBT person who is concerned about his or her rights. In addition, there are resources you will find listed in the next section of this book that are local to you. Support them. Send them all checks. Send them regularly. Without that, the future becomes less certain.

Legal and Political Gay, Lesbian, Bisexual, and Transgender Timeline

What follows is a list of notable events. Not all of them are strictly gay/lesbian events, but they may have either affected gay and lesbian rights or demonstrated the lengths to which other minorities have had to struggle, thereby putting gay and lesbian rights struggles into some context. They are not meant to encompass comprehensively all cultural and sociological events that have affected gay and lesbian life in America, but are listed here as important in relation to the legal and political issues discussed in the chapters of this book.

1610 – In what will later be known as the Land of Liberty, what will later become the Commmonwealth of Virginia passes the first sodomy statute imposing a death sentence for offenders. During the rest of the early part of the century, other colonies follow suit and pass anti-sodomy statutes, also making it a capital offense. It is the first time we are mentioned in this country in a statute. Welcome to America.

1776 – The United States serves notice of the break from Great Britain by issuing a Declaration of Independence stating that "all men are created equal," which begins a war with Great Britain in which gays will serve in the military.

1778 – Lieutenant Fredrick Gotthold Enslin is the first person to suffer court martial in the United States Army. He will not be the last.

1787 – The U.S. Constitution is drafted, though it counts slaves as only three-fifths of a person and fails to give women the right to vote. Though not specifically mentioned, gays do have the right to vote.

1791 – The U.S. Constitution, now amended with the first ten amendments that comprise the Bill of Rights, is adopted and made the supreme law of the United States.

1857 – The United States Supreme Court, in one of the worst decisions it has ever made, declares that under the United States Constitution, any slave that escapes from a master must be returned. (The other two worst decisions involve the internment of Japanese-Americans during World War II and the decision in 1986 that only homosexual sodomy is not protected under the U.S. Constitution.)

1865 – The United States abolishes slavery by passing the Thirteenth Amendment to the United States Constitution.

1868 – The Fourteenth Amendment to the U.S. Constitution is passed, which states that all persons are granted due process of law and that no person will denied the "equal protection of the laws." It also makes all people born in the United States citizens of the nation.

1869 – Karoly Maria Benkert (Kertbeny) coined the term homosexual. This marks the beginnings of identifying people within a class rather than classifying behavior of people. (A chance from "he likes to have his way with boys" to "he is a homosexual.")

1870 – Black men get the right to vote under the Fifteenth Amendment. Black women will just have to wait along with white women.

1914 – The first printed usage of the word "faggot" to refer to queers is published.

1919 – During World War I, the criminalization of homosexuals is codified in U.S. military law.

1920 – The American Civil Liberties Union, which will work to help gays and lesbians establish basic rights, is founded.

1924 – The Society for Human Rights was founded in Illinois and is believed to be the first organized gay rights organization in the United States.

1929 – The publisher of *The Well of Loneliness* featuring a lesbian relationship and written by Radclyffe Hall is convicted of obscenity.

1930 – The Motion Picture Production Code forbids all references to homosexuality.

1943 – Regulations are issued ordering psychiatrists to separate homosexuals from "normal" recruits, and homosexuals are banned from all branches of the military.

1948 – Kinsey publishes his report. You know the rest of that story.

1951 – Gay and lesbian people in America finally have an organization called the Mattachine Society, and it is formed in Los Angeles.

1954 – In a sensible moment during an insensible time, the U.S. Supreme Court unanimously rules that the practice of having separate schools for white and black children is unconstitutional. Perhaps this bodes that one day, maybe a hundred years from now, a not-yet-sitting U.S. Supreme Court will rule that having separate but equal institutions of marriage and union for straights and gays is also unconstitutional. Who knows?

1955 – The first lesbian organization is founded in San Francisco – The Daughters of Bilitis.

1961 – Illinois becomes the first state in the United States to repeal its ban on sodomy. No other state will follow suit for a decade.

1964 – The United States Congress passes the Civil Rights Act, which makes employment discrimination illegal if based on race, sex, national origin, or religion and establishes the Fair Housing Law. It guarantees access to public accommodation for those classes mentioned in the statute. It does not mention women or gay people.

1968 – Thirty women try to have lunch in the Oak Room at the Plaza Hotel in New York City. They are escorted out by the police, because women were not allowed to lunch at the Oak Room at the Plaza Hotel.

1969 – One word – Stonewall. The demonstration following the raid of a gay bar in New York City becomes the touchstone for the gay rights movement, which escalates during the 1970s. This is routinely identified as a watershed moment.

1972 – The first ban against gay discrimination in hiring by a city is enacted in East Lansing, Michigan.

1973 – The National Gay and Lesbian Task Force is founded, and the first national gay-and-lesbian-interest law firm, Lambda Legal Defense and Education Fund, overcomes a ruling stating that it is not a charitable organization, allowing it, too, to come into being. I will become a primary tool in advancing the rights of the lesbian and gay community. and it too, comes into being. Also during this year, the American Psychiatric Association removes homosexuality from its catalog of mental disorders, depriving opponents of gay and lesbian rights of a major tool. It is a banner year for national professional associations: the American Bar Association votes to recommend the repeal of the sodomy statutes in the United States.

1974 – The very first piece of federal legislation to prohibit discrimination against lesbians and gays is introduced into Congress. Needless to say, it does not pass.

1977 – The National Center for Lesbian Rights is founded in San Francisco. Nationally, gay and lesbian rights become a national focus after an enormous effort staged by Anita Bryant, formerly a singer and promoter of orange juice, who leads a successful effort to repeal the Miami-Dade County gay and lesbian anti-discrimination law. Ms. Bryant was also a former Miss America, leading one to the conclusion that her answer in the question competition was not that she would be working for world peace.

1978 – Openly gay San Francisco supervisor Harvey Milk is assassinated along with Mayor George Moscone by a former county supervisor in City Hall.

1979 – The first gay and lesbian march on Washington occurs.

1980 – The Human Rights Campaign Fund, organized to work for political achievements in our national government, is founded.

1981 – In July, *The New York Times* reports on a disease, described as cancer, being reported in gay men (even though the newspaper has an official policy that forbids the use of the word gay), reflecting reports a month earlier to the Centers for Disease Control in Atlanta. Later in the fall, the new disease is declared an epidemic.

1982 – In January, the Gay Men's Health Crisis, the first organization formed in response to the epidemic, is founded in New York City.

1983 – The first AIDS discrimination suit is filed by Lambda Legal Defense and Education Fund. The state of Wisconsin passes the nation's first statewide ban on gay and lesbian discrimination.

1985 – Rock Hudson announces his diagnosis of AIDS.

August 1985 – fourteen year-old Ryan White is barred from school because he has AIDS. Also that year, Los Angeles County becomes the first jurisdiction to pass a law against HIV/AIDS discrimination.

1986 – Incredibly, and through the most twisted logic, the Supreme Court of the United States declares that sodomy laws can be considered consitutional, prompting one to wonder whether or not any of the Supreme Court justices has ever had any fun at all.

1987 – The AIDS Coalition to Unleash Power (ACT UP) is formed, changing advocacy for patients and health policy forever. A second national march on Washington, D.C., occurs and enjoys record attendance.

1988 – Despite a veto by Republican President Ronald Reagan, the Civil Rights Act is expanded to include coverage of institutions that receive federal dollars.

1989 – The U.S. Army is ordered by a federal court to reinstate a gay soldier.

1990 – President George Bush signs into law the Americans with Disabilities Act, including people with HIV as people with disabilities who cannot be discriminated against under the law.

1991 – A study is released that states that the basis for homosexuality may be biological, not environmental and not a choice.

1992 – The voters of Colorado pass Amendment 2, which states that no municipality within its borders may pass gay and lesbian anti-discrimination laws, prompting a boycott of the state. Eventually, Amendment 2 is found to be unconstitutional by the Supremes.

1993 – Following up on a campaign promise, President Bill Clinton attempts to lift the ban on gays in the military. He is vilified for this and compromises by issuing a new policy entitled "Don't Ask, Don't Tell," which leads to increased numbers of gays and lesbians expelled from the armed services, rather than fewer. Also during this year, in a decision that would scare the hell out of married homophobes across the United States and result in the passage of anti-gay marriage statutes to "protect" heterosexual marriage, the Hawaii Supreme Court issued a ruling in favor of same-sex couples seeking a marriage license.

1994 – A lower court decision that awarded custody of lesbian Sharon Bottom's children to her mother is overturned by the Virginia Court of Appeals, which states that it was wrong of the lower court to award custody simply based on the mother's sexual orientation.

1995 – Then Congressman Robert Dornin (Republican – CA) offers legislation in the House of Representatives to automatically discharge all HIV-positive personnel (dishonorably?) from the Armed Forces. Also that year, when gay and lesbian representatives arrive at the White House for a meeting, Secret Service personnel are wearing gloves in fear of them, typifying homophobia that morphs into fear of contagion. During the last month of the year, protease inhibitors are introduced into the formularies of HIV patients, causing a sudden and widespread drop in the mortality of people with AIDS.

1998 – Matthew Shepard is beaten and dies in Wyoming.
Across the country in Vermont, three gay/lesbian couples who apply for marriage licenses and are denied bring suit, stating that they are being denied equal protection under the law.

1999 – In a stunning decision, the Vermont Supreme Court declares that the state legislature of Vermont must extend the benefits offered to married couples to gay and lesbian couples under the constitution of that state.

2000 – The legislature of Vermont crafts and passes a bill providing same sex couples with a legal institution called a civil union that confers the same rights as marriage under the laws of the state, and the bill is signed into law by the governor. The day it goes into effect, a lesbian couple become the first legally recognized same sex couple in the United States of America.

2002 – Maryland offers protection against discrimination to homosexuals. A movement to repeal is announced by a group called Take Back Maryland, and is later abandoned.

As you can see in this timeline, events that affect the gay and lesbian community are occurring more broadly and deeply than ever before. At the end of the twentieth century, gays and lesbians have emerged as a community in force, with solid organizations working to defend our rights. As one views the timeline, it is evident that there has not only been dramatic progress, but an incredible and almost insatiable movement to establish ourselves as equal citizens.

Glossary

Administrator – The person who is in charge of an estate when a person dies intestate, or without a will. The Administrator must pay all debts and expenses, collect any funds due the estate and distribute property in accordance with the direction provided by the laws of the state where the deceased person lived.

Advance Directive – See Living Will.

Adoption – A legal proceeding whereby a child and prospective parent or parents are joined in a permanent legal relationship that confers all the rights and duties of a biological parent-child relationship, including but not limited to rights of inheritance. In order for adoption to be legal, the biological parent or parents must relinquish their rights and responsibilities. Some states may bar gay adoption by statute or court action.

Alimony – A right of support won in family court that requires one spouse to provide another with a set amount of financial support in consideration of the marriage and its dissolution.

Alternate Beneficiary – A person named in a last will and testament who inherits a designated bequest if and only if the first-named beneficiary either pre-deceases or declines the bequest.

Alternate Executor – A person who shall serve as executor if and only if the named executor of the last will and testament is unable or unwilling to act.

Artificial Insemination – A procedure, preferably performed by a licensed physician, of placing donor sperm in a woman with the object of creating a pregnancy. This differs from in vivo fertilization in that the surrogate mother will be carrying a child of her own biological makeup in addition to that of the sperm donor.

Beneficiary – Any person named in a will who is to inherit property (a bequest) or act in an official capacity, such as an executor.

Bill of Rights – The Bill of Rights comprises the first ten amendments to the U.S. Constitution, and they enunciate the most basic of our civil liberties. You are familiar with many of these, including the right to free speech, First Amendment; The Right to Bear Arms, Second Amendment.

Civil Union – A legally recognized and sanctioned joining of domestic couples designed to confer almost all of the benefits of marriage without calling it marriage – available only in the State of Vermont.

Co-Executor – You can appoint more than one person to act as the Executor of your will, in which case they act jointly, as opposed to alternatively.

Contingency Fee – This is one of the ways that a lawyer charges for his or her services, allowing you to proceed with a case, but having the fee payable to the lawyer out of any proceeds realized as a result of winning the case, meaning that the fee is contingent upon some sort of recovery. Contingent fees can run from one-fourth to one-half of the recovery.

DOMA – The Defense of Marriage Act passed by Congress that exempts states from having to recognize any other state action that legalizes gay marriage and which defines marriage as an institution between one man and one woman only.

Domestic Partner Benefits – When either an employer or municipality allows for unmarried individuals to register as co-habiting partners, conferring certain and limited benefits for the couple, such as insurance coverage or, in the case of government sponsored domestic partner registration, the right to take over the lease of an apartment the two had shared.

Equal Protection – That part of the United States Constitution that states that all persons shall be afforded the equal protection of and access to the laws of the United States. This means that you cannot pass a law that states that people shall have the right to be married and then deny that right to marriage to certain people, but allow others to have it. (This is, of course, a subject of debate.)

Entrapment – A defense offered by an arrested person, often in connection with a drug or sex violation, whereby the defendant asserts that the arresting officers went beyond providing opportunity to commit a crime, but rather, caused the defendant to commit a crime he or she would otherwise not have committed.

Executor – Similar to an administrator, the executor is the person in charge of administering an estate when there is a written and legally executed last will and testament. An executor must pay all debts and expenses of the state, collect all monies due the estate, and distribute the property according to the wishes of the testator. If more than one is appointed in a will, there can be co-executors, and if a second is appointed to serve in case the first cannot, then he or she is the alternate executor.

Foster Care – A temporary care arrangement whereby a person or persons take charge of the well-being of a child for a period of time until the child can return to his or her biological or adoptive parents or legal guardian.

Full Faith and Credit Clause – This is a clause in the Fifth Amendment of the

United States Constitution which states that the state governments of the United States shall recognize each other's state laws. For example, a couple who is married in the state of Illinois will still be considered man and wife should they move across the Mississippi River to Missouri.

Galimony – See PALIMONY below.

Hate Crime – A usually violent crime (assault, battery, murder) motivated by the general identity of the victim – his or her race, creed, color, religion, gender, or sexual orientation.

Health Care Proxies – The designation of another individual to make health care decisions for you in the event you are unable to make them for yourself.

Impact Litigation – Tjese are lawsuits the outcomes of which will test an existing statute, regulation or policy to the point that if the litigation is successful, then the outcome will be changed for all affected by the statute, regulation or policy. In other words, it has a significant impact and goes beyond the immediate plaintiff and defendant in its effect.

Inter Rorem Clause. A statement in a will that sets forth the condition that anyone who is named in the will who challenges the validity of the will and loses, loses any bequest made to them within the will.

Intestate – When a person is without a written and legally executed last will and testament.

In Vitro Fertilization – The procedure, performed by a licensed physician, whereby a fertilized egg is placed into a woman for the purpose of creating a pregnancy. This differs from artificial insemination in that the child born to the woman will not be of biological relation to her, but rather solely the biological child of the donors of the sperm and the egg.

Joint Tenants – A form of property ownership that allows people to jointly own property that will automatically pass to the survivor among them upon the death of one of the owners, which is different than when property is owned as Tenants in Common (see below).

Legatee – A person who would inherit property under the laws of intestacy (if you died without a will); a next of kin.

Letters of Administration – when a person dies without a will (intestate) and someone is declared the administrator of the estate by the court, letters of administration are issued by the court that empower the administrator to act on behalf of the estate.

Letters Testamentary – When you have a will and you have appointed an executor, that person is not able to act as executor until the court issues him or her letters testamentary through the probate process.

Live-Together Agreement – A contract between persons who are going to establish their domicile together that outlines the conditions and arrangements for running their household and property.

Living Will – A written instrument, sometimes called a physician directive, medical directive or advance directive, stating one's wishes with respect to extraordinary means or life support in the event of catastrophic illness or accident.

Medical Directive – See living will.

Palimony/Galimony – This is not alimony, despite the fact that they sound a lot alike. This represents support for one partner from an ex-partner in a non-marital relationship. This differs from alimony in that alimony is written into the marriage laws of every state in consideration of a possible divorce and is therefore a right, whereas palimony/galimony is based not on such a right, but on a contract, either written or, in some cases, implied. Alimony is administered through family court in a divorce proceeding, whereas palimony/galimony is won through a contract action in civil court.

Parenting Agreement – A contract that can be stand alone, or part of a larger live-together agreement or other contract of understanding, that sets out the rights and responsibilities of a biological/legal parent and the non-biological partner with respect to the raising of a child, outlining how visitation might be handled in the event of a dissolution of the partnership, rights, responsibilities in raising the child, and/or custodial preferences in the event of the death of the biological/legal parent.

Parenting Decree – Available in only a few jurisdictions, a decree issued by a court recognizing that a child was brought into the world through a decision of a couple who cannot be married, with the intention of raising that child as co-parents, thereby conferring legal parent status on the non-biological partner in a relationship.

Physician Directive – see living will.

Power of Attorney – A written instrument that delegates your legal authority to another individual to do an activity or set of activities, often used in finances. In medical care these are often referred to as health care proxies.

Pre-Nuptual Agreement – A contract that in the past has been between heterosexual couples that, prior to marriage, defines the terms of the marriage, particularly regarding matters of finance and property, though not exclusively. In the wake of the Vermont Civil Union, a pre-nuptual agreement among gays and lesbians entering into that union is also possible.

Probate – the process by which a last will and testament is examined by a court and declared valid, whereupon the court issues the executor letters testamentary. It is then an only then that your executor can act on behalf of the estate.

Psychological Parent – When a non-biological parent forms a bond with a child of a partner who is the legal guardian and performs significant parenting functions and has lived with the child – a relationship fostered by the legal guardian – then a court may recognize that relationship as one of a parent who is deemed important enough to win visitation rights to the child in the event of a break up.

Residuary Beneficiary – There is a person who will get to inherit your residuary estate (see below). This person is very important, because they could conceivably wind up inheriting the entire estate, and are likely to inherit the bulk of it. It is advisable to name a residuary beneficiary as well as an alternative residuary beneficiary, so that if he or she dies before you, your will is not outdated. Note that the residuary beneficiary can be one and the same person as your executor, i.e., your domestic partner/lover/friend.

Residuary Clause – The part of a will that disposes of any and all property not already dealt with in the will and leaves it to an individual or set of individuals.

Restraining Order – An order of the court that protects a victim of domestic abuse by intervening and ordering the abusive person to stay away from the victim. The order can be pervasive and can include ordering the perpetrator to stay away from the victim in any and all venues, even if it is a home that they share. It can also order that the victim be compensated for medical expenses related to the violence. This is also called a Temporary Restraining Order (TRO), Stay Away Order or No Contact Order.

Second Parent Adoption – A procedure available in many, but less than half of the states, whereby an unmarried partner of an adoptive parent is allowed to also adopt the adopted child of the partner. For example, if Jane has adopted a baby, her partner Joan may elect a second-parent adoption, ensuring that the child will not be orphaned in the event of Jane's death.

Stalking – A felony in many states, stalking encompasses behavior that ranges from following a person, to passing by their home, to telephone calling with the intent to terrorize or harass a person. Being found guilty of stalking could bring a jail sentence or fine or both. **Surrogate Mother** – A woman who agrees, on behalf of another couple, to become pregnant, either by in vivo or artificial insemination, and bears a child on behalf of a couple to whom she yields parental rights.

TRO – Temporary Restraining Order – see Restraining Order.

Tenants in Common – A form of property ownership under which people together own property but there is an ability for one of the co-owners to sell or convey through a will his or her interest in the property to another.

Testamentary Substitutes – Types of property (real estate, insurance policies, joint bank accounts) that can be set up so that upon the death of the owner, the property passes automatically, by operation of law, to the person designated as the beneficiary of that property, without having to go through the estate that is created by a last will and testament.

Testate – When a person has a written and legally executed last will and testament.

Testator – A person who has written and legally executed a last will and testament.

Resources

How to Hire a Lawyer

Choosing a lawyer. Looking for a lawyer is a little bit like looking for a doctor. You want someone with whom you are comfortable and who you feel you can be honest with and who, in turn, you feel is honest with you. You also want to find someone who knows what they are doing when it comes to meeting your needs. Do not be afraid to ask an attorney you are considering hiring for an overview of their experience in a particular area of law and whether or not they regard the area as a specialty. You wouldn't go to a neurologist for an in-grown toenail, and neither should you go to a lawyer for advice on creating a surrogacy contract when he or she only practices criminal law.

Paying a lawyer. It is very important that you understand the fee structure that a lawyer offers and what it is that you are paying for. This will depend largely on the type of service you are seeking. There are basically three ways for a lawyer to charge a fee. The first is a flat fee – a fee that is designed to cover the time and expense to accomplish a particular task. For example, in hiring a lawyer to write a will, you may find that the charge is a flat fee of $500, for example, for a simple will. Another way that lawyers charge for their services is through an hourly charge, meaning that they will charge you for exactly the number of hours it takes to accomplish a task. This might be applicable in a circumstance where a lawyer is negotiating on your behalf and the time and expenditure cannot be set at the beginning of the work. Lastly, lawyers can be paid by contingency fee. This necessarily involves a lawsuit in which there is the prospect of a recovery of funds on your behalf and the lawyer's fee will come out of those funds. In the meantime, you will be responsible for paying expenses of the suit (filing fees, for example), but the lawyer's fee for service will be taken from your recovery. While this may sound like a bargain, you should know that contingency fees may run anywhere from one-fourth to one-half of the recovery. Make sure you understand at the outset what kind of fee you are being charged for the services being rendered.

Affording legal help. You may not be in a financial position to hire a lawyer, but still have a legal problem. There are resources available to you; however, they may limit their services to certain types of practice and be available only to those who are considered below the poverty line. If you are in this position, it is worth investigating your local Legal Aid societies, as well as finding out whether or not there are services involving sliding fee scales. If there is a local lesbian-or-gay- services center near you, or in your state, you might contact them to determine whether or not there are services you can explore. Another alternative is to telephone your state or local bar association to ask what alternatives may exist for you, since many law firms are registered with associations as firms that will take on pro bono (no charge) work. Note that if you are being charged in a criminal matter, if you cannot afford an attorney, you have a constitutional right to have one appointed for you.

Resources for finding a lawyer. There are a number of resources available to you in finding a lawyer with the type of specialty you seek. If in particular you wish to hire a lesbian or gay attorney, there are also resources that can help you there. The most obvious method is by reading advertisements. Many lesbian and gay attorneys advertise in the large number of free lesbian and gay community weekly newspapers. If, however, you would rather know more about a prospective attorney you are hiring, you may want to go through a referral process or get the advice of a bar association. What follows are avenues that are open to you in seeking help.

In General

American Bar Association. www.abanet.org – This Web site contains good information on nearly every aspect of your relationship with a lawyer (from hiring to firing), as well as providing you with parameters with respect to issues such as cost. You will also find nationwide links to free attorney-referral services, and you can obtain a referral for the type of lawyer you want (criminal law, for example) as well as the contact information for local and state bar associations that can assist with referrals in your area. This information is available under the section of the home page that links to services for the general public. However, the site is not set up to help you find a gay or lesbian lawyer specifically, though you may find one by specialty of discrimination. You cannot get legal advice from the Association or through the site. The American Bar Association is located at 750 North Lake Shore Drive, Chicago, Illinois 60611, Telephone 312-988-5000.

GayLawNet. www.gaylawnet.com This is an excellent e-resource offering an international and state-by-state directory of attorneys serving the gay, lesbian, bisexual, and transgender community. You will find the information on obtaining a lawyer under the Attorney Listings link on the home page. You can search by your geography and obtain the names, contact information, and specialties of the attorneys listed. Local organizations are also displayed in this search. In addition, there is information available on different laws affecting the community throughout the world and, state by state, as well as updates on the latest news affecting the legal interests of the gay, lesbian, bisexual, and transgender community. GayLawNet does not give out legal advice, nor are they able to respond to inquiries by email.

Martindale-Hubbell. www.lawyers.com This commercial organization publishes a national directory of attorneys and allows you to search on their Web site for attorneys in your geography by specialty, for free. However, there is no capability for designing a search that focuses on finding a lesbian, gay, bisexual, or transgendered attorney.

National Lesbian and Gay Law Association. www.nlgla.org While this organization does not make referrals, you can call them or visit their Web site to determine whether or not there is a gay or lesbian law association near you. NLGLA also holds annual conferences for attorneys who specialize in practices for the gay, lesbian, bisexual, and transgendered community. They are located at 200 East Lexington Street, Suite 1511, Baltimore, Maryland 21202, Telephone 508-982-8290, Fax 410-244-0775. You can e-mail them at info@nlgla.org.

By Geography

While there are many lesbian and gay bar associations in the country, the only resources included here are those with Web sites offering contact information. The following organizations either make legal referrals, list gay and lesbian attorneys on their site, or can direct you to resources that can identify legal professionals in your region.

CALIFORNIA

Los Angeles

The Los Angeles Gay and Lesbian Center – Legal Services Department. www.laglc.org This legal clinic offers a wide range of legal services at no or low cost, including advice on landlord/tenant, immigration, name change, and temporary-restraining-order issues. The can provide legal referrals as well. They are located at 1625 N. Schrader Boulevard, Los Angeles, California 90028; e-mail legalservices@laglc.org. Telephone the legal services department at 323-993-7670.

San Francisco

Bay Area Lawyers for Individual Freedom. www.balif.org
BALIF founded an AIDS/HIV legal referral panel and may be of help in directing you to resources if you are in need of an attorney. They can be contacted at P.O. Box 421983, San Francisco, California 94142-1983, 415-956-5764.

Bay Area Transgender Law Association. www.batlaw.org The primary mission of this organization is to educate policy-makers on the legal rights of the transgendered community; however, they can assist in legal referrals. They are located at 4960 Almaden Expressway, San Jose, California 95118; telephone 408-265-9681.

DISTRICT OF COLUMBIA

GayLaw (Gay and Lesbian Attorneys of Washington). www.gaylaw.org – This professional association provides many of the services of a bar association, including attorney referral. They can be contacted at P.O. Box 34072, Washington, D.C.; telephone 202-842-7723. Leave a message in the attorney-referral mailbox.

ILLINOIS

Lesbian and Gay Bar Association of Chicago. www.chilagbac.org – You can identify some members of the association at the Web site, or you can telephone for a legal referral. The site also contains a number of links to other Illinois GLBT resources, as well as essential civic resources and legal resources for those who cannot afford attorneys. They can be reached at 3712 N. Broadway, #415, Chicago, Illinois 60613; telephone 773-404-9574; e-mail contact@chilabbac.org.

MASSACHUSETTS

Massachusetts Lesbian and Gay Bar Association. www.melegal.org – MLGBA provides justice, advocacy, and education support and lists attorney members on their site. The site also provides links to other lesbian and gay bar associations, both locally and nationally, as well as local community resources. They also provide copies of important court decisions. They can be reached at P.O. Box 9072, Boston, Massachusetts 02114; telephone 617-984-0535.

NEW YORK

Lesbian & Gay Law Association of Greater New York. www.le-gal.org Providing a low-income law clinic as well as a weekly walk-in clinic and a trans-legal clinic, the association also publishes *Lesbian and Gay Law Notes* as well as providing a referral service. They are located at 799 Broadway, #340, New York, New York 10003 and can be reached by telephone at 212-353-9118 or by fax at 212-353-2970. Their email address is le-gal@earthlink.net.

NORTH CAROLINA

North Carolina Gay and Lesbian Attorneys. www.ncgala.org This association has an excellent Web site that overviews a wide variety of legal issues specific to the state of North Carolina which you can either read online or order as a paper copy (e-mail guide@ncgala.org). They also publish a directory of attorneys that is available free to organizations. They can be reached at P.O. Box 2164, Durham, North Carolina 27702-2164; telephone 919-990-1951. The e-mail contact regarding the directory is referral@ncgala.org.

OHIO

Ohio Human Rights Bar Association. www.ohrba.org This organization is located at P.O. Box 10655, Columbus, Ohio 43201; Telephone 614-443-5150.

OREGON

Oregon Gay & Lesbian Law Association. This association can be reached at P.O. Box 876, Portland, Oregon 97207; Telephone 503-229-3988.

PENNSYLVANIA

Gay and Lesbian Lawyers of Philadelphia. www.libertynet.org/gallop – You can obtain a referral by dialing extension 1 after reaching them by telephone. They also run Lavender Connections from their site, which connects a vast array of legal and non-legal resources on a wide variety of topics. They are located at P.O. Box 58279, Penn Central Station, Philadelphia, Pennsylvania 19102; telephone 215-627-9090.

TEXAS

Texas Human Rights Foundation. www.thrf.org This site contains links to many other Texas organizations, as well as offering attorneys the ability to sign on to their referral network. They are located at P.O. Box 667157, Houston, Texas 77266; telephone their state-wide legal hotline at 800-828-6417.

WASHINGTON

Lesbian and Gay Legal Society – They provide legal referrals and are located at 1122 E. Pike, #1258, Seattle, Washington 98122; their referral line is 206-292-5116.

General Legal and General Services Resources

Reading

GENERAL – HISTORICAL

Chauncy, George. *Gay New York – Gender, Urban Culture and the Making of the Gay Male World, 1890-1940.* BasicBooks, New York, 1994.
Kaiser, Charles. *The Gay Metropolis – The Landmark History of Gay Life in America Since World War II.* A Harvest Book, New York. 1998.
Marcus, Eric. *Making History – The Struggle for Gay and Lesbian Equal Rights – 1945-1990.* Harper Collins, New York, 1992.
Spencer, Colin. *Homosexuality in History.* Harcourt Brace & Company, New York, 1995.

HISTORICAL E-RESOURCES

GLBT Historical Society. www.glhs.org With an eye towards building a museum to house GLBT history and culture, this organization maintains a Web site offering links to other historical entities as well as archives that offer a rich assortment of publications and oral histories.

GLBT LEGAL SERVICE ORGANIZATIONS

The following organizations are legal organizations serving the GBLT community in defending and protecting legal rights. They do so by involving their assets in "impact litigation," which means that they undertake representation of cases that offer an opportunity to change law categorically. They are not able to act as law firms for the GBLT community, meaning that even if your case involves a real legal issue, if it is not impact litigation, they may not be able to represent you.

American Civil Liberties Union. www.aclu.org The ACLU maintains a lesbian and gay rights project and has been an essential asset in the protection of rights for the GLBT community. The Web site offers a wealth of information about the state of law as well as information about current cases involving a wide variety of legal needs, including issues around GLBT families, discrimination, the military, and hate crimes. The ACLU is located at 125 Broad Street, 18th Floor, New York, New York 10004.

Gay & Lesbian Advocates & Defenders. www.glad.org Despite the fact that they operate in New England, GLAD is an organization that tackles a broad range of national issues. The region that is the focus of the organization includes

Massachusetts, Connecticut, Rhode Island, Vermont, Maine and New Hampshire. Some of their recent work has included lawsuits to secure organ transplantation for HIV positive persons, securing family benefits for gay and lesbian families, and attacking New England's last sodomy statute. They are located at 294 Washington Street, Ste. 301, Boston, Massachusetts 02108; telephone 617-426-1350.

Lambda Legal Defense and Education Fund. www.lambdalegal.org LLDEF is involved in litigation in employment, housing, and public-accomodation discrimination. They have also brought ground-breaking lawsuits involving the military; HIV/AIDS-related discrimination, parenting and relationship issues; equal marriage rights; equal employment and domestic partnership benefits; "sodomy" law challenges; immigration issues; anti-gay initiatives; and free speech and equal protection rights. They have a national office located in New York as well as regional offices throughout the United States.

National Headquarters
120 Wall Street, Suite 1500
New York, NY 10005-3904
212-809-8585 phone
212-809-0055 fax
Western Regional Office
3325 Wilshire Boulevard, Suite 1300
Los Angeles, CA 90010-1729
213-382-7600 phone
213-351-6050 fax
Midwest Regional Office
11 East Adams, Suite 1008
Chicago, IL 60603-6303
312-663-4413 phone
312-663-4307 fax
Southern Regional Office
1447 Peachtree Street, NE, Suite 1004
Atlanta, GA 30309-3027
404-897-1880 phone
404-897-1884 fax
South Central Regional Office
3500 Oak Lawn Avenue, Suite 500
Dallas, TX 75219-6722
214-219-8585 phone
214-219-4455 fax

National Center for Lesbian Rights. www.nclrights.org The NCLR is a legal resource center whose primary mission is to advance the rights and safety of lesbians and their families through a variety of activities. It also provides representation and resources for gay men and bisexual and transgendered individuals. The organization has special projects focused on elder law, transgender law, immigration, and family law. They are located at 870 Market Street, Ste. 570, San Francisco, CA 94102; telephone 415–392-6257; fax 415–392-8442.

E- RESOURCES

Human Rights Campaign. www.hrc.org – More politically oriented as an organization than legally, HRC nevertheless provides a huge amount of information on a wide range of topics dealing with hate crimes, HIV/AIDS, family law, immigration, lesbian health, marriage law, transgender, and workplace issues. Their Web site contains important lists and links to other organizations by topical area. They can be reached at 919 18th Street, N.W., Ste. 800, Washington, D.C. 20006; Telephone 202-628-4160, fax 202-347-5323.

Lesbian and Gay Law Notes. This is an extraordinary resource published by the Lesbian & Gay Law Association of Greater New York and is available for anyone wishing to research a history of court cases affecting the rights of the GLBT community. Professor Arthur Leonard of New York Law School has organized this comprehensive resource. An archive of the Law Notes can be found at www.qrd.org/www/usa/legal/lgln, or you can subscribe by contacting the law association (see above for contact information).

National Association of Lesbian, Gay, Bisexual and Transgender Community Centers. www.lgbtcenters.org – while not an organization dispensing legal advice, they do provide a wide range of referrals for services to the lesbian, gay, bisexual and transgendered community. Some of their member organizations do provide legal services and do provide referrals to professionals within a particular community. Their referral service is only available on the Internet or you can email them at infor@lgbtcenters.org

Resources by Subject

In the following pages, you will find resources listed for further reading, organizations that may be able to help you, and Web sites that will provide you further insight into the issues you are facing. The resources are listed by chapter subject matter; however, you may find that some organizations are mentioned for more than one chapter because of the scope of services and information they provide.

Respecting the e-resources, the Web sites mentioned here do not imply an endorsement of any organization mentioned. Nor should you consider that these represent the entire span of Web resources on the topic. In legal practice, many private attorneys and law practices sponsor Web sites that often provide a wealth of information. However, for these purposes, the Web sites listed represent organizations rather than law firms.

Chapter 1. Goin' to the Chapel – Legal Ceremonies

READING

Curry, Hayden; Clifford, Denis; Hertz, Frederick. *A Legal Guide for Lesbian & Gay Couples*. Nolo Publishers, Eleventh Edition, Berkeley, March 2002.

Ihara, Toni Lynne; Warner, Ralph E.; Hertz, Frederick. Living Together: *A Legal Guide for Unmarried Couples*. Nolo Publishers, Berkely.

Sullivan, Andrew (ed). *Same-Sex Marriage: Pro and Con – A Reader.* Vintage Books, New York, 1997.

ORGANIZATIONS

Each of the national organizations (American Civil Liberties Union, Gay & Lesbian Advocates & Defenders, Human Rights Campaign, Lambda Legal Defense and Education Fund, the National Center for Lesbian Rights and the National Gay and Lesbian Task Force) is active in some capacity to create greater legal recognition for gay and lesbian unions. The following listings include additional resources dedicated to this issue as well as some regional resources available. Many have excellent Web sites, and you can find the URLs in the E-Resources section following this list:

Freedom to Marry Collaborative. Headed by one of the pre-eminent legal experts on this issue, Evan Wolfson, this coalition of organizations is in the process of launching an education and advocacy effort to support the right to marry. They are located at 116 West 23rd Street, Suite 500, New York, New York 10011; telephone 212-851-8418; fax 646-375-2069; E-mail evan@freedomtomarry.org

Freedom to Marry Coalition of Massachusetts. www.ftmmass.org – It is the aim of this organization to be active in grassroots education, advocacy, and lobbying in support of civil marriage rights for same-sex couples.

Love Makes a Family. www.lmfct.org This is a Connecticut organization working to expand that state's laws to include same-sex couples. They can be reached at 44 Wright Drive, Avon, Connecticut 06001; telephone 860-674-8942; e-mail info@lmgct.org.

Marriage Equality California. www.marriageequalityca.org This organization is dedicated to passage of civil unions in California and has an extensive Web site devoted to issues related thereto. They can be reached at P.O. Box 8, Venice, California 90294; telephone 877-356-4125.

New Hampshire Freedom to Marry Coalition. www.nhftm.org This is a coalition with state chapters devoted to changing marriage laws in this state. They can be contacted at P.O. Box 4064, Concord, New Hampshire 03302-4064; telephone 603-223-0309.

Vermont Freedom to Marry Task Force. www.vtfreetomarry.org This is a coalition made up of both individuals and organizations. They can be reached by writing to P.O. Box 1312, Middlebury, Vermont 05753; telephone 802-388-2633.

E-RESOURCES

The following Web sites contain information on legal aspects of gay and lesbian family and marriage issues as well as many historical descriptions of the gay and lesbian marriage struggle. Many of these organizations are actively working in support of greater marriage rights. You will also find texts of bills related to civil unions and domestic partnerships.

Gay and Lesbian Alliance Against Defamation. To see a list of newspapers that print same-sex announcements; http://www.glaad.org/publications/resource_doc_detail.php?id=3144

Human Rights Campaign. www.hrc.org Their site contains issues updates on marriage and family law and advocacy.

Lambda Legal Defense and Education Fund. www.lambdalegal.org You will be able to see progress on cases in which the organization is involved.

National Center for Lesbian Rights. www.nclrights.org The site contains information on the family law project of NCLR.

National Gay and Lesbian Task Force. www.ngltf.org

Vermont Secretary of State – Guide to Civil Unions in Vermont – www.sec.state.vt.us/otherprg/civilunions/civilunions.html

Chapter 2. Having a Family

The resources available to lesbians and gays who are considering parenthood have both breadth and depth and are quite extensive.

READING

Benkov, Laura. *Reinventing the Family – The Emerging Story of Lesbian and Gay Parents.* Crown Publishers, New York. 1994.

Martin, April. *The Lesbian and Gay Parenting Handbook – Creating and Raising Our Families.* Harper Perennial, New York, 1993.

Loving Journeys. P.O. Box 755, Peterborough, New Hampshire 03458; telephone

603-924-7489. This resource has produced a book ***Loving Journeys: Guide to Adoption*** – that contains a directory of adoption agencies throughout the country that accept lesbian and gay applicants.

ORGANIZATIONS

Family Pride Coalition. www.familypride.org FPC is an organization formed to support gays and lesbians who are considering becoming or are parents through advocacy, education, and providing venues for events and parenting groups. They are located at P.O. Box 65327, Washington, D.C.; telephone 202-331-5015, fax (202)-331-0080; E-mail info@familypride.org.

National Adoption Information Clearinghouse. www.calib.com/naic This Web site offers a wide ranging wealth of information for prospective adoptive parents and is set up by the Children's Bureau, Administration on Children, Youth and Families, Administration for Children and Families, Department of Health and Human Services. They are located at 330 C Street, S.W., Washington, D.C. 20447; telephone 703-352-3488 or 888-251-0075; fax 703-385-3206; e-mail naic@calib.com. Within their site, they have resources that are especially important for lesbian and gay parents:

> www.calib.com/naic Run by the National Adoption Information Clearinghouse, this essential site provides a wealth of information and links that will assist you in finding an agency and learning about all of the hurdles you will have to clear in choosing adoption. It is run as a national resource by the Children's Bureau, Administration on Children, Youth and Families Administration, Administration for Children and Families, Department of Health and Human Services. You can also find up-to-date information on your state's licensing specialists, your state's foster-care specialists and your state's adoption specialists. There is information available for adoptive parents and adoptees, for professionals and the layperson. There are statistics on adoption and databases for finding further information and there are summaries of state laws.
>
> www.acf.dhhs.gov. At this Web site sponsored by the Department of Health and Human Services – Children's Bureau Programs, you can get important links to information regarding the specialists in your state who can tell you if an adoption agency you are working with is licensed (www.acf.dhhs.gov/programs/cb/parent/licspc.htm) as well as adoption specialists in the state (www.acf.dhhs.gov/programs/cb/parent/adopt.htm) and also for foster care (www.acf.chhs.gov/programs/cb/parent/fostersp.htm)

The American Surrogacy Center, Inc. (TASC). www.surrogacy.com Offers a wide variety of resources for those considering surrogacy, including chat capabilities, message boards, and support groups as well as legal, medical, psychological, and agency resources.

E-RESOURCES

The following Web sites contain information on adoption and issues related to having a family:

Alternative Family Magazine. www.altfammag.com Includes an overview of statistics regarding lesbian and gay families.
Family Pride Coalition. www.familypride.org (formerly the Gay & Lesbian Parents Coalition International).
Human Rights Campaign. www.hrc.org
Lambda Legal Defense and Education Fund. www.lambdalegal.org
National Center for Lesbian Rights. www.nclrights.org
National Lesbian and Gay Task Force. www.ngltf.org

U.S. Department of State. http://travel.state.gov/adopt.html For information on foreign adoptions, this Web site will link you to very valuable government resources, such as the Office of Children's Issues. You can find congressional testimony regarding foreign adoptions and links to country-specific flyers for eighty-five nations.
http://www.ins.usdog.gov U.S. Immigration and Naturalization Service
www.adopting.org. For gays and lesbians – Adoption Information and Support – This site will supply you with a bibliography on gay adoption (www.adopting.org/gaybib.html), some of which are hot-linked to the source. They also provide information regarding adoption agencies in various states that can provide information specific to lesbians and gays (www.adopting.org/gaystate.html).

Chapter 3. Family Feuds

READING

Hertz, Frederick. *Legal Affairs – Essential Advice for Same-Sex Couples.* Henry Holt and Company, New York, 1998. (This book contains advice on a range of legal topics, including issues related to living together as well as those involved in the dissolution of relationships.)

ORGANIZATIONS

Regarding matters involving domestic abuse or the prevention of violence in your home, see the Resources section for chapter 9 (hate crimes) below for a list of gay and lesbian organizations that have anti-violence projects.

E-RESOURCES

Human Rights Campaign. www.hrc.org The Web site has a section where you can submit questions and ask experts on a wide range of topics, including issues related to breaking up.

Chapter 4. Till Death Do You Part

Many of the needs you will have around issues related to this chapter involve working with a private attorney. Therefore it is suggested that you review the How to Find an Attorney section above. In addition, there are a host of resources available to respond to the needs of the dying, many of which are not law organizations but are nonetheless knowledgeable about legal issues involved in advance directives and related matters.

READING

ORGANIZATIONS

In addition to the following resources, if you live near an HIV/AIDS organization or a large lesbian and gay services center, you may find that they have information or referrals regarding end-of-life issues. The following are organizations that, while not serving the lesbian, gay, bisexual and transgender community exclusively, are devoted to end-of-life issues.

Hemlock Society USA. A non-profit membership organization with state chapters that provides services to those seeking information on death and dying as well as acting as an advocate to change or challenge laws that affect end-of-life choice. They provide telephone counseling for members as well as services related to filing health care instruments with providers. The mailing address is P.O. Box 101810, Denver, Colorado 80250-1810; telephone 1-877-Hemlock; e-mail at hemlock@hemlock.org There is an annual cost for membership.

Partnership for Caring. This is a non-profit that provides services related to death and dying, including counseling, education services, and a hotline. At their Web site, you can download and print medical directive forms for the state in which you live. They also have a legal services director, in case you have questions about the laws in your state, and a hotline that is available to help those who are experiencing difficulty in a death- and-dying situation. They are located at 1620 Eye Street, N.W., Suite 202, Washington, D.C. 20006; telephone 202-296-8071; fax 202-296-8352; hotline 800-989-9455; e-mail pfc@partnershipforcaring.org.

E-Resources

The following Web sites contain information on legal death and dying issues for same sex/unmarried couples:

Hemlock Society. www.hemlock.org
Partnership for Caring. www.partnershipforcaring.org

Chapter 5. Discriminating Tastes

READING

Hunter, Nan; Michaelson, Sherryl E.; Stoddard, Thomas B. *The Rights of Lesbians and Gay Men – The Basic ACLU Guide to a Gay Person's Rights, Third Edition*. Southern Illinois University Press, Carbondale, Edwardsville, 1992.

ORGANIZATIONS

Naturally, each of the national organizations provide information regarding the matter of discrimination and offer an abundance of resources. In addition, you may wish to contact your state or city office for human rights.

ALABAMA
Department of Human Resources
Civil Rights/Equal Employment Office
50 Ripley Street
Montgomery, AL 36130
Tel: (334) 242-1550
http://www.dhr.state.al.us/default.asp

ALASKA
Alaska State Commission for Human Rights
800 A Street, Suite 204
Anchorage, AK 99501-3669
In Arkansas: (800) 478-4692
TTY (800) 478-3177
Tel: (907) 274-4692
TDD: (907) 276-3177
http://www.gov.state.ak.us/aschr/aschr.htm

ARIZONA
Arizona Civil Rights Division
Office of the Arizona Attorney General
1275 W. Washington Street
Phoenix, AZ 85007-2926
Tel: (602) 542-5263 (Intake Officer)
TDD: (602) 542-5002
http://www.attorney_general.state.az.us/civil_rights/index.html

CALIFORNIA
California Department of Fair Employment and Housing (DFEH)
Toll-free in California: (800) 884-1684

Outside California: (916) 227-0551
TTY IN California: (800) 700-2320
Fax: (916) 227-2859
http://www.dfeh.ca.gov/

COLORADO
Colorado Civil Rights Division Commission
1560 Broadway, Suite 1050
Denver, CO 80202-5143
In Colarado: (800) 262-4845 Toll-free
Tel: (303) 894-2997
Fax: (303) 894-7830
TDD: (303) 894-7832
http://www.dora.state.co.us/Civil-Rights/

CONNECTICUT
Connecticut Association of Human Rights (CAHR)
c/o CCHRO
21 Grant Street
Hartford, CT 06106
In Connecticut (800) 477-5737
Tel: (860) 541-3400
Fax: (860) 246-5068
TDD: (860) 541-3459
http://www.state.ct.us/chro/index.html

DELAWARE
Delaware Division of Human Relations
820 N. French Street, 4th Floor
Wilmington, DE 19801
Tel: (302) 577-5050

DISTRICT OF COLUMBIA
Department of Human Rights & Minority Business Development
One Judiciary Square
441 4th Street, NW, Suite 570 N
Washington, DC 20001
Tel: (202) 727-4559
http://ohr.washingtondc.gov/

FLORIDA
Florida Commission on Human Rights

325 John Knox Road, Bldg. F, Suite 240
Tallahassee, FL 32303-4149
In Florida: (800) 342-8170
Tel: (904) 488-7082
Fax: (904) 488-5291
TTY: (800) 955-8770
http://fchr.state.fl.us/

GEORGIA
Georgia Human Relations Commission
1720 Peachtree Street NW, Suite 333
North Tower
Atlanta, GA 30309
Tel: (404) 206-6320
Fax: (404) 206-6322
http://www.state.ga.us/ghrc/

HAWAII
Hawaii Civil Rights Commission
830 Punchbowl Street, Room 411
Honolulu, HI 96813
Tel: (808) 586-8636
Fax: (808) 586-8655
http://www.state.hi.us/hcrc/

IDAHO
Idaho Human Rights Commission (IHRC)
P.O. Box 83720
1109 Main Street, Fourth Floor
Boise, ID 83720-0040
Tel: (208) 334-2873
Fax: (208) 334-2664
TDD: (208) 334-4751
http://www2.state.id.us/ihrc/ihrchome.htm

ILLINOIS
Illinois Department of Human Rights
100 W. Randolph Street, Suite 10-100
Chicago, IL 60601
Tel: (312) 814-6200
TDD: (312) 263-1579
http://www.state.il.us/dhr/

INDIANA
Indiana Civil Rights Commission
100 N. Senate Avenue, Room N103
Indianapolis, IN 46204-2211
Toll-free: (800) 628-2909
Tel: (317) 232-2600
Fax: (317) 232-6580
TDD: 1 (800) 743-3333
http://www.state.in.us/icrc/

IOWA
Iowa Civil Rights Commission (ICRC)
211 E. Maple Street, 2nd Floor
Des Moines, IA 50319-1858
Toll-free: (800) 457-4416
Tel: (515) 281-4121
Fax: (515) 242-5840
http://www.state.ia.us/government/crc/_

KANSAS
Kansas Human Rights Commission
900 SW Jackson, Suite 851-S
Landon State Office Building
Topeka, KS 66612-1258
Tel: (785) 296-3206
Fax: (785) 296-0589
TDD: (785) 296-0245
http://www.state.ks.us/public/khrc/

KENTUCKY
Kentucky Commission on Human Rights
332 W. Broadway, Suite 700
Louisville, KY 40202
Toll-free (800) 292-5566
Tel: (502) 595-4024
Fax: (502) 595-4801
TDD: (502) 595-4084
http://www.state.ky.us/agencies2/kchr/

LOUISIANA
Louisiana Commission on Human Rights

P.O. Box 94004
1001 N. 23rd St., Suite 262
Baton Rouge, LA 70802-9004
Tel: (225) 342-6969
Fax: (225) 342-2063
TDD: 1-888-248-0859
http://www.gov.state.la.us/depts/lchr.htm

MAINE
Maine Human Rights Commission
51 State House Station
Augusta, ME 04333-0051
Tel: (207) 624-6050
Fax: (207) 624-6063
TDD: (207) 624-6064
http://www.state.me.us/mhrc/index.shtml_

MARYLAND
Maryland Commission on Human Relations
6 St. Paul Street, Suite 900
Baltimore, MD 21202-2274
Toll-free: (800) 637-6247
Tel: (410) 767-8600
Fax: (410) 333-1841
TDD: (410) 333-1737
http://www.mchr.state.md.us/

MASSACHUSETTS
Massachusetts Commission Against Discrimination (MCAD)
One Ashburton Place, Room 601
Boston, MA 02108-1518
Tel: (617) 727-3990
http://www.state.ma.us/mcad/

MICHIGAN
Michigan Department of Civil Rights
Service Center
State of Michigan Plaza Bldg., 6th Flr.
1200 Sixth Ave.
Detroit, MI 48226
Tel: (313) 256-2663
Fax: (313) 256-2167

TDD: (313) 961-1352
http://www.michigan.gov/mdcr_

MINNESOTA
Minnesota Department of Human Rights
Army Corps of Engineers Center
190 E. 5th Street, Suite 700
St. Paul, MN 55101
Toll-free: (800) 657-3704
Tel: (651) 296-5663
TDD: (651) 296-1283
http://www.humanrights.state.mn.us/

MISSOURI
Missouri Commission on Human Rights
P.O. Box 1129
3315 West Truman Boulevard
Jefferson City, MO 65102-1129
Tel: (573) 751-3325
Fax: (573) 751-2905
TDD: (573) 526-5091
http://www.dolir.state.mo.us/hr/

MONTANA
Montana Human Rights Commmission
P.M.S. Box 1728
1625 11th Avenue
Helena, MT 59624-1728
Tel: (406) 444-2884
http://erd.dli.state.mt.us/HumanRights/HRhome.htm

NEBRASKA
Lincoln Commission on Human Rights
440 S. 8th St., Suite 101
Lincoln, NE 68508
Enrique Brodsky, Executive Director
Tel: (402) 441-7624
Fax: (402) 441-6931
http://www.ci.lincoln.ne.us/city/mayor/human/

NEVADA
Nevada Equal Rights Commission

1455 E. Tropicana Ave, Suite 500
Las Vegas, NV 89119-6522
Tel: (702) 486-7161
Fax: (702) 486-7054
TDD: (702) 486- 7164
http://detr.state.nv.us/nerc/

New Hampshire
New Hampshire Commission for Human Rights
2 Chenelle Drive
Concord, NH 03301-8501
Tel: (603) 271-2767
Fax: (603) 271-6339
http://www.state.nh.us/hrc/

New Jersey
New Jersey Department of Law and Safety
Division of Civil Rights
31 Clinton Street
Newark, NJ 07102
Tel: (201) 648-2700
Fax: (201) 648-4405
http://www.state.nj.us/lps/dcr/

New Mexico
New Mexico Human Rights Commission
New Mexico Department of Labor – Education Bureau
1596 Pacheco Street, Suite 103
Santa Fe, NM 87505
Toll-free: (800) 566-9471
Tel: (505) 827-6838
Fax: (505) 827-6878
http://www3.state.nm.us/dol/dol_hrd.html

New York
New York State Division of Human Rights
One Fordham Plaza
Bronx, NY 10458
Tel: (718) 741- 8400
http://www.nysdhr.com/

North Carolina
North Carolina Human Relations Commission

1318 Mail Service Center
Raleigh, NC 27699-1318
Toll-free: (866) 324-7474
Tel: (919) 733-7996
http://www.doa.state.nc.us/doa/hrc/hrc.htm

NORTH DAKOTA
North Dakota Department of Labor
600 E. Boulevard Avenue, Dept. 406
Bismarck, ND 58505-0340
Toll-free in North Dakota: (800) 582-8032
Tel: (701) 328-2660
Fax: (701) 328-2031
TTY Relay in ND (800) 366-6889
http://www.state.nd.us/labor/

OHIO
Ohio Civil Rights Division
1111 E. Broad Street, Suite 301
Columbus, OH 43205
Toll-free: (888) 278-7101
Tel: (614) 466-2785
http://www.state.oh.us/crc/

OKLAHAMO
Oklahoma Human Rights Commission (OHRC)
Jim Thorpe Building, Room 408
2101 N. Lincoln Boulevard
Oklahoma City, OK 73105
Tel: (405) 521-2360
Fax: (405) 522-3635
TDD: (405) 522-3993
http://www.onenet.net/~ohrc2/

OREGON
Oregon Civil Rights Division
Bureau of Labor & Industries
800 N.E. Oregon, Suite 1070
Portland, OR 97232
Tel: (503) 731-4200
http://www.boli.state.or.us/civil/committee.html_

PENNSYLVANIA
Pennsylvania Human Relations Commission (PHRC)
301 Chestnut Street, Suite 300
Harrisburg, PA 17101
Tel: (717) 787-4410
TDD: (717) 783-9308
http://www.phrc.state.pa.us/

RHODE ISLAND
Rhode Island Commission for Human Rights
10 Abbott Park Place
Providence, RI 02903-3768
Tel: (401) 222-2661
Fax: (401) 222-2616
TDD: (401) 222-2664

SOUTH CAROLINA
South Carolina Human Affairs Commission
2611 Forest Drive, Suite 200
P.O Box 4490
Columbia, SC 29240
Toll-free (800) 521-0725
Tel: (803) 737-7800
TDD: (803) 253-4125
http://www.state.sc.us/schac/

SOUTH DAKOTA
South Dakota Division of Human Rights
118 W. Capitol Avenue
Pierre, SD 57501
Tel: (605) 773-4493
Fax: (605) 773-6893
http://www.state.sd.us/dcr/hr/HR_HOM.htm

TENNESSEE
Tennessee Human Rights Commission
530 Church Street, Suite 400
Nashville, TN 37243-0745
Toll-free: (800) 251-3589
Tel: (615) 741-5825
Fax: (615) 532-2197
http://www.state.tn.us/humanrights/

TEXAS
Texas Commission on Human Rights
P.O. Box 13006
6330 Highway 290 East, Suite 250
Austin, TX 78711
Toll-free in Texas: (888) 452-4778
Tel: (512) 437-3450
Fax: (512) 437-3478
TDD: (512) 371-7473
http://tchr.state.tx.us/

UTAH
Utah Anti-Discrimination Division
160 E. 300 South, 3rd Floor
Salt Lake City, UT 84114-6640
Toll-free: (800) 222-1238
Tel: (801) 530-6801
Fax: (801) 530-7609
TDD: (801) 530-7685
http://www.labor.state.ut.us/Utah_Antidiscrimination_Labo/utah_antidiscrimination_labo.htm

VERMONT
Vermont Human Rights Commission
135 State Street
P.O. Drawer 33
Montpelier, VT 05633-6301
Toll-free: (800) 416-2010
Tel: (802) 828-2480
Fax: (802) 828-2481
TDD: (802) 828-2480
http://www.hrc.state.vt.us/

VIRGINIA
Virginia Council on Human Rights
Washington Building, Suite 1202
1100 Bank Street
Richmond, VA 23219
Tel: (804) 225-2292
http://chr.vipnet.org/

WASHINGTON
Washington State Human Rights Commission(WSHRC)
711 S. Capitol Way, Suite 402
Olympia, WA 98504-2490
Toll-free: (800) 233-3247
Tel: (360) 753-6770
Fax: (360) 586-2282
TDD: (800) 300-7525
http://www.wa.gov/hrc/

WEST VIRGINIA
West Virginia Human Rights Commission
1321 Plaza East, Room 108A
Charleston, WV 25301-1400
Toll-free: (888) 676-5546
Tel: (304) 558-2616
Fax: (304) 558-0085
http://www.state.wv.us/wvhrc/

WISCONSIN
Wisconsin Equal Rights Division, Civil Rights Bureau
1 South Pinkney Street, Room 320
P.O. Box 8928
Madison, WI 53708-8928
Tel: (608) 266-6860
Fax: (608) 267-4592
http://www.dwd.state.wi.us/er/discrimination_civil_rights/fair_employment_law.htm

WYOMING
Wyoming Department of Employment/Fair Employment Programs
6101 Yellowstone, Room 259C
Cheyenne, WY 82002
Tel: (307) 777-7261
Fax: (307) 777-5633
http://wydoe.state.wy.us/doe.asp?ID=247

E-RESOURCES

The following Web sites contain extensive information on discrimination issues:

American Civil Liberties Union. **www.aclu.org**
Lambda Legal Defense and Education Fund. **www.lambdalegal.org**
National Gay and Lesbian Task Force. **www.ngltf.org**

Chapter 6. A Kinder Gender Nation

READING

There are a large number of books on the shelves by and about transgendered persons. The following is noted as a historical reading.

Jorgensen, Christine. *Christine Jorgensen – A Personal Autobiography*. Cleis Press, San Francisco, 1967.

ORGANIZATIONS

Bay Area Transgender Lawyers Association. www.batlaw.org

National Transgender Advocacy Coalition. www.ntac.org – an activist group centered on advancing the rights of transgendered persons by affecting social and legal outlooks. The Web site contains statistical information as well as providing action alerts and notices of sponsored lobby days. They are located at 14252 Culver Drive, Suite 904, Irvine, California 92604-0326, and you can e-mail them at info@ntac.org

E-RESOURCES

The following Web sites contain information on transgender issues:

Human Rights Campaign. www.hrc.org
Lambda Legal Defense and Education Fund. www.lambdalegal.org
National Center for Lesbian Rights. www.nclr.org
National Gay and Lesbian Task Force Transgender Civil Rights Project. www.ngltf.org

Transgender Law & Policy Institute. www.transgenderlaw.org This site offers comprehensive information and articles on hate crimes, company and university transgender policies, and the latest on jurisdictions with protection laws enacted for transgendered people. You can contact the organization by e-mail at info@transgenderlaw.org.

Transparentcy. www.transparentcy.org This organization works with transgender parents and their children and supplies lists of resources, including those for custody, hate crimes and legal resources. You can reach them by email at paula@transparentcy.org.

Chapter 7. Serving Your Country

READING

Benecke, Michelle M.; Osburn, C. Dixon; Gilberd, Kathy. *How to Survive Under "Don't Ask, Don't Tell, Don't Pursue"*. Servicemembers Legal Defense Network. Washington, D.C.

Scott, Wilbur J.; Stanley, Sandra Carson (eds). *Gays and Lesbians in the Military – Issues, Concerns and Contrasts*. Aldine de Gruyter, New York, 1994.

Shilts, Randy. *Conduct Unbecoming*. St. Martin's Press, New York, 1993.

Sobel, Stacey L.; Cleghorn, Jeffery M.; Osburn, C. Dixon. *Conduct Unbecoming – The Seventh Annual Report on "Don't Ask, Don't Tell, Don't Pursue, Don't Harass."* Servicemembers Legal Defense Network, Washington, D.C.

NOTE OF CAUTION: While the publications produced by the Servicemembers Legal Defense Network are free, excellent resources that can be downloaded from the organization's Web site (see below), if you are using a computer on base, you should wait and use a computer that is personal, not a base computer.

ORGANIZATIONS

Human Rights Campaign. www.hrc.org

Servicemembers Legal Defense Network – www.sldn.org – The pre-eminent organization assisting gays and lesbians in the military, last year SLDN helped with over 500 cases for service members who were facing investigations. They have a legal department staffed with four attorneys, and their Web site contains a wealth of essential information for any gay or lesbian serving in the military. There, you can download the latest copies of their survival handbook, as well as their annual report entitled *Conduct Unbecoming* and even consult their "e-law" library. They can be reached at

P.O. Box 65301, Washington, D.C. 200356-5301; telephone
202-328-3244.

E-RESOURCES

The following Web sites contain information on gays, lesbians, and the military:

American Veterans for Equal Rights. www.glbva.org Formerly known as the Gay, Lesbian and Bisexual Veterans Association, this is an organization dedicated to equal treatment for all members of the military and U.S. veterans. Their Web site contains links to governmental offices handling veteran's affairs, and they have launched a project to document the stories of lesbian and gay service people. You can reach them by email at **glbva@glbva.org**

Center for the Study of Sexual Minorities in the Military. http://www.gaymilitary.ucsb.edu/index.htm Located at the University of California, Santa Barbara, the center promotes the interdisciplinary analysis of lesbian, gay, bisexual, and transgendered persons in the armed forces. There are a number of academic articles written on various aspects of sexual minorities in the military, as well as press releases and media articles.

Don't Ask, Don't Tell, Don't Pursue Database. http://dont.stanford.edu Housed at Stanford University, this resource offers a look at primary materials regarding U.S. policy on gays and lesbians in the military from World War I to the present, including litigation, legislation, hearings and a number of policy documents.

Chapter 8. Crimes of Passion

The Triangle Foundation.*www.tri.org* To read the *Bag a Fag* report, you can go to the Web site for the Michigan Triangle Foundation. They are located at 19461 West Seven Mile, Detroit, Michigan; telephone 313-537-3323; fax 313-537-3379.

E-RESOURCES

The following Web sites contain information on sodomy:

www.sodomylaws.org – At this Web site, you can get information about changes in the status of sodomy laws around the country, as well as read research and historical articles.

Chapter 9. Hate Crimes

If you are the victim of a crime, you may wish to contact an organization with experience in counseling gay and lesbian people. The following organizations are all part of the National Coalition of Anti-Violence Programs (NCAVP) and can provide assistance to you if you are the victim of a crime.

ARIZONA
Anti-Violence Project/Valley of the Sun Gay & Lesbian Community Center
PO Box 33367
Phoenix, AZ 85067-3367 [check web]

ARKANSAS
Women's Project
2224 Main Street
Little Rock, AR 772206
Tel: 501 372-511??????? GET PHONE NUMBER, check web

CALIFORNIA
Anti-Violence Empowerment Committee
Project of the Central Coast
PO Box 241
Santa Barbara, CA 93102
Tel: 805-569-0561

Fax: 805-569-0526

Community United Against Violence
973 Market Street, Suite 500
San Francisco, CA 94103
Tel: 415-777-5500
Fax: 415-777-5565
www.xq.com/cuav

Los Angeles Gay and Lesbian Center
Anti-Violence Project
1625 North Shrader Blvd.
Los Angeles, CA 90028
Tel: 323-993-7645
Fax: 323-993-7699
www.lagic.org

Gay and Lesbian Center of Long Beach
2017 East Fourth Street
Long Beach, CA 90814
Tel: 562-434-4455
Fax: 562-433-6428

The Lesbian and Gay Men's Community Center
P.O. Box 3357
San Diego, CA 92163
Tel: 619-692-2077
Fax: 619-260-3092

Woman, Inc.
333 Valencia Street, Suite 251
San Francisco, CA 94103
Tel: 415-864-4777
Fax: 415-864-1082

COLORADO
The Anti-Violence Program of Equality Colorado
P.O. Box 3000476
Denver, CO 80203
Tel: 303-839-5540
Fax: 303-839-1361
www.equalitycolorado.org

CONNECTICUT
Connecticut Women's Education and Legal Fund

135 Broad Street
Hartford, CT 06105
Tel: 860-247-6090
Fax: 860-524-0804

District of Columbia
Gays and Lesbians Opposing Violence
1712 16th Street, N.W.
Washington, D.C. 20009

FLORIDA
Gay, Lesbian & Bisexual Community Center of Central Florida
P.O. Box 533446
Orlando, FL 32853
Tel: 407-425-4527
Fax: 407-423-9904
www.glbcc.org

IDAHO
Idaho Anti-Violence Project
P.O. Box 768
Boise, ID 83701
Tel: 208-344-4295
Fax: 208-344-4458

Horizons Anti-Violence Project
961 West Montana
Chicago, IL 60614
Tel: 773-871-CARE (hotline)
Fax: 773-427-6643
www.horizonsonline.org

KENTUCKY
Lesbian and Gay Services Organization
Box 11471
Lexington, KY 40575-1471
Tel: 606-257-3530
LOUISIANA
Lesbian and Gay Community Center of New Orleans
2114 Decatur
New Orleans, LA 70116
Tel: 504-945-1103

MASSACHUSETTS
Fenway Community Health Center

Violence Recovery Program
7 Haviland Street
Boston, MA 02115
Tel: 617-267-0900
Fax: 617-267-3667
www.fchc.org

MICHIGAN
Triangle Foundation
19641 West Seven Mile Road
Detroit, MI 48219
Tel: 313-537-3323
Fax: 313-537-3379
www.tri.org

MINNESOTA
Out Front Minnesota
310 East 38th Street, Suite 204
Minneapolis, MN 55409
Tel: 612-822-0127
Fax: 612-822-8766

MISSOURI
St. Louis Lesbian & Gay Anti-Violence Project
C/o University of Missouri
Department of Psychology
St. Louis, MO 63121
Tel: 314-826-7067
Fax: 314-516-5392

NEW YORK
New York City Gay and Lesbian Anti-Violence Project
240 West 35th Street, Suite 200
New York, NY 10001
Tel: 212-714-1184
Fax: 212-714-2627
www.avp.org

OHIO
Buckeye Region Anti-Violence Organization
P.O. Box 82068
Columbus, OH 43202
Tel: 614-268-9622
Fax: 614-262-9264

Lesbian and Gay Community Service Center of Greater Cleveland
6600 Detroit Avenue
Cleveland, OH 44102
Tel: 216-651-5428
Fax: 216-651-6439

Stonewall Cincinnati
P.O. Box 954
Cincinnati, OH 45201
Tel: 513-651-2500
Fax: 513-651-3044

OKLAHOMA
Tulsa Oklahomans for Human Rights
4021 South Harvard Avenue, Suite 210
Tulsa, OK 74135-4600
Tel: 918-747-5466
Fax: 918-747-5499

RHODE ISLAND
Rhode Island Alliance for Lesbian and Gay Civil Rights
41 12th Street
Providence, RI 02906
Tel: 401-331-6671
Fax: 401-272-4374

TEXAS
Montrose Counseling Center
701 Richmond Avenue
Houston, TX 77006
Tel: 713-529-0037
www.neosoft.com/-mcc/
Other Organizations to assist victims of crime:

Gay and Lesbian National Victims Assistance Hotline
The National Center for Victims of Crime
2111 Wilson Boulevard, Ste. 300
Arlington, Virginia 22201
Tel: 703-276-2880
Fax: 703-276-2889
www.ncvc.org

The National Crime Victim Bar Association
2111 Wilson Boulevard, Ste. 300
Arlington, VA 22201

Tel: 703-276-0960
Fax: 703-276-2889
e-mail: victimbar@ncvc.org
www.victimbar.org

Online Resources
www.hatecrime.org This site carries news developments in hate crimes as they affect the lesbian and gay community and directs people to ways they can become involved in advocating for hate crime legislation.

www.partnersagainsthate.org This Web site, run by an organization of the same name, offers information and statistics as well as a calendar of events regarding hate crimes in America. The site follows legislation as well as current events and profiles promising programs to deal with the problem.

Other Lesbian and Gay OnLine Reading Materials on Hate Crimes Legislation

Campaign to End Homophopbia. www.endhomophobia.org
Human Rights Campaign. www.hrc.org
International Hate and Violence Education Foundation. www.ihave.org
Lambda Gay and Lesbian Victims' Assistance. www.lambda.org
National Lesbian and Gay Task Force. www.ngltf.org
StopViolence.com. www.stopviolence.com

Chapter 10. Conclusion – What's Your Problem?

If you are interested in learning more about the political issues and legal struggles associated with lesbian and gay rights, the following are organizations you may wish to learn more about.

American Civil Liberties Union. www.aclu.org (see above)
Gay and Lesbian Victory Fund. www.victoryfund.org
Human Rights Campaign. www.hrc.org (see above)
Lam*bda Legal Defense and Education Fund.* www.lambdalegal.org (see above)
Log Cabin Republicans. www.lcr.org
National Center for Lesbian Rights. www.nclu.org (see above)
National Lesbian and Gay Task Force. www.ngltf.org (see above)
National Lesbian Political Action Committee. www.lesbian.org/nlpac
National Organization for Women – Lesbian Rights Project. www.now.org/issues/lgbi
National Stonewall Democratic Federation. www.stonewalldemocrats.org

Index